The birth of modern London

MANCHESTER
UNIVERSITY PRESS

STUDIES IN
DESIGN
AND
MATERIAL
CULTURE

general editor
Christopher Breward

The birth of modern London

The development and design of the city
1660–1720

Elizabeth McKellar

Distributed exclusively
in the USA by
St. Martin's Press

Manchester University Press

Manchester and New York

Published by Manchester University Press
Oxford Road, Manchester M13 9NR, UK
and Room 400, 175 Fifth Avenue, New York, NY 10010, USA
http://www.man.ac.uk/mup

Distributed exclusively in the USA by
St. Martin's Press, Inc., 175 Fifth Avenue, New York,
NY 10010, USA

Distributed exclusively in Canada by
UBC Press, University of British Columbia, 6344 Memorial Road,
Vancouver, BC, Canada V6T 1Z2

British Library Cataloguing-in-Publication Data
A catalogue record for this book is available from the British Library

Library of Congress Cataloging-in-Publication Data applied for

ISBN   0 7190 4075 2   *hardback*
        0 7190 4076 0   *paperback*

First published 1999

05 04 03 02 01 00 99   10 9 8 7 6 5 4 3 2 1

Typeset in Stone Serif with Sans display
by Carnegie Publishing, Lancaster
Printed in Great Britain
by Bookcraft (Bath) Ltd, Midsomer Norton

For Suzanne and Ian

Contents

Illustrations

Every effort has been made to trace copyrightholders. If any have inadvertently been overlooked the publisher would be very happy for them to come forward to make the necessary arrangements.

Preface

This book is the outcome of a number of preoccupations and experiences. Firstly, my interest in the architecture of the period began at Oxford where I studied it as an undergraduate. But whereas the flamboyant buildings of the English Baroque have a secure place in the architectural canon, it quickly became apparent that the crucial importance of the 1660-1720 period in the development of London - although generally acknowledged - has been little researched. Secondly, my investigations into the topic of urban housing are attributable to a stubborn intellectual perversity. This ensured that when I was informed by one of my tutors there that architectural history was only concerned with the great buildings of the past, I immediately began to explore their opposite - anonymous, everyday buildings - and they have remained my primary concern ever since. Finally, my absorption with London is part of a long-term love affair with the city in which I live and work, and which like all relationships is a complex mixture of frustrations and fascinations but one which I find endlessly engrossing and rewarding.

The existing secondary literature on the subject largely dates from the 1930s and 1940s and there have been few published works since then.[1] In 1934 the Danish architect and town planner Steen Eiler Rasmussen published his compelling but highly individualized account of London's growth, *London: The Unique City*, which is more in the nature of an architectural and planning treatise than a historical study.[2] The following year Norman Brett-James gave a generalized account of London's expansion in the seventeenth century, which provided a pioneering and still immensely valuable topographical survey of growth.[3] This was followed by T. F. Reddaway's *The Rebuilding of London after the Great Fire* of 1940, which is a thorough examination of the Fire's impact, although largely confined to the City.[4] The definitive account of late seventeenth- and eighteenth-century speculative development in London remains to this day Sir John Summerson's classic, *Georgian London*, first published in 1945.[5]

Summerson's book, written at the end of the war, was in part an emotional response to the destruction of London that lay all around him. It is a masterpiece of architectural interpretation and imaginative reconstruction. From the very first chapter when he presents an air view of London over several centuries, the reader is made part of an exciting journey through the capital's expansion. But it was also a book with a serious historical purpose, an attempt to discover a model for urban growth. Summerson found this in a dialectical relationship between two constituent parts: 'taste' and 'wealth'. He explained the relationship between the two in a loosely Marxist way using the base and superstructure idea. He acknowledged this in an interview in 1987 when he said, 'Marxist history, materialism interested me and it influenced *Georgian London*'.[6] Although the model is somewhat simplistic and the terms 'taste' and 'wealth' and their origins are never fully explained, the book remains one of the most ambitious attempts to convey the totality of a city's development for this period, or indeed any other.

After reading *Georgian London* it in itself became another impetus towards carrying out my own research. I wanted to discover if Summerson's analysis of the period was correct. This was hard to verify as, until the revised version came out in 1988, the work had no footnotes and a very small bibliography. At first I imagined that Summerson would only provide a starting point. Yet as time went on I found my work taking on the form of a sustained dialogue with him. Sometimes he provided the source of inspiration, at others he became the point of opposition. It is remarkable, given the small amount of space he devotes to the period, the extent to which I found many of Summerson's throw-away lines and sweeping pronouncements to be correct. Although my work is a critique of Summerson, it is also a homage to the first British architectural historian who tried to place design developments within a broader historical context. *Georgian London* then is a leitmotif which recurs throughout this book. The fact that it exerts so powerful a pull, even today, is testimony to its enduring depth and richness.

Like Summerson my interest in this subject was aroused by contemporary debates and circumstances. I wanted to offer an alternative view to the dominant voice of the self-styled 'new georgians' and classical revivalists among those writing on eighteenth-century architecture. They espouse a contemporary, conservationist stance which takes a romantic approach to the Georgian city, highlighting its urbane qualities and aesthetic harmony in contrast to the fragmentary nature of many twentieth-century towns.[7] The Georgian city and its buildings continue to be presented in much architectural writing as redolent of an era of social and political harmony, despite the fact that social and economic history has radically revised this interpretation over the past twenty years or so. At a time when classical architecture and a return to craft-based production is once again being proposed by a small group as a paradigm for the ills of the twentieth-century city, it seemed important to me to investigate not just the physical landscape which resulted but the processes that lay behind its creation.

The reviews which greeted the new edition of *Georgian London* in 1988 were evidence of this tendency. Simon Jenkins' review in the *Sunday Times* was entitled 'First of the Neo-Georgians', a title which would have been difficult to apply to Summerson in 1945 when he had only just left the ultra-modernist MARS group.[8] Towards the end of his life Summerson's modernist instincts were still to the fore when he gave evidence for Peter Palumbo at the Mansion House inquiry. The whole of Jenkins' review, apart from one paragraph, was devoted to a résumé of the triumphs and disasters of the Georgian conservation lobby and finished with a war cry from Jenkins for the continuing battle ahead. Summerson's book then has been accepted as a masterpiece, but only by completely emasculating its radical message, and instead treating it as simply a conservationist tract.

Summerson's interest in the development of London was heightened by its destruction. Mine by contrast was awakened in the 1980s (when most of the research for this project was carried out) by the expansion of the City eastwards into Docklands and at Broadgate, which fringed the borough of Hackney where I was then working. The frenzied speculation and often inadequate building that one could see taking place, often literally over night, made me question whether development in the equally frenetic conditions of the late seventeenth-century building boom had really proceeded along the relatively calm avenues of planned and controlled estate development that Summerson had outlined. And could it truly have been carried out by bands of craftsmen, who according to the existing literature, happily sub-contracted with one another, operated a form of barter, and seem to have been nothing less than an up-dated version of the brotherhoods of medieval builders whom the Arts and Crafts were so fond of recalling? The realities of the extremely competitive property and building industries with which I was working on a daily basis made me question whether early modern London could have been built in such a way.

In order to go beyond the existing literature it was essential to examine new documentary sources. One reason that urban development is much better understood for the eighteenth century onwards is the greater availability of primary material: there are no district surveyors in the seventeenth century; no drainage plans - which are a good record for nineteenth- and twentieth-century buildings; no censuses or often even ratebooks, both easy ways of pin-pointing new building. The Middlesex Deeds Register, a crucial source for London, is not indexed until 1720 and is very difficult to use prior to that date. The major archives for the growth of the capital in the 1660–1720 period are in the Guildhall (particularly for City development), in the London Metropolitan Archives and in the Public Record Office. It was from the latter that the major source for my doctorate came (on which this book is based), which was legal accounts of property and building disputes from the Court of Chancery.[9] It was only in the courts of Equity, of which Chancery was one, that circumstantial evidence was possible, which has made them a valuable source for historians. However, there are formidable obstacles to using these records which are voluminous, have never been properly indexed and consequently large tracts of them remain unexplored.[10]

I worked with a sample of 221 cases initially brought together by Mr Frank Kelsall, previously of English Heritage. He extremely generously made his transcripts of the proceedings available to me. I then checked a sample against the originals, analysed them and entered them on a computer database under various categories to extract the maximum information on as wide a range of areas relating to building as possible.[11] The cases are generally concerned with matters of property ownership and financial or contractual disputes regarding land and construction, rather than matters of style or the usage of buildings. Their great strength lies in the variety of information and level of detail that they offer. All stages of development are covered from acquiring the site and raising the finance, through the building process, to the finished house and the arrival of the first occupants. Their main disadvantage is disentangling the relevant information from the often complex and lengthy surrounding legal context. Frequent reference is made in the text to this source as 'Chancery evidence' or 'cases in Chancery'. Through using this new material, in conjunction with other contemporary written and drawn evidence, I hope to be able to offer a more detailed account of the speculative building world and the growth of the capital at this time.

Notes

1 Two recent exceptions are: Stephen Porter, *The Great Fire of London*, Stroud, Sutton, 1996 and Jules Lubbock, *The Tyranny of Taste: The Politics of Architecture and Design in Britain, 1550-1960*, New Haven and London, Yale University Press, 1995, in which late seventeenth- and early eighteenth-century London forms one of the case studies through which Lubbock develops his theme, see, pp. 3-18, 21-42, 96-9.

2 Steen Eiler Rasmussen, *London: The Unique City*, 1934, Cambridge, Mass. and London, MIT Press, 1982.

3 Norman Brett-James, *The Growth of Stuart London*, London, London and Middle-sex Archaeological Society with George Allen & Unwin, 1935.

4 T. F. Reddaway, *The Rebuilding of London after the Great Fire*, London, Jonathan Cape, 1940.

5 John Summerson, *Georgian London*, 1945, Harmondsworth, Penguin, 1962 and subsequent editions (the edn referred to throughout is the 1978 Penguin edn).

6 John Summerson interviewed by Martin Pawley, *Architects' Journal*, 16 and 23 November 1987, pp. 28-30.

7 For the definitive guide to this particular sub-culture see, Alexandra Artley and John Martin Robinson, eds, *The New Georgian Handbook*, London, Ebury Press, 1985. For critiques of Georgian romanticism see: David Matless, 'Ages of English Design: Preservation, Modernism and Tales of their History, 1926-1939', *Journal of Design History*, Vol. 3, No. 4, 1990, pp. 203-12; Patrick Wright, *A Journey Through Ruins: The Last Days of London*, London, Radius, 1991, especially Ch. 8; and more generally Patrick Wright, *On Living in an Old Country*, London, Verso, 1985.

8 Simon Jenkins, 'First of the Neo-Georgians', *Sunday Times*, 28 August 1988.

9 The cases consulted came from PRO classes C5-10, Six Clerks Series, mainly *c.* 1660-1720.

10 The best introduction to Chancery is, Henry Horwitz, *Chancery Equity Records and Proceedings, 1600-1800: A Guide to Documents in the Public Record Office*, London, HMSO, 1995. I am grateful to Professor Horwitz for discussions about the work of Chancery.

11 I am grateful to Charles Harvey and especially to John Styles for advice and help with the establishment of the database. Peter Denley and Deian Hopkins, eds, *History and Computing*, Manchester, Manchester University Press, 1990 was also useful.

Acknowledgements

Writing a book, like designing a building, is more of a collaborative process than is generally realized. In the course of ten years of researching and writing this book, and its predecessor my Ph.D., I have received the help of a large number of colleagues and friends. My first acknowledgement must be to my postgraduate tutors Adrian Forty, Charles Saumarez Smith and John Styles from whom I have learnt so much and whose continuing support and friendship, long after their official responsibilities have ceased, are greatly valued. I must also thank my colleagues in a number of the institutions where I have worked over the period of this book: to Patrick Hammill and David Heath for opening my eyes to the possibilities of the landscape of London in general and Hackney in particular; to Howard Martin for introducing me to lecturing; to my colleagues in the Architecture Department at the University of North London, particularly Jos Boys, Colin Davies, Robert Harbison, Julian Holder, Joe Kerr and Rose Nag; in my current post I have received immense encouragement from my department, especially from those in the Research Group, whom I would like to thank for awarding me a grant towards the cost of illustrations. I am particularly grateful to Charles Saumarez Smith for reading the manuscript and to Neil Burton, Todd Longstaffe-Gowan and Michael Symes for their comments on the sections of the text relating to gardens and open spaces. I benefited greatly from the advice and enthusiasm of the two external examiners of my Ph.D., Peter Borsay and Mark Girouard. I would also like to thank my various editors at Manchester University Press: Katherine Reeve, Matthew Frost and Monica Kendall. Thanks are also due to the following for information, invitations to speak, discussions and help of all kinds, in alphabetical order (with apologies for any who may have been missed): Dana Arnold, Malcolm Baker, Susie Barson, William Cannell, Zöe Croad, Jonathan Elliott, Tom Faulkener, Christopher Frayling, Vanessa Harding, Julian Harrap, Michael Harris, Negley Harte, Stephen Heywood, Tanis Hinchcliffe, Anne MacMurdie, Helen Mallinson, Andrea Michell, Chris Miele, Elizabeth Newlands, Jo Oulton, Katrina Royall, Richard Stables, Robert Thorne, Suzanne Waters, Clive Wainwright, Edward Woodman, Jackie Wullschläger. I am especially grateful to my family, particularly Shona for editorial expertise and John for help with Latin and Chancery sleuthing, and above all my parents to whom this book is dedicated. Finally I must thank Frank Kelsall previously of English Heritage for so generously sharing with me evidence of the highest quality. Although I am sure that he would have made very different use of the material I hope he approves of this work which is greatly indebted to him. I look forward one day to reading his book on Barbon.

Abbreviations and notes on the text

All dates have been converted to the modern calendar. Spellings and punctuations in quotations, however, have been kept as in the original source, apart from changing 'long s' to 's'. The units of measurement and money have not been modernized and are given respectively in feet and inches, and pounds, shillings and pence.

Abbreviations used in the notes

BL	British Library
BM	British Museum
CSP(Dom)	*Calendar of State Papers (Domestic)*
DNB	*Dictionary of National Biography*
EH	English Heritage
HMSO	Her Majesty's Stationary Office
OED	*Oxford English Dictionary*
PRO	Public Record Office
RCHM	Royal Commission on the Historic Monuments
RIBA	Royal Institute of British Architects
VCH	Victoria County History

Introduction

Constructing Classicism: architecture in an age of commerce

This book is about the making of London in the period 1660-1720, by which I mean 'making' in a number of senses. It is concerned with how people built, the ways in which they organized themselves to do so, the manner in which they did so, who those people were, and the methods by which buildings were both conceived and physically realized. It proceeds from the assumption that it is only by research into the processes by which architecture is produced, as well as by the more traditional examination of form, that a full understanding of the creation of architecture in any period can be reached. The purpose of the work is not solely to investigate methods of building practice but through this to attain a deeper knowledge of architecture and design overall at this time. The decision to focus on practice should therefore be seen as part of a wider trend within architectural history to move away from an analysis centred on style alone, to a more wide-ranging socio-economic approach as a means of explaining architecture and its place within the wider culture.

The first part 'The development of the city' discusses the processes and methods by which the development of the city was financed and organized. It considers the leading developers and questions to what extent the traditional model which attributes responsibility for the development of London to aristocratic land-lords is a viable one. It looks at the structure of the building industry and assesses how this was adapted to meet the demands of the production of speculative housing on a scale and at a pace never previously experienced. The second part 'The design of the city' goes beyond the first in examining not just the transformation of money and materials into built form but the translation of ideas also. The first two chapters in this part outline how concepts concerning the form of the new terraces were communicated and transmitted through the building chain and finally realized in the built product. Was this done through drawings or were traditional non-drawn design methods still used? And how important was the growing architectural literature in the spread of the new housing type? The final chapters focus on the style and layout of the new developments and ask to what extent they can be categorized, as they have often been, as a 'modernizing' phenomenon.

The core of the book is therefore concerned with issues of production and practice, rather than issues of representation and consumption. It seeks to explore the relationship between process and form. The decision to focus on architectural practice was made out of a belief that it provides an arena in which to explore the various constituent parts of architecture. The production of architecture involves a range of financial, organizational, technical, legal, constructional and design procedures through which a building emerges into built reality. The study of practice therefore offers a chance to examine the critical interface between the physical, social and economic realities within which architecture exists, and the prevailing ideologies that shape the design genesis and conception. It provides a fulcrum upon which we can posit a relationship between the forms employed and the society from which they came.

The purpose of this Introduction is to outline the main themes in the text and the historiography which it addresses. The book has been conceived within the discipline of architectural history and is primarily concerned with architectural and urban design issues. However, it attempts to place these within the broader historical context of late seventeenth- and early eighteenth-century London. It therefore draws on a range of material and relates to a number of debates in different specialisms, the most important of which are outlined below. Such an interdisciplinary approach has many pitfalls and perils, of which I am only too painfully aware. But I hope that the inevitable superficialities which result will be counterbalanced by the new insights to be gained from adopting a broader perspective on a subject area which, particularly for periods prior to the nineteenth century, has fallen behind other branches of cultural and historical studies through maintaining an overly insular outlook.

The first and perhaps most obvious area of relevance is urban studies, particularly for the early modern city. There have been a growing number of works examining towns in eighteenth-century society. Historians have stressed their function as generators of economic growth and social mobility for their surrounding regions, and London, in particular, has been seen to have played an important national role in this respect.[1] It is a commonplace among historians today that the eighteenth century 'began' not in

1700 but in terms of broad political, social and economic trends around 1660, what has become known as 'the long eighteenth century'. In terms of long-term developments this is undoubtedly correct. However, it has had the unfortunate effect of eliding the Restoration and late Stuart years with the post-1714 Georgian era, even though, as the most cursory examination will show, the previous period had individual and separate characteristics as well, not least in the cultural sphere. In London the restoration of the monarchy in 1660 released a revitalization of the city and an explosion of the economy, which had been arrested by the turmoil and strife of the 1640s and 1650s. The late 1660s to the 1680s saw the beginnings of a building boom in the capital which laid the foundations of the modern city and introduced a townscape which was to dominate, first in the capital and then throughout the country, for the next century and a half. The decades up until 1720 witnessed the birth of modern London as both a physical and commercial entity. But crucial as this pre- Hanoverian period was it has generally been written about merely as a forerunner to the better known eighteenth-century urbanism which succeeded it. The first object of this study is to reclaim the late seventeenth- and early eighteenth-century metropolis and its buildings as a distinctive and unique phase in its own right, and not simply as a precursor to the Georgian town.

With regard to architectural practice the late seventeenth and early eighteenth century in Britain has traditionally been seen as a transitional period between the medieval and the modern. It was the time at which the building process changed from being a locally organized craft-based activity into a commercial industry. Alongside this the post-1660 era is notable for another development, the introduction of classicism on a widescale for the first time in Britain. The classical style was transformed in this period from being the exclusive possession of the Court, as it had been in the sixteenth and earlier seventeenth century, into the predominant manner for both the upper and middling sorts. Most historical attention has been focused on the rise of the architect in relation to these two developments. However, the role of the craftsman, still the main figure in the building and design worlds, has remained largely ignored. Did the changes in the building industry and the introduction of classicism necessarily inhibit the design and organizational roles of the craftsman as has generally been assumed? And how was a knowledge of classicism spread among those working in the building industry, particularly in speculative housing, with which architects were not involved? The relationship between such shifts in practice and changes in style will be another major theme of this work.

The exact nature of the brand of classical design used in this period is also problematic. It has long presented an obstacle for those seeking to construct histories of British architecture. The term 'Renaissance' has never sat very comfortably on English architecture (Scottish architecture having a separate history at this date). The chronology of this island does not accord with the rest of Europe. It is not until the mid-seventeenth century that an Italian style of classicism is used by Inigo Jones and then there is a jump from his few Palladian buildings straight into the Baroque. Nor do the earliest phases, in which a selection of Renaissance ideas and motifs were incorporated into existing building types, follow a clear chronological path nor a consistent pattern of development. Earlier generations of historians, such as Reginald Blomfield and Bannister Fletcher, got round this problem by presenting the Renaissance as extending all the way from the sixteenth through the seventeenth and eighteenth to the early nineteenth century. More recent works tend to differentiate between the Tudor and early Stuart periods and the eighteenth century, leaving the late seventeenth century in an uncomfortable, intermediate position.

This creates a difficulty in the literature which for the most part uses a Wölfflinian notion of style to create a history that defines English architecture in terms of how closely it follows recognizable Italian or other European models and adopts identical designs. Both Serlio and Palladio, in particular, are used as canonical texts against which designs and motifs can have their classical credentials checked and certified. Besides the search for respectable precedents to validate 'native' architecture many historians have gone one step further and attempted to create a coherent classical tradition within England. Blomfield in his history of the English Renaissance written in 1900 presented it as a developmental process which peaked in the seventeenth century with Jones and Wren (whom he identified as the two outstanding English architects), and then suffered a morbid decline throughout the eighteenth century. As he wrote, 'The fifty years from the Restoration to the death of Queen Anne were, in fact, the culminating point of modern English architecture.'[2]

John Summerson in what remains the main textbook on the subject, *Architecture in Britain, 1530-1830* of 1953, developed an alternative history of British (as opposed to English) architectural design which moved the emphasis firmly on to the eighteenth century and to Palladianism. He himself was writing in opposition to the generation before him, principally Sir Reginald Blomfield and Sir Thomas Jackson. In the bibliography for his book he criticized their biological interpretations and their dismissal of post-Renaissance British classicism, 'To Blomfield and Jackson the

Romantic and Neo-Classic movements were merely the nameless aftermath of the Renaissance, the beginnings of an arid epoch of "archaeology" and "revivalism". The present work owes nothing consciously either to Blomfield or Jackson.'[3] In focusing on the Georgian period, and in particular Anglo-Palladianism, Summerson was reflecting a wider interest among modernist historians in an architectural approach which with its undecorated surfaces, geometricity and the primacy of the plan as form-generator chimed in with their own aesthetic preferences.[4]

The desire to smooth out and explain away the inconsistencies in British classicism was evident more recently in Giles Worsley's book, *Classical Architecture in Britain: The Heroic Age*, of 1995, in which the late seventeenth century becomes an 'interlude' in his version of British classicism.[5] Worsley asserts that his book is an attempt to overturn Summerson's teleological modernist assumptions. But in so doing he merely replaces one teleology with another, arguing for Palladianism as a constant presence from Jones in the mid-seventeenth century until the end of the eighteenth century.[6] Worsley also owes more to Summerson than he realizes for in *Georgian London* Summerson argued strongly for Palladianism as *the* paradigm for English classicism. This is discussed in Chapter 8 below.

Blomfield called the red and white style of the late seventeenth and early eighteenth century a 'vernacular architecture'.[7] It was these brick and wood structures, which ranged from large country seats and institutions to modest town terraces, which formed the majority of buildings of the time. The subsequent evolution of this style into a form of national vernacular contributed towards their exclusion from a traditional classical trajectory. But they were not considered vernacular buildings in their day, which were generally of wood, or stone in the case of churches. The new brick architecture of the town house has received particularly scant attention as it falls between the two categories into which architecture is generally divided, those of polite and vernacular. This study explores buildings below the level of the elite but still informed by the values of polite architecture. Urban housing in this period has generally been presented as little more than a poor relation to the better known glories of the Georgian terrace. The purpose of this investigation is to examine it in its own time and as far as possible on its own terms, rather than through an eighteenth-century prism. In placing such commonplace structures within a history of English architecture I am seeking to challenge accepted notions about the introduction and use of classicism and instead I hope to contribute towards the beginnings of an alternative history of architectural reception and perception in Britain.[8]

Until relatively recently there had generally been a bifurcation between historical studies of the town on the one hand and architectural ones on the other. The former concentrated on the developmental processes or social history of the town,[9] while the latter tended to focus on the individual house and present the town as a product of architectural style alone.[10] However, since the late 1980s there have been attempts to link architectural and social analyses. Dan Cruickshank and Neil Burton in *Life in the Georgian City* and Mark Girouard in his book *The English Town,* both of 1990, utilized a similar approach for the urban sphere to that taken in the latter's classic text *Life in the English Country House: A Social and Architectural History* of 1978.[11] But it is Peter Borsay, above all, who has established the pattern for what has come to be called, after the title of his book, the English Urban Renaissance, relating new ideas of beauty, comfort and convenience to the profound economic and social changes of the period.[12] He places the architecture of the town in the context of a wider process of social readjustment. Borsay argues that there was a realignment of the social strata in the period, in which the traditional elite widened to embrace the growing ranks of increasingly wealthy middling groups. This consisted of a continuous interchange between status and wealth, in the process of which definitions of gentility were redrawn. Central to the cohesion of this new social divide between polite and popular was a shared cultural identity and environment, in other words gentility was conferred through the possession of certain cultural objects and attributes (behavioural as well as physical), and in this way the wealth of the middle class could be transferred into status. Culture, including architecture, was crucial in this process. He sees the provincial town house as the means by which the middling ranks, through the copying of an aristocratic architectural language, enhanced their status and displayed their own cultural knowledge. At the same time their adoption of classical architecture differentiated them from the poor and non-gentle who inhabited the older urban areas where vernacular buildings predominated.

The new town architecture, according to Borsay's analysis, played a key role in the creation of a new polite society both through the profound physical transformation which it wrought in urban planning and scenography and through its deployment of the universalizing language of classicism. Art historians have taken a similar approach, in particular David Solkin writing about Vauxhall Gardens and David Bindman discussing Westminster Abbey. They both utilize Habermas's notion of the public sphere to emphasize the role of the city in creating new forms of building types and public spaces in which a distinctive urban culture was formed.[13] The exciting new directions opened up by Borsay and Solkin's writings on the formation of social identities in the eighteenth-century city have advanced our understanding of the subject. However, once again we need to be careful in applying the concept of the long eighteenth century to a socio-cultural development which was embryonic at best even by the 1720s. Although the relationship between the gentry and the middling ranks was an issue in the 1660-1720 period a widespread concordance with the mediating notion of politeness had not yet occurred. There is also a tendency in these works to underestimate the malleability of architectural classicism which was an evolving language rather than a static one, which changed its vocabulary and meanings throughout the period.

In 1982 McKendrick, Brewer and Plumb published their pioneering treatise *The Birth of a Consumer Society: The Commercialization of Eighteenth-Century England*, which has been enormously influential on many subsequent writers, including Borsay, and was centred around what has become known as 'emulation theory'.[14] This postulates that in the eighteenth century the growing ranks of the middle class adopted upper-class culture and consumption patterns as a matter of course. The theory assumes that copying the habits of those of a higher social rank is a normative behaviour pattern, and this has been used to explain the increase in consumer goods in the eighteenth century and hence industrial growth. Other historians have contested the social emulation pattern, doubting that the process was the simple aping of their social superiors that it is sometimes depicted to be.[15] Its critics have questioned the means by which people both acquired, understood and used their material possessions and argued that they were far more complex than the simple emulation model allows. Borsay does allow for this, as he says that one of the advantages of classicism was what he calls its 'linguistic richness', which permitted wide variations in status to be expressed while maintaining a common cultural form.[16]

This present book also takes a sceptical line towards the emulation model. Instead I have been more influenced by Peter Earle in his works *The Making of the English Middle Class: Business, Society and Family Life in London, 1660-1730* and *A City Full of People: Men and Women of London, 1650-1750* in which he argues for the emergence of a separate and distinct middle class in this period who created a culture and identity of their own.[17] This issue is explored in this study largely in relation to the producers rather than the consumers of London housing, although it also has ramifications for notions of space and its 'ownership' in the city which are discussed in Chapter 9 below. In attempting to uncover something of the speculative building world and its operations I am hoping to emphasize the crucial importance and contribution of the middling sort, as well as the gentry, in the creation of the city through a new kind of mass architecture for a society and an economy undergoing rapid transformation.

Notes

1 The best introductions to the subject are: P.J.Corfield, *The Impact of English Towns, 1700-1800*, Oxford, Oxford University Press, 1982; A.L.Beier and Roger Finlay eds, *London 1500-1700: The Making of the Metropolis*, London and New York, Longman, 1986; Peter Borsay, ed., *The Eighteenth-Century Town: A Reader in English Urban History 1688-1820*, London and New York, Longman, 1990.

2 Reginald Blomfield, *A Short History of the Renaissance Architecture in England, 1500-1800*, London, George Bell, 1900, p.297.

3 John Summerson, *Architecture in Britain, 1530-1830*, Harmondsworth, Penguin, 1983 edn, p.580.

4 The most influential work in stimulating the connection between classical and modernist design was Rudolf Wittkower's, *Architectural Principles in the Age of Humanism*, 1949, London, Academy Editions, 1973 but also his collection of lectures and essays which later appeared as *Palladio and English Palladianism*, London, Thames & Hudson, 1974; and Colin Rowe's, 'The Mathematics of the Ideal Villa', *Architectural Review*, No. 101, 1947, pp.101-4. For subsequent analyses see: Henry A.Millon, 'Rudolf Wittkower, "Architectural Principles in the Age of Humanism": Its Influence on the Development and Interpretation of Modern Architecture', *Journal of the Society of Architectural Historians*, Vol. 31, 1972, pp.83-91; Alina A.Payne, 'Rudolf Wittkower and Architectural Principles in the Age of Modernism', *Journal of the Society of Architectural Historians*, Vol. 53, 1994, pp.322-42. Eva-Marie Neumann, 'Architectural Proportion in Britain, 1945-1957', *Architectural History*, Vol. 39, 1996, pp.197-221.

5 Giles Worsley, *Classical Architecture in Britain: The Heroic Age*, New Haven and London, Yale University Press, 1995, Ch. 4. 'Late Seventeenth Century Architecture and the Baroque Interlude'.

6 See my review of Worsley, *Classical Architecture*: Elizabeth McKellar, 'Palladianism via Postmodernism: Constructing and Deconstructing the "English Renaissance"', *Art History*, Vol. 20, No.1, March 1997, pp.154-7.

7 Blomfield, *Renaissance*, p.297.

8 For an excellent book for the previous period offering just such an alternative approach see, Lucy Gent, ed., *Albion's Classicism: The Visual Arts in Britain, 1550-1660*, New Haven and London, Yale University Press, 1995.

9 For example: C. W.Chalkin, *The Provincial Towns of Georgian England: A Study of the Building Process, 1740-1820*, London, Edward Arnold, 1974; R. S.Neale, *Bath 1680-1850: A Social History*, London, Routledge & Kegan Paul, 1981.

10 For example: Dan Cruickshank and Peter Wyld, *London: The Art of Georgian Building*, London, Architectural Press, 1975.

11 Dan Cruickshank and Neil Burton, *Life in the Georgian City*, London, Viking, 1990; Mark Girouard, *The English Town*, New Haven and London, Yale University Press, 1990.

12 Peter Borsay, *The English Urban Renaissance: Culture and Society in the Provincial Town, 1660-1770*, Oxford, Clarendon Press, 1989.

13 David H.Solkin, *Painting for Money: The Visual Arts and the Public Sphere in*

Eighteenth-Century England, New Haven and London, Yale University Press, 1993, Ch. 4; David Bindman and Malcolm Baker, *Roubiliac and the Eighteenth-Century Monument*, New Haven and London, Yale University Press, 1995, Ch. 2; Jürgen Habermas, *The Structural Transformation of the Public Sphere: An Inquiry into a category of Bourgeois Society*, 1962, trans. Thomas Burger with the assistance of Frederick Lawrence, Cambridge, Mass., Polity Press, 1989.

14 See N. McKendrick, J. Brewer and J. H. Plumb, *The Birth of a Consumer Society: The Commercialization of Eighteenth-Century England*, London, Europa, 1982; H. J. Perkin, 'The Social Causes of the British Industrial Revolution', *Transactions of the Royal Historical Society*, No. 18, 1968, pp. 123-43.

15 For example, Lorna Weatherill, *Consumer Behaviour and Material Culture, 1660-1760*, London and New York, Routledge, 1988. For a more recent evaluation of the consumption debate containing a range of approaches see, J. Brewer and R. Porter, eds, *Consumption and the World of Goods*, London and New York, Routledge, 1993; on attitudes to consumption see particularly Part III, 'Production and the Meaning of Possessions', pp. 177-301, which also includes a contribution by Weatherill, pp. 206-27.

16 Borsay, *English Renaissance*, p. 232.

17 Peter Earle, *The Making of the English Middle Class: Business, Society and Family Life in London, 1660-1730*, London, Methuen, 1989; Peter Earle, *A City Full of People: Men and Women of London, 1650-1750*, London, Methuen, 1994.

I The development
of the city

Surveying the scene: conflicting perspectives on the modern city

1

Some have compared it to a Carpenter's Rule; but it much resembles the Shape (including *Southwork*) [sic] of a great *Whale*, Westminster being the under Jaw, *St James's Park* the Mouth; the *Pall mall* &c. Nd, the upper Jaw; *Cock and Pye Fields*, or the meeting of the 7 *Streets*, the Eye; the rest of the City and *Southwork* to Eastsmithfield, the Body; and thence Ed to Limehouse, the Tail; and 'tis probably in as great a Proportion the largest of Towns, as that is of Fishes. [Nd = North, Ed = East, the 7 Streets = Seven Dials]

(Edward Hatton, *A New View of London*, 1708, Introduction, p. ii)

London in the seventeenth century was one of the most important and rapidly expanding capitals in Europe. From the 1660s onwards it was transformed from an essentially medieval town of wooden buildings located within the City walls to a modern metropolis of brick and stone which broke its traditional bounds and spilled out in all directions (figures 1 and 2). Within a remarkably short space of time a new townscape of spacious streets and squares replaced the tightly packed buildings of the old City. New parks, theatres, coffee-houses and other fashionable meeting places sprang up to cater for the leisure demands of an increasingly prosperous society. Towering above them all rose St Paul's and the spires of the City churches, the twin symbols of London's triumphant survival of the disasters of the 1640s to 1660s - Civil War, Plague and Fire.

Daniel Defoe in his *A Tour through the Whole Island of Great Britain* of 1724–26 praised London as the new Rome: 'New squares, and new streets rising up every day to such a prodigy of buildings, that nothing in the world does, or ever did, equal it, except old Rome in Trajan's time.'[1] The analogy with Rome was a deliberate one, part of the ancients versus the moderns argument of the seventeenth century. In this debate it was the moderns who eventually won and contemporary London was seen as not just the equal of its great classical forebear, but as having surpassed it in its role as a commercial and productive urban entity.[2] Edward Hatton in his *A New View of London* of 1708 stressed both its ancient roots and its contemporary world economic supremacy as a trading entrepôt and the dominant financial centre of the world from the late seventeenth century onwards.

> London is generally believed, not only to be one of the most Ancient, but the most Spacious, Populous, Rich, Beautiful, Renowned and Noble Citys that we know of at this day in the World: 'Tis the seat of the *British* Empire, the Exchange of *Great Britain* and *Ireland;* the Compendium of the Kingdom, the Vitals of the Commonwealth, and the Principal Town of Traffic ... and was of so great Esteem in the time of the *Roman* conquest, as to be honoured by them with the Title of *Augusta*.[3]

The result of London's commercial pre-eminence was a new kind of metropolis; as Jules Lubbock puts it, 'the candlestick had supplanted the triumphal column and the armchair the imperial palace ... [it] was the first modern city'.[4]

London experienced phenomenal growth in the period 1500–1700, in comparison with both other parts of Britain and its continental rivals. The capital's exceptional growth arose from its expanding international trading role and was given added impetus by domestic developments. Upheavals in the provincial economies led to rural depopulation and migration to the capital, the centre of the nation's political and economic life.[5] London according to Roger Finlay and Beatrice Shearer's population analysis grew from a city of 120,000 in 1550, to 200,000 in 1600, to 375,000 in 1650, and 490,000 in 1700.[6] Other studies give a slightly different pattern with lower figures for the earlier period and estimates ranging from 556,000 to 641,000 for *c.* 1700, which accentuate still further the late seventeenth-century growth.[7]

There has been a great deal of debate about the role of urban development in early modern Europe, and its contribution to social and economic change.[8] Some of the literature has sought to minimize the impact of urbanization as a generator of cultural and economic development and has instead emphasized the contribution of the rural environment to the processes of capitalism, economic growth and increased social mobility in the early modern period.[9] Other historians, such as Penelope Corfield, have argued forcibly for the role of towns as powerful forces in the shaping of England, in particular.[10] London occupied a special and distinctive place within the country, one that, whatever its relationship to rural areas, set it apart from other urban centres and gave it a unique importance in national life.[11] In the period 1550–1700 the population of England as a whole less than doubled, whereas that of the metropolis increased fourfold. This differential in growth was especially pronounced in the second half of the seventeenth century, when the population overall declined slightly but that of London continued to increase. Some indication about the importance London assumed nationally can be gained from the fact that in 1600 nearly 5 per cent of people were Londoners; this had risen to 7 per cent in 1650 and almost 10 per cent by 1700.[12] As John Evelyn commented in 1664, London was 'a citty, by far too disproportionate already to nation'.[13]

Finlay and Shearer show that while London's population was always increasing it did not do so in an even manner. While the population in the old area of the City remained relatively stable that of London as a whole increased fourfold. The suburbs north of the river grew rapidly throughout the period, until by 1700 they contained over three times the population of the City. Whereas in 1560 the City contained three-quarters of the population and the suburbs a quarter, by 1680 it was the other way round with a quarter of the population in the City and the rest in the suburbs. Finlay and Shearer suggest that by 1650 London was already operating as a multi-centred conurbation. This picture of considerable

1] Wenceslaus Hollar, *London, A Long View*, 164 This section of Hollar's famous panorama depic the City before the destruction of the Fire Winchester House is visil in the foreground while t skyline is dominated by Paul's and the hills of Highgate and Hampstea behind. The view show the predominant form c pre-fire housing of timber-framed construction with projecting bays, steepl pitched roofs and gable and mullioned leaded windows.

suburban expansion is also borne out by Michael Power's researches on East London.[14] The population history of London is still evolving but what is even more unclear is its relationship to topographical growth. The ratio between housing supply and population is not a constant one, and this aspect of the early modern city is very little understood.[15] We should not therefore expect that the population changes outlined above resulted in a supply of houses in equal ratio in the different suburbs. Our knowledge of the topographical development of London in this period is still partial and imperfect. No precise mapping of the growth of the capital is attempted here but instead the the main areas of development will be outlined, the broad reasons for their growth discussed and their differing characteristics delineated.[16]

The first requirement for building development to take place is a plentiful supply of land. C. W. Chalkin in *The Provincial Towns of Georgian England* showed how differences in the type of land

available for development led to variations in the building pattern followed by individual towns. For example, differences in the physical nature of the ground available for building meant that marshy or low-lying land was less valuable than higher well-drained land.[17] In London the east and south of the river were generally boggier and lower than the north and the west, contributing to higher land values and a preponderance of building in the west rather than the east. The other factor Chalkin identified as being a possible constraint on expansion was the type of land-ownership, which determined the supply of land available for building. Most land at this time was held either by the Crown or

by private owners with considerable freedom of action. There was a great deal of mobility in the ownership of land following the Restoration, and many estates changed hands or were granted by the King in return for support during the Interregnum. The political situation therefore created an unusual fluidity in the land market, which helped to establish a climate in which development could take place. Lawrence Stone in his article 'The Residential Development of the West End of London in the Seventeenth Century' commented on the frequency with which large London houses were exchanged in the late seventeenth and eighteenth centuries. He suggested that this was because the nobility's primary affiliation was to their country seats, whereas their London estates did not generate the same psychological attachment.[18]

After the Restoration the most pronounced movement was in a westerly direction and this created a new and important area for the capital. It can be seen by comparing Hollar's map of 1664 with Strype's of 1720 (figures 3 and 4). Brett-James characterized the growth of the western suburbs in the seventeenth century as taking place in two stages. Up to 1660 building took place on Lincoln's Inn Fields and the ground between Chancery Lane and Drury Lane, also at Covent Garden and on land between Drury Lane and St Martin's Lane. The second phase from 1660 to 1700 saw changes in the Strand, and the growth of Westminster, St James's, St Giles's, Soho and the area to the north of Holborn.[19] There was also development to the east, particularly around Spitalfields, Stepney and Mile End New Town (figure 5).

Building spread westwards along the river to join up with the old judicial and parliamentary centre of Westminster, now the home of the Court as well, with Charles II's decision to base himself at St James's. The revival of the Court led to a stream of aristocrats, officials and gentry returning to London seeking preferment and this exacerbated the existing shortage of upper-class housing in the 1660s. Exclusive housing had always been located on the western fringes of the capital with poorer areas to the east, partly because of the higher quality of land, but also because the prevailing wind was from a westerly direction. This meant that noxious fumes were blown eastwards, while at the same time sewage and rubbish in the river floated downstream also to the east.

Lawrence Stone tried to outline why the expansion of the western suburbs occurred at this time, and why in his view this was entirely due to an increased demand for upper-class housing in the late seventeenth century.[20] He explained the demand for exclusive housing as arising from a threefold process: firstly, a great expansion in the numbers of the gentry; secondly, a growing professional class; and thirdly, an increasing tendency for both to

2] John Kip, *A Prospect of City of London, Westminster and St James's Park*, 1710. This shows the view from St James's Park looking eastwards. In the foreground is St James's Palace and Square, the market stalls to the east of the square are just visible. The curve of the Strand can be seen to the south with the spoke of Seven Dials and Lincoln's Inn Fields prominent to the east. The dense nature of the new developments of regular brick houses can be clearly seen, as can the varied nature of most of the terraces, including those of St James's Square.

live in London. The latter group made the city their permanent place of residence, while the gentry spent proportionately longer periods in town in comparison with the earlier part of the century. They came for reasons of business, politics and law, and for the social season. During the course of the seventeenth century London became safer and more attractive to the upper classes so that by the end of the 1600s it was the centre for all these activities. Adminstratively late seventeenth-century England was the most decentralized nation in Europe but culturally, legally, economically and politically it was the most centralized of all.

The clearest evidence of the requirement for gentry housing is provided by the St James's Square scheme situated next to the royal palace. The Earl of St Albans in his petition to the Crown in 1663 for the grant of the freehold wrote that:

> ye beauty of this great Towne and ye convenience of your Court are defective in point of houses fitt for ye dwellings of Noble men and other Persons of quality, and that your Majesty hath thought fitt for some Remedy hereof to appoint yt ye Place in St James Field should be built in great and good houses.[21]

St James's Square was finished in the 1670s and further developments took place around the Piccadilly area in the 1680s. However, despite the success of St James's these later developments were often presented as strange incursions into an area not previously considered part of the urban milieu. The sense of wonder that they

3] Wenceslaus Hollar, *London, Westminster and Southwark*, 1664. This map provides the clearest view of London just prior to the fire showing the well-established growth of the city in the northern and eastern suburbs plus the beginning of expansion to the west.

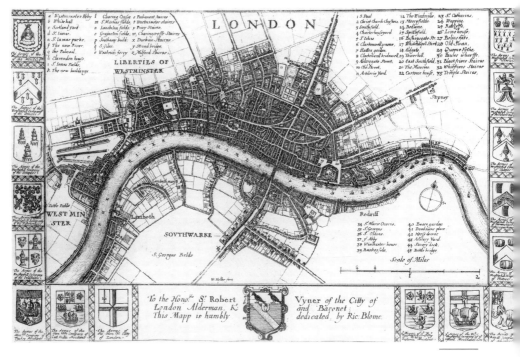

4] John Strype, *A New Plan of the City of London, Westminster and Southwark*, frontispiece to his edition of Stow's *Survey*, 1720. Strype's map meticulously details the new developments. There has been considerable expansion in the east, while to the north there are new buildings in Hoxton and Bloomsbury. The greatest area of growth is to the west where Strype includes the just completed Hanover Square scheme as well as the first developments to the north of the Oxford road on the Harley-Cavendish estate, at that time unfinished.

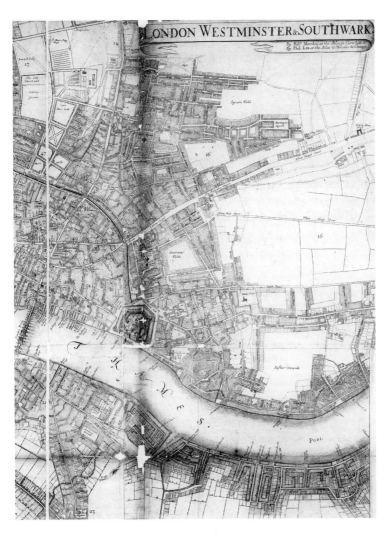

5] Robert Morden and Philip Lea, *London, Westminster and Southwark*, 1690. This section of the map shows the growth of the eastern suburbs. The major area of expansion was to the north in Spitalfields with other developments taking place in Whitechapel, Wapping and East Smithfield. Barbon's square at Wellclose is visible above Ratcliffe Highway, while in the north-west corner the open spaces of Moore Fields with its planted avenues of trees and Bunhill Fields stand out.

engendered and the huge potential risks associated with building are conveyed by John Evelyn's comments on the development of the nearby Albemarle House in the 1680s:

> certain rich bankers and mechanics, who gave for it and the grounds about £35,000; they designe a new towne as it were, and a most magnificent piazza. 'Tis said they have already material towards it with what they sold of the house alone, more worth than what they paid for it, see the vicissitudes of earthly things. I am astonished at the demolition, nor less at the little army of labourers and artificers levelling the ground, laying foundations and contriving great buildings, at an expense of £200,000 if they perfect their design.[22]

The pre-Civil War developments had largely taken place in an area abutting the City centred around Lincoln's Inn Fields and Covent Garden. This led to subsequent infill building between Chancery Lane and Drury Lane up to St Martin's Lane. However, not all the post-1660 building focused on Westminster, and other areas adjacent to the existing urban core also expanded, particularly to the north of Holborn in Bloomsbury and along the Strand. For a time it was unclear as to where the dominant focus would be. Even within the short period covered by this book some areas had already undergone a rise and fall in their fortunes, particularly in the central zone. John Strype in his 1720 updating of Stow's *Survey of London* provided a commentary on the social standing of the different areas he described, through his use of the terms 'well', 'good' and 'poor'. His work can be used to construct a social morphology of the city in a similar fashion to that of Charles Booth in his great book *Life and Labour of the People of London* of 1889–90.

The Bloomsbury area to the north was considered as exclusive as St James's and maintained its fashionability throughout the period. The neighbourhood was much prized for healthiness and airiness, and development was continuing in the 1720s on the Rugby estate and in Lamb's Conduit Fields. Other places such as Soho with its large, transient, cosmopolitan population and chaotic street plan saw a greater fluctuation in their fortunes. F. Colsoni in his tourist guide to London of 1693 recommended his European readers, 'Souvez vous fur tout d'aller voir la belle place de Soho, qui s'appelle aussi Kings Square & Monmouths Square.'[23] John Strype writing in the 1720s praised the square but commented on the nearby messy Newport House redevelopment as follows: 'It is for the Generality Inhabited by the French; as indeed are most of these Streets and Alleys, which are ordinarily built and the rents cheap.'[24]

As new areas developed, contemporaries began to differentiate between them and to comment on their distinctive characteristics. Celia Fiennes in her *Journeys* wrote that, 'London is the Citty properly for trade, Westminster for the Court'.[25] Defoe in his *Tour* observed that London fell into three distinct parts, 'the city, the Court, and the out-parts':

> The city is the centre of its commerce and wealth. The Court of its gallantry and splendour. The out-parts of its numbers and mechanics; and in all these, no city in the world can equal it. Between the Court and city, there is a constant communication of business to that degree, that nothing in the world can come up to it.[26]

Others such as Addison saw the essential division as being into two main parts:

> When I consider this great city in its several quarters and divisions, I look upon it as an aggregate of various nations, distinguished from each other by their respective customs, manners and interests. The Courts of

two countries do not so much differ from one another as the Court and the City in their peculiar ways of life and conversation. In short the inhabitants of St. James's, nothwithstanding they live under the same laws and speak the same language, are a distinct people from those of Cheapside, who are likewise removed from those of the Temple on the one side and those of Smithfield on the other by several climates and degrees in their way of thinking and conversing together.[27]

Addison as a propagandist for a new form of polite urban culture naturally emphasized the gap between Court and City, whereas Defoe, with a sharper eye for the economic pulse of the town, discerned the umbilical cord which linked the two worlds, namely money. He made explicit the relationship between the financial operations of the City and the presence of the nobility in town:

> stock-jobbing: a trade, which once bewitched the nation to its ruin, and which, though reduced very much, and recovered from that terrible infatuation, which once overspread the whole body of the people, yet is still a negotiation, which is so vast in its extent, that almost all the men of substance in England are more or less concerned in it ... and this is one thing which makes such a constant daily intercourse between the Court part of the town, and the city; and this is given as one of the principal causes of the prodigious conflux of the nobility and gentry from all parts of England to London, more than ever was known in former years, viz. that many thousands of families are so deeply concerned in those stocks, and find it so absolutely necessary to be at hand to take advantage of buying and selling, as the sudden rise or fall of the price directs, and the loss they often sustain by their ignorance of things when absent, and the knavery of brokers and others, whom, in their absence, they are bound to trust, that they find themselves obliged to come up and live constantly here, or at least, most part of the year.[28]

Defoe wrote that there had been rivalry between the Court and the City in Charles II's reign.

> But the city, I say, had gained the ascendant, and is now made so necessary to the Court (as before it was thought rather a grievance) that now we see the Court itself the daily instrument to encourage and increase the opulence of the city, and the city again, by its real grandeur, made not a glory only, but an assistance and support to the Court, on the greatest and most sudden emergencies ... The equality, however, being thus preserved, and a perfect good understanding between the Court and city having so long flourished, this union contributes greatly to the flourishing circumstances of both, and the public credit is greatly raised by it; for it was never known, that the city, on any occasion, was so assistant to the government, as it has been since this general good agreement. No sum is so great, but the Bank has been able to raise.[29]

The opulence and grandeur of the City that Defoe stressed was not, unlike other parts of London, the result of expansion but

6] W. Lodge and
. Tempest, *The Monument*,
c. 1677 (detail). The
Monument, 1671–77, was
designed to commemorate
he tragedy of the Fire and
multaneously to celebrate
London's triumphal
covery from the disaster,
depicted through the
arrative of rebirth shown
in the bas-relief on the
edestal. This view shows
he newly rebuilt City with
its wide roads, paved
sidewalks and thriving
commercial enterprises.
Besides the prominent
shop fronts and displays,
the main premises on
ither side of 'the Square'
e also businesses, evident
by the low band of
continuous windows on
he right and the enclosed
display window and
warehouse-type building
on the left. The
alustraded roof terraces,
enthouse projections and
alconies were all common
features at the time.

rather of rebuilding necessitated by the Fire of 1666. This led to the transformation of the commercial heartland from a tightly packed warren of medieval buidings into a modern landscape of regularized streets of brick-built properties: a metamorphosis that literally helped blur the boundaries between the old and the new part of the capital (figure 6). Defoe also realized that a bipartite division of the city was too simplistic a model and he mentioned the existence of intermediate areas, particularly around the Strand: 'Charing-Cross is a mixture of Court and city; Man's Coffee-house is the Exchange Alley of this part of the town, and 'tis perpetually thronged with men of business, as the others are with men of play and pleasure'.[30] The Strand area, along with Bloomsbury, was the first to see large-scale redevelopment after the Restoration. This was largely pioneered by Nicholas Barbon and provides interesting examples of the mixing of residential and commercial functions. Adjacent to the City at the eastern end of the Strand the redevelopment of Essex House took place from the mid-1670s onwards. This involved the conversion of a large aristocratic mansion and its grounds on the riverfront into a series of streets. A similar approach was taken at York and Arundel Houses and today Somerset House is the sole survivor of this earlier settlement pattern. Brett-James commenting on this trend says it is hard to say exactly why it occurred, but in these three cases the owners were all Royalists who had grown poor in the King's service. It was also of course part of the wider shift to the west, and as the aristocratic palaces that lined the Thames from the Temple to Westminster were destroyed, a new enclave of palaces along Piccadilly rose to take their place.

The Strand developed as a major commercial nexus linking the City and the Court. Strype wrote: 'That Part of the Strand, which is in this Parish, is the best Part of it, both for Largeness of the Street and the Goodness of the Buildings, and Ability of the Inhabitants, who drive a considerable Trade, being so near the Court ... This parish of St Clement Danes is large, well built and inhabited, by many Persons both of the Nobility and Gentry, as well as rich Tradesmen.'[31] The mixed residential and commercial nature of the area was planned from the beginning. The Duke of Beaufort who redeveloped his land and bought Buckingham House at Chelsea as his new home, had a smaller house built for himself on the Strand site 'to dispatch business in'.[32] The routes to the river were of the utmost importance and some streets such as Milford Lane became principally traffic routes to and from the wharfs. Nicholas Barbon's device of a triumphal arch to hide the commercial waterfront from the streets behind was the most dramatic architectural expression of the attempt to unite residential and commercial functions in one scheme (figure 7).

7] The Essex Street Arch WC2, c. 1675. The Arch cleverly provides a grand terminating feature to the view along Essex Street, while at the time masking the transition between the residential street on one side and the wharfs and commercial activity situated by the Thames on the other.

The City recognized the threat from the development of an adjacent commercial area and in 1675 presented a petition against the Essex House scheme protesting against:

> the great Mischief and Inconveniences dayly arising to the Citty from ye multitude of New Building erected in the Outparts thereof, by which meanes the Citty is deprived of many Thousands of her Inhabitants and a vast number of new Built House within the same stand empty and unemployed; that beside those buildings erected upon new foundations, the houses of many noblemen situate in the Strand and other places near the said city are now converting into private hands and intended to be so employed, which, if permitted will tend to the ruine of said citty already languishing under great decay of their Retayle Trade.[33]

The City also petitioned against various other schemes in the 1660s and 1670s and their sense of unease was recorded by Pepys who mentioned the opposition from them to the proposed building at St James's in 1663: 'the building of St. James's by my Lord St Albans, which is now about, and which the city Stomach, I perceive highly, but dare not oppose it'.[34]

Besides these large-scale projects small schemes were being built everywhere involving pocket-handkerchief-sized plots. Such developments have been less recognized, partly because they are less well documented, and also perhaps because they are generally less immediately identifiable as new buildings on maps. They were particularly common in areas squeezed between existing buildings as at St Giles-in-the-Fields and St Martin-in-the-Fields which lay between the already urbanized strip along the river and around Covent Garden, and the more major developments taking place to the north. Small-scale redevelopment was common along existing thoroughfares such as St Martin's Lane where existing houses were replaced by newer, more up-to-date ones. It also predominated in the outlying villages and settlements on the fringes of London.

It seems natural to us that the house-building boom at the end of the seventeenth century was a necessary and welcome phenomenon. It provided new houses with increased standards of space and comfort, such as can be seen in figure 8. It stimulated economic growth by providing investment opportunities for some and employment opportunities for many. Finally, it ensured the expansion of London beyond the old City walls, which no longer contained sufficient space for an international trading capital.

However, to contemporaries the rapid despoliation of what had so recently been green fields by rows and rows of houses was a less benign phenomenon. The astonishingly rapid rate at which building took place must have been troubling to many, even those who appreciated its benefits, as their accustomed habitat was transformed so abruptly and irrevocably before their eyes. The experience of the city did not end at the point on the map which shows the limit of building. The open spaces surrounding the city were equally important as sites of recreation, food production, industry and military training. Contemporaries saw the green fields which they named, had long acquaintance with and used for various activities as part of their day-to-day environment; not as left-over areas waiting to be developed, as historians have tended to interpret them. We should not therefore see the development process or the growth of London as either an inevitable or an inexorable process. There remained powerful obstacles to new building both ideological and institutional.

From the late sixteenth century onwards building was prohibited in London by legislation and Royal decree, leading to proclamations against the practice in 1580 and 1602 and an Act of Parliament in 1593.[35] These early proclamations seem to have arisen from a genuine anxiety that new building would lead to an influx of the poor and that this in turn would lead to food shortages, famine, plague, and potential political and social unrest. However, for most of the seventeenth century, at least from the time of Charles I onwards, the restrictive building policy seems to have been a more cynical ploy to raise revenue. There is, as Brett-James says, a fundamental paradox in the fact that although new buildings were forbidden, for example under the proclamations of 1625 and 1630, yet at the same time these edicts issued regulations for controlling construction and brickmaking. Jules Lubbock deduces from this that their secondary objective was to to regulate the appearance and materials of new buildings and in so doing they established a new model for urban housing.[36]

This set the pattern for the rest of the century. Draconian legislation against new building was passed under the Protectorate in 1657. It was followed after the Restoration by less extreme measures outlined in proclamations in 1661 and 1671. If the primary motive was financial this would explain the continuation of the restrictions, even under Charles II, when large planned developments became commonplace. Thus there grew up a dual system. Firstly the official one, whereby large developers petitioned the Crown for a licence prior to building. The scheme was then submitted to the Surveyor General, most particularly to ensure compliance with the building regulations, and if approval was received a licence would be granted. At the same time the illegal system of unlicensed building continued, which was subject to fines, when the authorities chose to investigate.

The 1671 proclamation was followed by a spate of petitions to the Privy Council for both large and small schemes. These range from one Peter le Caine who requested permission to finish

building three houses in Stepney 'for a Work Shopp to sett up severall Broad Looms in'[37] to grandees such as the Earl of Exeter and the Duke of Buckingham seeking to redevelop their mansion sites.[38] The system made it easier for aristocrats who had the ear of the King to petition for permission for large-scale developments. The one person who doesn't feature in the Privy Council records as requesting permission to build is Nicholas Barbon, the major developer of the day. The Crown tried unsuccessfully to stop two of Barbon's schemes at Essex House (where building had already begun) and at Red Lion Fields, suggesting that the authorities were relatively powerless in controlling unlicensed building, especially once it was underway.[39]

However, although the building restrictions must have provided the Crown with a tidy revenue sum, they are also evidence of more deep-seated fears about what a free market in housing might produce. The desire to regulate and control building can be seen as part of a much more widespread anxiety about the growth of the city. The physical reshaping of the urban landscape led to a concomitant disruption of patterns of land usage, accessibility to various amenities and a reordering of spatial and mental boundaries.

The first and most immediately obvious way in which the new developments were unsettling was their environmental impact. Complaints regarding new houses varied from the blocking of the 'ancient lights' of established properties,[40] to the disturbance of the existing infrastructure of roads and water supplies. At Golden Square a licence to build was initially refused by the Crown because of its anxiety that the sewers of the newly built area might interfere with the water supply to Whitehall and St James's Palace.[41] In relation to building on Little Lincoln's Inn Field in 1693 owners of houses in Chancery Lane worried about their access claimed that, 'for time out of mind the owners and occupiers have enjoyed foot and vehicle way through a piece of waste ground on the west of their houses', which Sir Thomas Cooke and Nicholas Barbon were now threatening to build over.[42]

The opposition at Lincoln's Inn Fields demonstrates the psychological disruption caused by changing patterns of land use. In their evidence protesting against the development the members of Lincoln's Inn stressed the public benefit that such common land provided:

> The inhabitants of those parts of the Cities of London and Westminster near adjoining to the said Little Lincolns Inn Fields as also all other his Majesty's liege people have time out of mind had the free use of the said Little Lincolns Inn Fields to divert, walk and air themselves in at their wills and pleasures at all times and all seasons.[43]

A similar dispute arose between the Society of Gray's Inn and Nicholas Barbon over his plans for Red Lion Fields in 1684. The lawyers again couched their complaint not just in terms of their own interest, which lay in certain common ways they had over the Fields, but also in terms of the loss of an amenity for the wider public. They said that the new development would be to the prejudice not only of the Society, but also of 'persons of quality that resort there'. The proposed development would prevent their walks in the Fields for their health and recreation and would result in the loss of their 'wholesome air'.[44] But Barbon dismissed these comments saying that they came, 'principally from the private interest or design of some gentlemen of the Inn who have houses near the field in Holborn or Bloomsbury, backing on to the field'.[45]

It was this dispute which led to the famous battle in Red Lion Fields between Barbon's workmen who tried to dig trenches before the matter had been settled and the lawyers, 'whereof the said Society came forth in a body and wounded several of the workmen and beat them out of possession'.[46] This was however following considerable provocation, as the following representation to the Privy Council of 24 July 1684 indicates:

> The said Barbon did of late and particularly upon the 11th day of June last march about the fields in the head of two hundred men, shouting and hallowing within the hearing of Grays Inn, and waving their hats

as by way of challenge to the gentlemen of the Society to come out and encounter them, the said Barbon himself exhorting them that they should not be discouraged for he would back them with a thousand the next morning.[47]

Housing developments led to a reordering of boundaries and priorities which threatened the existing use of land around the city for common purposes. As the outer edge of the city constantly increased, those who had been accustomed to living within easy reach of green fields found an ever-expanding belt of new housing between them and the countryside beyond. Unhappiness about this is evident in the representation to the Privy Council about the Red Lion Fields development, in which it is said that Barbon's scheme will, 'very much annoy all the buildings in and about Bloomsbury'.[48]

Londoners prior to the late seventeenth century were used to thinking of their city as a physical whole, in its entirety. This conception of the city as an entity can be seen in representations such as Hollar's and Sutton Nicholls' which present the city from a bird's-eye viewpoint as a perceptible, viewable and therefore comprehensible organism (see figures 1 and 53). Furthermore they present the city as situated within a precise landscape of hills, rivers and surrounding features. The city exists in relation to the country-side around it, which together form a recognized *locale*. What was disturbing about the new developments was that they disrupted established notions of spatiality and land use, not just within the built-up area, but also between the buildings and the landscape. Existing expectations became deordered and disorientated by the new developments which usurped present functions and replaced them with a physical world which did not correlate to traditional patterns of use in and around the city. The spatial continuity between built and unbuilt became disturbed in the process as old certainties disappeared.

This sense of dislocation is summed up by Defoe whose anxiety about the mushrooming of the metropolis is expressed in a desire for physical wholeness and completeness:

It is the disaster of London, as to the beauty of its figure, that it is thus stretched out in buildings, just at the pleasure of every builder, or undertaker of buildings ... and this has spread the face of it in a most straggling, confused manner, out of all shape; whereas the city of Rome, though a monster for greatness, yet was in a manner, round, with very few irregularities in its shape.[49]

This was the natural consequence of the new form of commercial city which grew in relation to the demands of the market, rather than in accordance with a preordained scheme. In this respect, at least, the ancient model was in Defoe's eyes superior to the modern one. Other opposition came from those who deplored not the fact of building, but rather the manner in which it was undertaken. Nicholas Hawksmoor writing to George Clarke in 1715 bemoaned the missed opportunity after the Fire both within and without the City:

> When London was Burnt in 1666, out of that fatall accidentall mischief one might have expected some good when ye Phoenix was to rise again, vitz. a convenient regular well built Citty, excellent, skillfull, honest Artificers made by ye greatness & Quality of ye worke in rebuilding such a Capital. but instead of these, we have noe city, nor Streets, nor Houses, but a Chaos of Dirty Rotten Sheds, allways Tumbling or takeing fire, with winding Crooked passages (Scarse practicable) Lakes of Mud and Rills of Stinking Mire Running through them.
>   The Workmen soe far from skill or honesty that ye Generall part of 'em are more brutall & Stupid then [sic], in ye remotest part of Britain and the longer they worke the worse they grow, as you may see in all ye Additional Scoundrell Streets they are Continuously Cobling up. to Sell by wholesale and this is not all in London, for this sort of Vermin has run, & Spread all over ye Country, and as they have Ruind ye Capitall Soe have they all ye Other Citys & Townes in Engld.[50]

John Evelyn gave more consideration than most of his contemporaries to the problems and planning of London. In the 1661 tract, commissioned by Charles II, *Fumifugium: Or the Inconveniencie of the Aer and Smoak of London Dissipated. Together with some Remedies humbly proposed*, Evelyn sketched his vision of a new city, well before the trauma of the Great Fire. He lambasted the existing conditions of the city and looked forward to the day when it might be rebuilt along the lines of Rome and the other European capitals with which he had become familiar in his exile during the Protectorate.

> That this Glorious and Antient City, which from Wood might be rendered Brick, and (like another Rome) from Brick made Stone and Marble ... should wrap her stately head in Clowds of Smoake and Sulphur, so full of Stink and Darknesse, I deplore with just Indignation. That the Buildings should be compos'd of such a congestion of mishapen and extravagent Houses, that the streets should be so narrow and incommodious in the very Centre, and busiest places of Intercourse: That there should be so ill and uneasie a form of paving under foot, so troublesome and malicious a disposure of the Spouts and Gutters overhead, are particulars worthy of Reproof and Reformation: because it is here by rendred a Labyrinth in its principal passages, and a continual Wet-day after the storm is over.[51]

However, when the expansion of the city came, Evelyn too was bitterly disappointed with the result. He wrote of 'Vulgar Workmen, who for want of some more solid Directions, Faithful and easy Rules in this Nature, fill as well whole Cities as Private Dwellings with Rubbish and a thousand Infirmities'.[52] It is interesting that even Evelyn, the great advocate of new buildings, as his solution to the problems of pollution in *Fumifugium*, suggested as his most radical proposal the creation of a series of 'plantations' around the city. These comprised belts of trees, orchards and gardens separating the city from the noxious industries which were to be sited beyond them, an early form of green belt and occupational zoning. Evelyn then, like Defoe, ultimately saw the solution to London's problems in terms of containment and control rather than *laissez-faire* expansion.

Unease about what seemed to be the uncontrollable growth of the metropolis sprang not only from legal and environmental concerns, but was linked to a broader debate about the growth of trade and consumption.[53] The effects of increasingly diverse economic activity and the production of an ever expanding range of material goods available to a wider sector of the population became a matter of acute concern in the late seventeenth and eighteenth century. It was felt that this had led to social competition, social and economic mobility and emulative consumption. All of these threatened both traditional ideas of social hierarchy and moral and ethical notions about values such as luxury, competition, emulation and vanity which were transformed by economic rationalists, such as Bernard Mandeville, from traditional moral sins into economic virtues.[54] The furore surrounding Mandeville's publication of *The Fable of the Bees* in 1724 demonstrates how fundamentally disturbing and how far from being resolved the argument was even by the early to mid-eighteenth century.

Neil McKendrick places the intellectual origins of the revolution in consumption in the 1690s, but the widespread acceptance of these ideas did not come until the second half of the eighteenth century.[55] In the late seventeenth and early eighteenth century this was a highly contentious matter. An interesting examination of the issues can be found in the writings of one of McKendrick's intellectual pioneers and a key figure as a developer in this book, Nicholas Barbon. It is interesting to consider the gap between economic speculators, such as himself, who welcomed the freedom that the new markets brought, and the majority of people who found such activity profoundly disturbing to their entire moral, social and political understanding of the world.[56]

In his *Discourse of Trade* of 1690 Barbon took on the mercantilists, such as Mun, who had argued that trade must be restricted in order to preserve a balance of payments, and instead advocated the benefits of elastic and expanding domestic demand. He emphasized the role of fashion in promoting consumption and creating new markets. This put Barbon in the vanguard of those formulating a new attitude to luxury and consumption.[57] Prior to this in 1685 he had published *An Apology for the Builder Or a Discourse Shewing the Cause and Effects of the Increase of Building*, written the year after his run-in with Gray's Inn. The disquiet that many felt about the expansion of London is clear from Barbon's opening remarks. He writes that: 'the Artists of this Age have already made the City of London the Metropolis of Europe, and if it be compared for the number of good Houses, for its many and large Piazzas, for its richness of Inhabitants, it must be allowed the largest, best built, and richest City in the world'.[58] But rather than admiration among people this has led to envy and astonishment, 'to see every year a new Town added to the old one … and are angry with the Builders for making her so great'.[59]

> The Citizens are afraid that the Building of new Houses will lessen the Rent and Trade of old ones, and fancy the Inhabitants will remove on a sudden like Rats that they say run away from old Houses before they tumble. The Country Gentleman is troubled at the new Buildings for fear they should draw away their Inhabitants, and depopulate the Country … And both agree that the increase of Building is prejudicial to the Government, and use for Argument a simile from those that have the Rickets, fansying the City to be the Head of the Nation, and that it will grow too big for the Body.[60]

In other words the same arguments were applied to housing as had been to trade. That is, that there was a finite amount of trade or houses to go round, and an obvious increase of houses or trade in one direction would unbalance the system and lead to decreases elsewhere. Put in this ideological context one can understand the immense hostility and unease that the new housing developments provoked.

In *An Apology for the Builder* Barbon sought to counter this argument, firstly, by arguing that there is a natural population growth, so that the need for houses is not static but is constantly increasing. Secondly, by arguing, as he does in *A Discourse of Trade*, that trade is 'the making and selling all sorts of commodities to supply their occasions'.[61]

> But this is certain, that there are no more Houses built every year than are occasion for; because there are Tenants for the Houses, when built, and a continuance every year to build more. For the Builders will do as other Traders, who, when the Market is overstocked with their Commodities, and no occasion for those already made, forbear to make any more, or bring them to Market, till a new occasion requireth them. And when they find they cannot lett those already built, they will desist from building, and need no Act of Parliament to hinder them. So that we may as well complain that there is too much Cloth and Stuff made,

too much Corn sowed, too many Sheep or Oxen bred, as that there are too many Houses built; too many Taylors, Shoo-makers, Bakers and Brewers, as there are too many Builders.[62]

With his firm grasp of concepts such as the law of supply and demand, the operation of the markets and commodity value it is no wonder that Barbon's business operations were a mystery to his age. He went on to argue not only that house building would necessarily stay in a ratio to demand, but that new buildings far from being detrimental to a town were in fact beneficial to it. This was because they raised land values and hence rents not only in the new buildings, but in old properties which were adjacent as well.

> And the Rents in some of these Out-parts have been within this few years considerably advanced by the addition of New Buildings that are beyond them. As for instance, the Rents of the Houses in Bishopsgate-Street, the Minories etc. are raised from fifteen or sixteen pounds per annum, to be now worth thirty, which was by the increase of buildings in Spittle-fields, Shadwell and Ratcliff-Highway. And at the other end of the Town those Houses in the Strand and Charing Cross are worth now fifty and threescore pounds per annum, which within this thirty years were not lett for above twenty pounds per annum; which is by the great addition of buildings since made in St James's, Leicester Fields, and other adjoyning parts. But in those out-parts where no New Buildings have been added, as in Old Street, Grub Street, and all that side of the city which does not increase, Houses continue much of the same value, as they were twenty years ago.[63]

New development was also beneficial to the trade both of the city and of the country because they provided a new area 'for the Wholesale-Trader to traffick in. The inhabitants of these places do eat, wear clothes, and furnish their houses.'[64] It is upon building, he argues, that ultimately all the other trades depend. The growth of the capital is essential therefore for the development of the nation, and he cited Amsterdam as a contemporary example of a city made great through expansion. Finally Barbon looked forward to a day when London would not only be a European centre, but a 'metropolis of the world' based on a trading empire across the seas.

> For the Metropolis is the heart of a Nation, through which the Trade and Commodities of it circulate, like the blood through the heart ... and if that declines, or be obstructed in its growth, the whole body falls into consumption ... And if those Gentlemen that fancy the City to be the Head of the Nation, would but fancy it like the heart, they would never be afraid of its growing too big. For I never read of such a disease, that the Heart was too big for the Body.[65]

However, the majority of opinion at the time compared the swelling of London not to the natural circulation of the blood but to

a disease or malformation which distorted the body beyond its
natural shape. Tristram Shandy's father in his customary manner
in Laurence Sterne's novel discourses on decay and degeneracy in
relation to the corporeal and the urban:[66]

> He was very sensible that all political writers upon the subject had
> unanimously agreed and lamented, from the beginning of Queen
> Elizabeth's reign down to his own time, that the current of men and
> money towards the metropolis, upon one frivolous errand or another,—
> set in so strong,—as to become dangerous to our civil rights,—though, by
> the bye,—a current was not the image he took most delight in,—a
> distemper was here his favourite metaphor, and he would run it down
> into a perfect allegory, by maintaining it was identically the same in the
> body national as in the body natural, where the blood and spirits were
> driven up into the head faster than they could find their ways down:—a
> stoppage of circulation must ensue, which was death in both cases.[67]

Although Barbon might argue for the growth of London as a
'natural' phenomenon, the majority of opinion was not in favour
of free market growth but viewed such developments with great
suspicion and attempted to disrupt or control them through a
variety of means. The profound psychological and spatial displace-
ment which resulted from the swallowing up of open areas by new
building should not be underestimated. It marked the beginning
of that spatial segregation and privatization of the city which characterized London in the eighteenth and nineteenth centuries as a
result of estate development.[68] It created a conflicting dynamic in
the city both to maintain open space and to develop new areas of
housing; for on the one hand growth and expansion, and on the
other control and containment.

Notes

1 Daniel Defoe, *A Tour through the Whole Island of Great Britain, 1724-26*, ed. Pat
   Rogers, Harmondsworth, Penguin, 1971, p. 286.

2 For more on this see, Jules Lubbock, *The Tyranny of Taste: The Politics of Architecture and Design in Britain, 1550-1960*, New Haven and London, Yale University
   Press, 1995, pp. 3-7.

3 Edward Hatton, *A New View of London*, London, 1708, Preface, p. i.

4 Lubbock, *Taste*, p. 7.

5 A. L. Beier and Roger Finlay, eds, *London 1500-1700: The Making of the Metropolis*,
   London and New York, Longman, 1986, Introduction, pp. 11-14.

6 Roger Finlay and Beatrice Shearer, 'Population Growth and Suburban Expan-
   sion', in Beier and Finlay, *London 1500-1700*, pp. 37-59. Also see, E. A. Wrigley and
   R. S. Schofield, *The Population History of England, 1541-1871*, London, Edward
   Arnold, 1981.

7 For a summary see, Vanessa Harding, 'The Population of London, 1550-1700: A
   Review of the Published Evidence', *London Journal*, Vol. 15, No. 2, 1990, pp. 111-28.

8 Two useful texts are: Philip Abrams and E. A. Wrigley, eds, *Towns in Societies:*

Essays in Economic History and Historical Sociology, Cambridge, Cambridge University Press, 1978; P. Sweezy *et al.*, *The Transition from Feudalism to Capitalism*, London, Verso, 1978.

9 See for example: Fernand Braudel, *Capitalism and Material Life, 1400-1800*, London, Fontana, 1974; Peter Clark and Paul Slack, *English Towns in Transition, 1500-1700*, Oxford, Oxford University Press, 1976; Peter Clark and Paul Slack, *Crisis and Order in English Towns, 1500-1700*, London, Routledge & Kegan Paul, 1972.

10 P. J. Corfield, *The Impact of English Towns, 1700-1800*, Oxford, Oxford University Press, 1982.

11 E. A. Wrigley, 'A Simple Model of London's Importance in Changing English Society and Economy, 1650-1750', *Past and Present*, No. 37, 1967, pp. 44-70, reprinted in Abrams and Wrigley, *Towns in Societies*; Valerie Pearl, 'Change and Stability in Seventeenth-Century London', *London Journal*, Vol. 5, No. 1, May 1979, pp. 3-34; Beier and Finlay, *London 1500-1700*.

12 Finlay and Shearer, 'Population Growth and Suburban Expansion', p. 38.

13 John Evelyn, *Diary*, 12 June 1664, ed. E. S. de Beer, Oxford, Clarendon Press, 1955.

14 M. J. Power, 'Shadwell: The Development of a London Suburban Community in the Seventeenth Century', *London Journal*, Vol. 4, No. 1, 1978, pp. 29-46; M. J. Power, 'The East and West in Early-Modern London', in E. W. Ives, R. J. Knecht and J. J. Scarisbrick, eds, *Wealth and Power in Tudor England*, London, Athlone Press, 1978, pp. 169-70; M. J. Power, 'East London Housing in the Seventeenth Century', in Clark and Slack, *Crisis and Order in English Towns*, pp. 237-62.

15 Francis Shepherd, Victor Belcher and Philip Cottrell, 'The Middlesex and Yorkshire Deeds Registries and the Study of Building Fluctuations', *London Journal*, Vol. 5, No. 2, 1979, pp. 176-217, argue that it was the demographic cycle not the trade cycle which was the major determinant of the building pattern in eighteenth-century London.

16 For a detailed analysis of individual areas see, Norman Brett-James, *The Growth of Stuart London*, London, London and Middlesex Archaeological Society with George Allen & Unwin, 1935.

17 C. W. Chalkin, *The Provincial Towns of Georgian England: A Study of the Building Process, 1740-1820*, London, Edward Arnold, 1974, p. 70.

18 Lawrence Stone, 'The Residential Development of the West End of London in the Seventeenth Century', in B. C. Malament, ed., *After the Reformation*, Pennsylvania, University of Pennsylvania Press, 1980, pp. 167-212.

19 Brett-James, *Stuart London*, pp. 151-2.

20 Stone, 'Residential Development'.

21 PRO SP44/13 p. 340.

22 As quoted in Brett-James, *Stuart London*, pp. 383-4.

23 F. Colsoni, *Le Guide de Londres*, London, 1693, p. 17.

24 J. Strype, *The Survey of London*, London, 1720, Bk VI, Ch. 6, p. 86.

25 Christopher Morris, ed., *The Illustrated Journeys of Celia Fiennes 1685-c. 1712*, Stroud, Sutton, 1995, p. 222.

26 Defoe, *Tour*, p. 306.

27 Joseph Addison, *The Spectator*, No. 403, 12 June 1712.

28 Defoe, *Tour*, pp. 306-7.

29 Defoe, *Tour*, pp. 308-9.

30 Defoe, *Tour*, pp. 327-8.

31 Strype, *Survey*, Bk IV, Ch. 7, pp. 111, 116.

32 Strype, *Survey*, Bk IV, Ch. 7, p. 119.

33 PRO PC/2/64 p. 395.

34 Samuel Pepys, *Diary*, 2 September 1663, ed. Robert Latham and William Matthews, London, Bell & Hyman, 1970-83.

35 For more information on official restrictions on building see, Brett-James, *Stuart London*, Chs 3, 4, 12; Lubbock, *Taste*, pp. 25-9.

36 Lubbock, *Taste*, p. 28.

37 PRO PC/2/63 p. 4.

38 PRO PC/2/63.

39 PRO PC/2/64 pp. 394, 398, 404; PC/2/70 p. 208.

40 PRO C10/128/17, C8/352/47.

41 *Survey of London, St James Westminster*, Pt II, Vol. XXI, London, Athlone Press, 1960, pp. 138-9.

42 PRO C8/352/47.

43 PRO C8/379/4.

44 PRO C9/92/3.

45 PRO C9/92/3.

46 PRO C9/457/109, C10/230/7.

47 PRO PC/2/70.

48 PRO PC/2/70.

49 Defoe, *Tour*, p. 287.

50 Letter 17 February 1715 to Dr George Clarke, 'The Explanation', reproduced in K. Downes, *Hawksmoor*, London, Zwemmer, 1959, Appendix A, No. 58.

51 John Evelyn, *Fumifugium: Or the Inconveniencie of the Aer and Smoak of London Dissipated. Together with some Remedies humbly proposed*, London, 1661, 'To the Reader'.

52 John Evelyn, 'An Account of Architects and Architecture', Preface to his translation of Roland Fréart, *A Parallel of the Antient Architecture with the Modern*, London, 1707, p. 5.

53 See: Neil McKendrick, John Brewer and J. H. Plumb, *The Birth of a Consumer Society: The Commercialization of Eighteenth-Century England*, London, Europa, 1982; Lorna Weatherill, *Consumer Behaviour and Material Culture, 1660-1760*, London and New York, Routledge, 1988; J. Brewer and R. Porter, eds, *Consumption and the World of Goods*, London and New York, Routledge, 1993.

54 Bernard Mandeville, *The Fable of the Bees*, ed. Philip Harth, Harmondsworth, Penguin, 1989.

55 McKendrick, Brewer and Plumb, *Birth of a Consumer Society*, p. 13.

56 For an earlier version of this argument see Elizabeth McKellar, 'Architectural Practice for Speculative Building in Late Seventeenth-Century London', unpublished Ph.D., Royal College of Art, 1992, Ch. 1 'The Expansion of London: the Social and Ideological Context of Development', pp. 20-39. For a similar argument on Barbon see, Lubbock, *Taste*, pp. 13-15, 96-9.

57 On Barbon's economic theory see, William Letwin, *The Origins of Scientific Economics*, London, Methuen, 1963, pp. 48-78.

58 Nicholas Barbon, *An Apology for the Builder Or A Discourse Shewing the Cause and Effects of the Increase of Building*, London, 1685, p. 2.

59 Barbon, *Apology*, p. 2.

60 Barbon, *Apology*, pp. 2-3.

61 Barbon, *A Discourse of Trade*, London, 1690, p. 5.

62 Barbon, *Apology*, pp. 19-20.

63 Barbon, *Apology*, pp. 21-2.

64 Barbon, *Apology*, p. 22.

65 Barbon, *Apology*, pp. 30-1.

66 For more on the link between the wealth of nations and the health of nations see, Roy Porter, 'Consumption: Disease of the Consumer Society?', in Brewer and Porter, *Consumption*, pp. 58-81.

67 Laurence Sterne, *The Life and Opinions of Tristram Shandy*, 1759-67, ed. Graham Petrie, Harmondsworth, Penguin, 1967, p. 73.

68 See Donald J. Olsen, *Town Planning in London: The Eighteenth and Nineteenth Centuries*, New Haven and London, Yale University Press, 1964.

The developers: noble landlords and greedy speculators

2

his house in a morning like a court, crowded with suitors for money. And he kept state, coming down at his own time like a magnifico, in deshabille, and so discourse with them. And having very much work, they were loth to break finally, and upon a new job taken they would follow and worship him like an idol, for then there was fresh money.
(Roger North on Nicholas Barbon in his *Autobiography of the Hon. Roger North*, 1887, p. 57)

In *Georgian London* John Summerson outlined what he saw to be the classic development process in the late seventeenth century. He described the prime developer of the time as being 'the noble landlord with a greedy purse' and he gave as his two examples, the fourth Earl of Southampton and the first Earl of St Albans.[1] Summerson extracted various principles from their respective schemes at Bloomsbury Square and St James's Square of the 1660s and 1670s, which he claimed established the pattern for speculative building for the following century and a half.[2] Foremost among these were the idea of an aristocratic lead, through the development of their own estates, and the enabling of this through a process whereby the land was let off on leases to speculative builders who acted as middlemen and actually built the houses. This was made possible by the distinction between the landlord who owned the freehold and the builders who had a leasehold interest.

We have already encountered one major developer, Nicholas Barbon, who was not an aristocrat building upon his own estates but a speculator buying and selling land from and to others. Summerson was writing in the days before the increasing wealth and power of the commercial classes at this time, particularly in London, had been recognized.[3] But his model of estate development has not been re-examined in the light of changing historical perceptions of the period. This chapter sets out to discover whether Summerson's analysis is still sustainable or whether the new wealth of the City also played a significant role in the reshaping of the capital. In order to answer this question I will begin by looking at the types of landholdings upon which development is known to have occurred, the extent to which this took place upon noblemen's estates and the role they played within the development process.

One of the most easily identifiable group of sites are those where aristocratic houses and their grounds were vacated, pulled down, and rebuilt with a higher density of residential property, usually in the form of several streets. Among other places this happened at the great riverfront palaces of Exeter, Essex and Derby Houses and at Wild and Newport Houses situated either side of Covent Garden in the 1670s. Following Summerson's model we would expect all these areas to have been developed leasehold. In fact we find the opposite to be true and in only one instance of the five given above does this occur. This is at Great and Little Exeter Houses, which Nicholas Barbon leased from the Earl of Exeter for a term of forty years in 1676 at a cost of £500 p.a.[4] Barbon was in this instance acting as the middleman in developing the land. The Earl employed Sir Francis Child as an agent to handle the collection of ground rents from the lessees, for which he got 40s commission per pair of leases.[5]

In all the other schemes mentioned above, the freeholds of the land were sold by their noble owners to others for development. At Essex House, for example, Barbon purchased the freehold to carry out his development there for what he called 'a great sum of money',[6] which was somewhere between £13,000 and £15,000, according to the court records.[7] At Derby House he and Arnold Browne purchased the freehold from the Earl of Derby in 1683 for an unknown sum.[8] Newport House was also carried out as a freehold development by Barbon, who purchased the house from George Porter in 1681 for £9,500.[9] Wild House was developed by Isaac Foxcroft who bought the freehold from the previous owner Humphrey Wild, who had begun developing the site himself in the 1650s. He sold the site in 1688 for £7,000 to Foxcroft.[10] The majority of aristocratic landowners on fairly small sites did not it seems become involved in the development process, preferring to sell the land off completely.

If we move on to larger blocks of unbuilt land further removed from the existing urban core, we might expect to see a different pattern. Perhaps one in which landowners were less ready to alienate their holdings. These larger blocks of land fall into various types. Some of them were sites being sold off by the Crown. The authorities sold three sites to Barbon in the 1680s – the Old Artillery Ground, Wellclose and Tower Hill – all on the east side of the City and fairly close to existing buildings.[11] Here again Barbon was able to purchase the freeholds of the land in 1682 at prices of £3,200 for Wellclose,[12] and £5,700 for the Old Artillery Ground (the price for

Tower Hill has not been found).[13] Barbon was evidently slow to settle the purchase and a series of increasingly impatient letters were sent to him in January and February 1682 asking him to come to the Treasury and pay the money due immediately.[14] The willingness of the Crown to release land for development played a key role in the post-Restoration expansion of London.

Two other large schemes provide a more detailed picture of other types of development patterns. These are the Barbon developments to the north of Holborn in Lamb's Conduit and Red Lion Fields, and the Soho area of Soho Fields, Leicester Fields, the Military Ground, Gelding Close and the Pulteney Estate. All of these were large-scale developments on open ground. They were undertaken by their owners as a mixture of freehold and leasehold development. The procedure at Conduit Close is representative of the pattern. It was divided among a number of different owners and here Barbon carried out some of the building by a lease of 1686 from the Rugby estate for fifty years at a ground rent of £50 p.a.,[15] some of the rest of the ground he held freehold and in some areas his exact claim to the land was disputed.[16]

The other major area of development of the 1670s was in Soho. Here we can find more evidence of aristocrats maintaining the freeholds of their estates. The Military Ground was granted by Charles II to the Earl of Macclesfield, who let it to Nicholas Barbon and John Rowley to develop in 1677 by a lease of sixty-one years.[17] Further west in Windmill Fields the freeholder Sir William Pulteney let off blocks of land to developers to build on from 1666 onwards.[18] In one instance at Gelding Close (the Golden Square area), the land was developed by two men, Isaac Symball and James Axtell, who managed to acquire the freehold.[19]

The Earl of St Albans was also active in the area having been granted Soho Fields by the Crown until 1734.[20] He was not as directly involved here as he had been at St James's, as the ground was developed by Richard Frith, who obtained a lease from him for fifty-three and a quarter years in 1677.[21] The Earl of Leicester, however, did make building leases and controlled the development himself on his land at Leicester Fields and Swan Close from 1670.[22] The comparison between St Albans' earlier and later developments is a pertinent one. In many areas of large-scale development, or in the rebuilding of aristocratic houses, the pattern of development that Summerson emphasized on the St James's and Bloomsbury estates was not followed. Lord Southampton and the Earl of St Albans in choosing to develop their own land themselves and taking an active role in their schemes, were very much the exception and not the rule. Only the Earl of Leicester from this group followed their example.

Late seventeenth-century speculative building was not then on the whole co-ordinated estate development. It did not conform to the well-known eighteenth-century pattern in which landowners deliberately set out to maximize the return on their land through careful and planned control of the building that took place upon it. In comparison with eighteenth-century projects, such as those on the Grosvenor or Bedford estates, late seventeenth-century developments took place on much smaller land holdings that their owners were far more prepared to alienate than they were in the following century, when their value was better realized. The land market was more fluid and hence smaller plots of land were developed, usually by speculators, sometimes with the involvement of the landowner but more often without it. The development pattern even in the largest areas of the city under construction is therefore the exact opposite to that which came to predominate within the next fifty years or so.

Many medium and small developments took place, particularly in the City, and perhaps it is here that one is most likely to find small-scale development being carried out freehold. For example, Barbon's first schemes were carried out in the City on land he held in Mincing Lane, on what he described as being, 'a good estate'.[23] On this he built seven houses in 1674. This gave him his start as a speculative builder and as Roger North said, 'the fire of London gave him means of doing and knowing much of that kind'.[24] Elizabeth and Anthony Tasker can be found operating in a similar way at Love Lane, St Mary, Aldermanbury where they replaced property destroyed in the fire with three new houses in 1668.[25] An example of what must have been a typical City rebuilding pattern can be found near Newgate Street. Here Alice Gamble owned a small plot of land on a long lease which 'had lain waste and unbuilt' since the Fire. She contracted with Nicholas Daintrey to build a single brick house on the plot in 1670.[26]

Michael Power identified the main building pattern in East London in the seventeenth century, both before and after 1660, to be the development of small parcels of leasehold land by individual builders. Even where there were substantial estate holdings he found that they tended to be let off piecemeal for development.[27] Judging by the evidence in Chancery this kind of patchwork development was also common throughout the City and the West End with arrangements even within a single landholding varying considerably. Although development is easier to trace on fairly large plots of land, within these and between them many small, individual developments of a few houses also took place.

The pattern that emerges from this research is that in both the east and the west it was the exception and not the rule for landowners to develop their own holdings. Power suggests that the reason the largest landowners in east London, the Wentworth family, did not carry out development themselves was because they did not have the money with which to do so.[28] Lawrence Stone supports this analysis arguing that the nobility in the late seventeenth century were hit by a decline in rents and a rise in land taxes which may have caused the sale of outlying properties.[29] He proposes that the reason that so much development took place on land held by the aristocracy, was that they found it easier to obtain a licence from the Crown for building than those without connections at Court. However, they did not develop the land themselves as their greatest requirement was for ready cash, which their agricultural estates could only provide on a much more long-term basis.[30]

This need in conjunction with an attitude which saw their London landholdings as extraneous to their main country estates, explains the lack of landed involvement in urban speculation in this period. The elite were not so impoverished that they could not carry out new building altogether, as the significant amount of country house building at the time demonstrates.[31] However, they seem to have concentrated for the most part on the embellishment of their own individual houses, rather than large-scale property investment. Instead we see the commercial opportunities which land speculation offered being largely exploited by another sort. This group comprised for the most part financiers, professionals, merchants, a few tradesmen and some gentry. The commercial initiative here was being taken by a different stratum of society. In the development of London in the post-Restoration period we can see an instance of the rise of a newly powerful group in society, who contemporaries called speculators, adventurers, financiers and merchants and who today we might call businessmen.[32]

As John Summerson pointed out, there were two kinds of developers: 'those who speculated in land plus houses and those who speculated only in houses'.[33] In this chapter the focus will be on those in the former category, while the second type will be discussed in Chapter 5. Foremost among the first group was Nicholas Barbon (?1698). As he himself said to Roger North, the major source of biographical and anecdotal information about him, 'it was not worth his while to deal little; that a bricklayer could do'.[34] He was the son of Praise God Barbon a leather-seller, otherwise better known as the republican preacher and parliamentarian who gave his name to the Barebones Parliament. Nicholas trained as a doctor in Holland but although he did not practise medicine on his return to England, he was habitually referred to as Dr Barbon, and he obviously styled himself as such. This was all part of the great Barbon act which Roger North conveys so vividly in his account of the man. He compared Barbon's skills as a builder with those of his father as a preacher:

> He was bred in the practices as well as the knowledge, of working the people under his father in the late times … with his much dealing in building, and consequently transacting with multitudes, he was an exquisite mob master, and knew the arts of leading, winding, or driving mankind in herds as well as any that I ever observed.[35]

He was a larger than life figure who in his personality and the scale of his commercial operations both baffled and intrigued his contemporaries. North tells how he lived in Crane Court 'as lord of the manor'.[36] Barbon also employed his own particular methods in the development process. These were responsible for his figuring so prominently in the courts at the time. It is impossible to know how far others followed his example, but it seems he was unique in the unscrupulousness and brazenness of his business tactics. Roger North, obviously fascinated by Barbon, asked him about this, and Barbon quite openly outlined for him his business approach.

> I once asked him why he dealt so much in building and to overrun his stock, and be not only forced to discontent everyone, but be perpetually harrassed with suits. He said it was not worth his while to deal little; that a bricklayer could do. The gain he expected was out of great undertakings, which would rise lustily in the whole, and because this trade required a greater stock than he had, perhaps £30,000 or £40,000, he must compass his designs either by borrowed money or by credit with those he dealt with, either by fair means or foul. He said his trade would not afford to borrow on such disadvantage as he must, for want of sufficient security, be at, 10 per cent at least; so he was forced to take the other way of being in debt, which he said was very much cheaper to him than borrowing, for his way was to put men off from time to time by fair words, as long as they were current, and so he got one, two, and sometimes three years. And then perhaps they would begin to threaten most fiercely to arrest him, which at last they did. So he put in bail, for which end he had always a bank of credit with a scrivener and goldsmith or two. Perhaps for some carelessness of the plaintiff's attorney the suit baffled itself at first, but if it came so far as a trial he defended stoutly if he had colour, if not let it go by default, then brought a bill in Chancery, and perhaps got an injunction, and at the last, when the injunction was dissolved, and judgment affirmed upon a writ of error (which was one delay seldom omitted) and execution ready to come out, he sent to the party, and paid the money recovered, and costs, which might amount to three, four or perhaps five per cent, and seldom more than half the charge of borrowing … and so by contrivance, shifting, and many losses, he kept his wheel turning, lived all the while splendidly, was a mystery in his time, uncertain whether worth anything or not, at last bought a Parliament-man's place, had protection

and ease, and had not his cash failed, which made his works often stand still, and so go to ruin, and many other disadvantages grown, in all probability he might have been as rich as any in the nation.[37]

Nicholas Barbon and Sir John Parson's development of the three Crown properties they bought in 1682 – Wellclose, the Old Artillery Ground and Tower Hill – shows other aspects of Barbon's development procedures. One of these was to assign leases to an associate. The purpose of this was to make it seem as if all the ground was let, although in reality the person whose name was on the leases was a straw man and not expected to build. This happened on these three sites which were effectively run as one development, where building leases were made to William Prideaux and George Proctor. Prideaux and Proctor were subsequently described as 'agents or servants in trust for Barbon'.[38] The purpose behind employing them was to use the ground rents covenanted for in the leases as a means of raising money. Barbon began building on his own account and claimed to have spent £12,000 himself.[39] He then approached Edward Noell to lend him £5,000 as a mortgage on the premises. Noell arranged for Robert Breedon, brewer, and William Jarman, distiller, to lend the money, which they did 'by the much persuasion and importunities' of Barbon and Prideaux.[40] In return they were assigned Prideaux's leases as a mortgage. Barbon promised faithfully to finish the buildings. This of course he did not do and he spent the £5,000 elsewhere. Breedon and Noell then found that the value of the houses did not equal their debt, nor as they were unfinished could they derive an income from them by letting them out themselves. As Breedon complained, the leases were:

> so designed only for the benefit of the said Mr Barbon, and contrived to countenance the greater valuations of the premises whereby to enable him the said Mr Barbon, to raise money thereupon afterwards of other persons, and not really expected from the said William Prideaux by his improvement of the premises and performing such his extraordinary covenants which would have required a very great and considerable sum of money to have complied with and make good the same, and more than the said Prideaux was capable on his own account of disbursing as this defendant has reason to believe, he being informed that the said Prideaux was then a man of mean substance in the world and since proves insolvent ... he believes that such foundations as were laid, or houses built were very imperfect and at very little or inconsiderable charges, and done or contrived more for colour to borrow and raise money thereupon than any real design to make them capable of being a sufficient security for any considerable sum of money to be lent or borrowed thereupon.[41]

Meanwhile the freehold of the premises had been passed to the trustees of the Fire Office in 1683. They therefore proceeded to pursue Breedon, to whom Prideaux's leases had been assigned, in the courts for his failure to carry out the covenants in the leases, namely to build a certain number of houses by a certain date. By clever manipulation Barbon was able to raise a good deal of money on the ground, but at the same time he had sold off the freehold freeing him from ultimate responsibility for the ground rents. By mortgaging the building leases and then not finishing the houses he could continue with the scheme or not as he chose. Presumably he was waiting for the property market to pick up but he never lived to complete this project before his death. He did not mind waiting for a scheme to come to fruition, as Roger North said: 'If he got into an undertaking he mattered not time, for some would depend many years, and if money failed he would stand stock still, whatever ruin attended his works.'[42]

Barbon became MP for Bramber in 1690 and 1695. This meant that he was able to claim protection from prosecution under MPs' privileges. The later Chancery cases often contain frustrated claimants unable to bring Barbon to account. Breedon in his final case in 1699 after Barbon had died complained of him, 'being a Member of Parliament and insisting upon his privileges as such would never also be brought to answer your orators' bill', meanwhile Prideaux was, 'either dead, or insolvent and obscure'.[43]

The other tactic employed by Barbon which North described was his means of manipulating people in order to carry out his schemes. North called him 'an exquisite mob master'.[44] Evidence of intimidation by Barbon can be found in his handling of a number of existing tenants on the Essex House site.[45] Besides the house itself the site included a number of premises mainly used for businesses, on which new twenty-one year leases had recently been granted when Barbon bought the property. These were occupied by John Pride mercer and hosier, Rowland Woodyear skinner, John Coggs goldsmith of 'The Reindeer', John Ratford spectaclemaker, John Holland shoemaker, William Hanmer upholsterer, and Thomas Taylor watch and clockmaker. Some of the tenants seem to have come to an agreement fairly early on with Barbon, as their names disappear from the subsequent litigation. However, a hard core held out against Barbon claiming that he was, 'fraudulently intending to circumvent your orators and deprive them of the benefit of their said leases or to weary them out of possession thereof in order to some unjust ends of profit and advantage to himself'.[46] Barbon then used the tactics of divide and rule among those who refused to come to terms with him. William Hanmer, for example, was a sub-lessee to Henry Grice, a haberdasher. Barbon approached Hanmer to try to buy Grice's lease from him. However,

Hanmer had been warned of this possibility, and in his agreement with Grice it was stated that he should surrender the premises to no one but Grice, and especially not to Barbon.[47] Then Hanmer claimed that Barbon had 'cunningly prevailed' with Grice to give up his lease, so that Hanmer's business of over twenty-one years was threatened. Barbon had already pulled down the greater part of the premises and now he threatened 'to untile and pull down that house also upon your orator's head'.[48] So by a mixture of threats and cajoling Barbon got his way. Eventually both sides agreed to submit to arbitration to determine the amount of compensation that Barbon should pay to the tenants for loss of business and setting up trade elsewhere.[49] Barbon then refused to pay the money claiming that it was the responsibility of Samuel Vincent, who had purchased the site from him.[50]

Barbon was recognized as a phenomenon in his own age. He built and speculated and created on a scale way beyond that of any of his rivals. He dominated the late seventeenth-century London building world, but he was in no way a typical representative of it. Barbon's willingness to go to court as part of his habitual practice, and hence his very high representation in this book, should not obscure from us the fact that he was an exceptional figure in his time, or indeed in any time. Besides his building activities he set up the first Fire Insurance Office. He also tried to establish a Land Bank and an Orphans' Bank. He developed a scheme for raising water from the Thames to overcome increasing water shortages. This was not, however, commercially successful. He conducted a heated debate with John Locke in the 1690s over the debasement of the coinage, publishing in 1696 *Discourse concerning coining the new money lighter, in answer to Mr Lock's considerations about raising the value of money*. He was from a strongly anti-monarchist, unconventional background. He was an outsider who had no interest in becoming respectable and joining the establishment as his frequent clashes with the authorities demonstrate. Starting from a fairly modest inheritance he used the opportunity created by the Fire first to make and then to lose a fortune. In business terms, and in terms of his behaviour and code of conduct, he was a completely self-made man. Our first example of a leading developer could not be further from the aristocratic landowning figure than could be imagined.

Another example of an entrepreneur from a non-gentry background is Isaac Symball. He was described as a gentleman from St Anne Westminster after his death,[51] but also as a yeoman, brickmaker and corn chandler.[52] The *Survey of London* says that he was described as a person 'of no reputation' in 1689, and relates how he met a dramatic end stabbed over a game of cards in 1695. Symball was the joint-developer with James Axtell of a field called Gelding Close, which became Golden Square with its surrounding streets such as Warwick Street and Brewer Street.[53] A schedule of mortgages attached to a case provides evidence of where he was active and the scope and range of his business.[54] The schedule of mortgages on properties listed at his death in 1695 is given below:

A messuage occupied by Sir Charles Orby
Ground in Golden Square
Ground in Little Windmill Street
Messuage in Arlington Street
Ground in Golden Square
One house fronting Wardour Street in Old Soho, with eight stables
     backwards
Ground in Golden Square
2 houses in Red Lion Square with coach-house and stables
One house in Theobalds Way
One house
12 houses in Symball's Alley, Old Soho
5 houses in Coulston's Court, Drury Lane
3 houses in Russell Court, Drury Lane
4 houses in Almonry, Westminster
3 houses in Pulteney Street, Soho and 5 houses backwards
2 houses in Warwick Lane
1 house in Phoenix Court
5 houses in Liquorpond Street
3 houses in Frith Street
One messuage in Moore Street
8 houses, 6 stables, 5 coach-houses in Hog Lane, Soho
6 houses in Brewer Street
7 houses in Warwick Street [55]

Symball carried out one scheme where he acted as the lead developer at Gelding Close and purchased the land for building. Elsewhere he leased parcels of land from others on which he then made building leases, principally in the Soho area. Three of these mortgages were worth £800, four between £550 and £400, five were for £350–£300 and one was worth £180. This represents a total value of £6,080 which Symball was borrowing in mortgages at his death. Most of these were being paid back over a fairly long period of time with repayment averaging around £20 p.a., with ground rents varying enormously from 10s p.a. to £40 p.a. depending on the size and location of the plot.

At Wild House the Survey of London states that Isaac Foxcroft was the developer.[56] One of the Chancery cases confirms that he purchased the freehold of Wild House in 1688 paying £7,000 for it.[57] However, a closer reading of the case reveals that Foxcroft was not the developer at all. He is described as being from the Inner Temple, in other words he was a lawyer. Foxcroft was in fact providing the financial backing for a developer called Robert Rossington. In return for £8,050, to be paid by 1691, Foxcroft would convey the site to Rossington. In the meantime Foxcroft lent Rossington in partnership with his son George £7,000 to begin building and developing the site. Rossington like Symball seems to have been a substantial property developer. The case lists him as having interests in the following places besides Wild House:

> Sheen House and other houses near Richmond
> premises in Pall Mall and Park Place and around St James Palace
> many premises around Grays Inn Lane
> the two wing houses of Wild House
> houses in Cow Cross Street and Turneball Street, St Sepulchres
> Gunpowder Alley, Bishopsgate
> premises in Holborn [58]

It seems that Rossington's major development besides Wild House was the rebuilding of most of the Gray's Inn Road area in the 1680s, pulling down existing houses and building new ones. (Figure 29 shows a surving late seventeenth-century house in Gray's Inn Road.[59]) Nothing else is known about Rossington apart from the fact that he is described in the case as being a gentleman from Holborn, but his portfolio of small holdings is probably typically of many at the time.

The final example of a developer working on a large scale is Sir Thomas Neale. Unlike most of the other examples he was part of the establishment, holding the posts of Master of the Mint and Groom Porter to the King.[60] His duties in the latter post included: furnishing the King's lodgings; providing cards and dice; and deciding disputes at the card-table and on the bowling-green. These activities were in keeping with Neale's true talents and interests. He was a business buccaneer and adventurer in the Barbon mould. He was involved in speculative mining and carried out several successful public lotteries for the government.[61] Neale is best known for his Seven Dials development in Covent Garden of 1693 in which he acted as the chief developer. He can also be found having some brief involvement at Red Lion Fields where he held the lease on the Fields in 1683 from Sir Richard Fisher prior to Barbon.[62] Neale built a street in Whitechapel,[63] and developments in Shadwell, East London.[64] In 1695 he bought a large piece of land between Piccadilly and Hyde Park with the intention of developing it. However, like Barbon he fell victim to the financial instability of the 1690s and he died insolvent in c. 1699.[65]

This brief survey of some of the largest developers demonstrates two things. Firstly, many of them were self-made men and entrepreneurs, not wealthy gentry or landed aristocrats. Secondly, Summerson's characterization of them as '"amateurs" so far as the building industry was concerned', must to some extent be questioned.[66] Certainly they did not come from the ranks of the building industry, they were speculators and businessmen; but as these examples show they were not involved in one-off developments but in many places simultaneously. Many of them carried on other or related business activities as well, but this was normal practice at the time. The depth and scale of their involvement in property can in no way be characterized as that of dilettanti.

Summerson's term 'amateur' is perhaps more applicable to the financial backers and investors who were a part of every development but were less directly involved in the property world. The example of Wild House where Isaac Foxcroft provided the capital and Robert Rossington carried out the development is extremely unusual. The large sums of money required and the risk involved, meant that normally a consortium of financial backers was formed to finance the purchase and the development costs of a site. At Soho Fields, for example, Richard Frith and his co-developer Cadogan Thomas were able to develop the land largely through capital provided by William Pym and Benjamin Hinton. In 1677 when Frith obtained the lease and patent to build in the area Pym lent him £5,000 on the security of these, while in 1680 Benjamin Hinton lent £16,000 to Cadogan Thomas in the form of a mortgage on the land. Pym sold his interest in the Fields to Benjamin Hinton in 1681 leaving Hinton as the major backer. In 1683 Hinton's business crashed and he was declared bankrupt. At this point Thomas and Frith's combined debts to Hinton amounted to £60,000. His bankruptcy spelt disaster for them too and all their interests in the scheme passed to his creditors, effectively ending their involvement in the area.[67]

Benjamin Hinton was a goldsmith [68] who 'grew into great Esteeme and Creditt with very many Noblemen, Gentlemen and others'.[69] He was married to Elizabeth Madox, who had been brought up by Sir John Moore as his own child.[70] Moore was an extremely wealthy merchant and an investor in building projects. This may have come about through his becoming involved with Barbon at Mincing Lane. Moore lived in one of the houses which Barbon built there in 1674.[71] Whether he put money into this scheme is not known, but he can be found lending £4,000 to Barbon for work at St James's in 1675,[72] and purchasing land in the City at College Hill, St Michael Paternoster for £1,000 which Barbon was to develop.[73] Such alliances and connections are commonly found in the Chancery evidence, suggesting that the building world and its backers formed a relatively tightly knit group. As Richard Grassby says in his essay on 'Social Mobility and

Business Enterprise in Seventeenth-Century England', personal contacts within the business world were essential to success and 'the kinship group was the basis of all business dealings'.[74] William Pym also invested in the Arlington Street area.[75] Less is known about him but he was described as being a gentleman of St James, Clerkenwell.

Barbon's activities provide interesting evidence of the kind of people from whom he drew his finance. In the development of the Bedford Ground Barbon borrowed money from three sources. Firstly, he was lent money by Richard Webb, who was a lawyer, and Richard Chiswell, who was a stationer and bookseller in the City. They lent a total of around £6,000 to Barbon mainly to cover the cost of the lease from the Bedford Corporation. He then borrowed a further £8,000 from Richard Kent, a gentleman of London, and £5,500 from George White, a merchant of London.[76] This example shows a cross-section of the types of people from whom capital was normally obtained: a lawyer, a tradesman, a gentleman and a merchant. The involvement of the legal profession was widespread. Often they acted as agents for other people and in fact this was the case here, where Webb's name was being used in trust for Matthew Blucke, Esq. of Hunsden, Herts for £3,000 of the money.[77] Barbon borrowed the money as a mortgage, against the security of the land he was to build on or other land where he had an interest. This was the normal method of raising money.

At Exeter House where Barbon was 'intending to build an Exchange and other building upon part of the said demised premises, and having occasions to take up several thousand pounds for that purpose' he borrowed £7,000 from Thomas Browne in 1676-79, secured by a mortgage on Exeter House. Thomas Browne was a scrivener, a group who along with goldsmiths and bankers feature heavily in the cases as financiers of building. He reassigned his mortgage in 1677 to James Host Esq. of Mitcham, Peter Vandeput merchant of London, and Henry Cherry and William Millett gentlemen of London who lent further sums. All these people claimed to have used Browne because they were looking for a good security on which to lend out money. So initially Browne lent Barbon his own money, and then he lent out other people's money which had been placed with him.[78]

Sir Robert Clayton (1629-1707) is perhaps the prime example of a scrivener who expanded his existing roles to embrace property speculation as well. He was a leading City figure and Whig politician, becoming both Lord Mayor and an MP. He formed a partnership with John Morris in which moneylending and land conveyancing were their major transactions and through which he amassed a fortune.[79] He was one of the richest business tycoons in London and one of the few who left over £100,000 at their deaths, along with people such as Sir John Banks and Sir Josiah Child.[80] Evelyn described him as, 'this Prince of Citizens, there never having been any, who, for the stateliness of his palace, prodigious feasting, and magnificence, exceeded him'. D. C. Coleman in an article on the man cites him as an interesting example of a scrivener whose work expanded into the spheres of what would today be considered the work of estate agents, solicitors and accountants. Clayton and Morris obtained details of lands for sale and contacted likely purchasers. They also arranged mortgages and advanced money to borrowers. The intense activity in the land market after the Restoration settlement created a great deal of work for what Coleman calls 'the intermediaries of capital mobility', lawyers, scriveners, bankers and goldsmiths.[81]

Clayton did not just facilitate land transfers but he also invested in land and property as well. The following information about Clayton's property dealings can be found in Chancery suits. Firstly, he held an interest on Marshland, the site of what became Seven Dials, which he sold to Thomas Neale.[82] He also lent £5,000 jointly with John Morris to Barbon for the development of Essex House.[83] Frank Melton in his article outlining Clayton's building projects in the City after the Fire until 1672, lists the major ones at Austin Friars, Rood Lane, Hand Alley, Bartholomew Lane, Cornhill and Finch Lane. His brother William, a joiner by trade, was in-volved in some of these places. Melton asserts that the City projects were not a success overall and that:

> There was no dearth of capital for private building, but the great capi-talists – the bankers and other financiers – seem to have played little part either directly or as entrepreneurs in urban development. If rentiers were an insignificant class in post-Fire London, the implication is that arti-sans, shop-keepers and other petty capitalists rebuilt their own houses and shops, unencumbered with mortgage debts.[84]

As we have seen, the opposite seems to have been the case outside the City, where the majority of large-scale development was fin-anced by bankers and scriveners rather than by the gentry or money from agricultural estates outside London.

Roger North tells how Barbon, 'maintained a gang of clerks, attorneys, scriveners, and lawyers, that were his humble servants and slaves to command' in order to carry out his extensive oper-ations.[85] His associates included people such as Samuel Vincent, who was described as Esq. of Buckenham, Norfolk,[86] who set up the Fire Insurance Office with Barbon and others in 1681.[87] Another member of this group was Sir John Parsons who almost certainly provided the money to purchase the Old Artillery Ground, Tower

Hill and Wellclose in 1682 and was active in their development, jointly making building leases with Barbon.[88] Other investors in the insurance scheme and in Barbon's associated building projects included people such as John Hinde, a goldsmith and banker, who was declared bankrupt in 1685 and died in the Fleet Prison.[89]

A crucial element in the group Barbon built around him were his legal advisers. Two of those most closely associated with him were Edward Noell and George Bradbury. Edward Noell, gentleman of the Inner Temple, was another of the founders of the Fire Insurance Office and often acted as an agent for Barbon.[90] Bradbury acted in a similar capacity and susbsequently became a judge of some note.[91] The most active lawyer on Barbon's behalf was John Bland. The Chancery cases give the impression that he worked full-time for Barbon, and he is variously described as an agent for Barbon, measurer, gentleman, scrivener and as being of the Middle Temple. He was an executor of Barbon's estate after his death.[92] He had an involvement in nearly all of Barbon's projects: either acting as a trustee for him, as for example at the Newport Ground;[93] or disposing of building leases; and sometimes taking them himself. Sir Richard Fisher said that Barbon used Bland, 'whom he employed to make all his leases'.[94] He can also be found measuring the builder's work at Wellclose Square.[95] His work for Barbon even brought him to the point of being thrown into prison in 1689. Barbon owed money to Michael Scrimshire, a goldsmith. When Scrimshire became bankrupt his creditors had Barbon arrested in King's Bench. Barbon asked John Bland and George Proctor to stand bail for him. Proctor was also a servant or agent to Barbon. This they did with the consequence that the commissioners handling the bankruptcy had Bland and Proctor arrested for debt and committed to the Marshalsea.[96]

The development process relied on the skills of a variety of people: building speculators who understood the market and could raise finance; businessmen prepared to become part of a syndicate of investors; managers, such as John Bland, who could organize the operation; lawyers who could draw up contracts and understood how to manipulate the labyrinth of seventeenth-century property legislation; and scriveners who could provide finance and arrange transfers of money between parties and to employees. There is one example in the cases of another form of employment that the property market generated. This is an estate agent – one William Palmer, a broker of St Andrew Holborn, 'having considerable business of that nature'. He was described as:

> a person that gets his livelihood by procuring of purchasers for those that have estates in manors, lands, houses, tenements or hereditaments

to be sold, and by giving intelligence or information to purchasers of the same, for which he usually has and receives of the seller, in case your orator helps him to a purchaser, or gives intelligence to any person that buys of him, the sum of twenty shillings for every hundred pounds that any purchaser ... gives for his purchase, and also of the buyer the sum of twenty shillings for every hundred pounds he pays for any purchase.[97]

In conclusion one could say the following about the areas from which investment was drawn for the development process. Firstly, it seems mainly to have come from non-agricultural sources unconnected with the land. Secondly, it largely came from within London itself, although of course some of this money was generated by international trade. Thirdly, the majority of investors came from the financial and business community of self-made men, rather than from the gentry and aristocracy. Fourthly, although capital sums were sometimes paid, for example for the purchase of freehold land, the majority of financing was organized through credit networks particularly mortgages on land. The prime movers were not aristocrats who were generally remarkably passive in the process but entrepreneurs and adventurers looking to make their fortune. It was a new area of business which attracted new men.

Notes

1 John Summerson, *Georgian London*, 1945, Harmondsworth, Penguin, 1978 edn, p. 39.

2 Summerson, *Georgian London*, p. 42.

3 See: Roy Porter, *English Society in the Eighteenth Century*, Harmondsworth, Penguin, 1982, pp. 85–99; Peter Earle, *The Making of the English Middle Class: Business, Society and Family Life in London, 1660–1730*, London, Methuen, 1989.

4 PRO C8/26/391.

5 PRO C5/226/43.

6 PRO C6/77/19.

7 PRO C8/247/7, C8/269/79.

8 PRO C10/272/96, C10/294/65.

9 PRO C6/342/50, C8/555/84.

10 PRO C8/427/84.

11 PRO C6/326/51.

12 PRO C10/337/19.

13 *Survey of London, Spitalfields and Mile End New Town*, Vol. XXVII, London, Athlone Press, 1957, pp. 29–30.

14 PRO *CSP(Dom)*, Treasury Books VII, pp. 372–406.

15 PRO C5/148/21, C5/155/66, C5/218/38, C7/92/93.

16 PRO C7/92/93.

17 PRO C10/159/67; *Survey of London, St Anne, Soho*, Vol. XXXIV, 1966, p. 383.

18 *Survey of London, St James, Westminster*, Vol. XXXI, 1960, pp. 116-18.

19 C7/316/37; *Survey of London, St James, Westminster*, pp. 138-41.

20 *Survey of London, St Anne, Soho*, p. 27.

21 PRO C7/137/63.

22 *Survey of London, St Anne, Soho*, pp. 424-8.

23 PRO C7/543/52.

24 Roger North, *The Autobiography of the Hon. Roger North*, ed. Augustus Jessopp, London, D. Nutt, 1887, p. 53.

25 PRO C6/289/21, C6/289/34.

26 PRO C10/105/132.

27 Michael J. Power, 'The Urban Development of East London 1550-1770', unpublished Ph.D., University of London, 1971, pp. 122-9.

28 Power, 'Urban Development' p. 122.

29 Lawrence Stone and Jeanne Fawtier Stone, *An Open Elite? England 1540-1880*, Oxford, Oxford University Press, 1986, p. 281.

30 Lawrence Stone, 'The Residential Development of the West End of London in the Seventeenth Century', in B. C. Malament, ed., *After the Reformation*, Pennsylvania, University of Pennsylvania Press, 1980, p. 197.

31 John Summerson, 'The Classical Country House in 18th-Century England', *Journal of the Royal Society of Arts*, No. 107, July 1959, pp. 539-87; Charles Saumarez Smith, 'Supply and Demand in English Country House Building, 1660-1740', *Oxford Art Journal*, Vol. 2, No. 2, 1988, pp. 3-9.

32 For more on this see, Richard Grassby, 'Social Mobility and Business Enterprise in Seventeenth-Century England', in Donald Pennington & Keith Thomas, eds, *Puritans and Revolutionaries: Essays in Seventeenth-Century History Presented to Christopher Hill*, Oxford, Clarendon Press, 1978, pp. 355-81.

33 Summerson, *Georgian London*, p. 42.

34 Jessopp, *Roger North*, p. 55: information on Barbon from: *DNB*; Norman Brett-James, *The Growth of Stuart London*, London, London and Middlesex Archaeological Society with George Allen & Unwin, 1935, pp. 325-4.

35 Jessopp, *Roger North*, pp. 52-3.

36 Jessopp, *Roger North*, p. 53.

37 Jessopp, *Roger North*, p. 55-7.

38 PRO C7/169/99.

39 PRO C7/169/99.

40 PRO C9/245/3.

41 PRO C7/148/37.

42 Jessopp, *Roger North*, p. 57.

43 PRO C9/245/3.

44 Jessopp, *Roger North*, p. 53.

45 PRO C5/491/85, C6/62/95, C6/77/19, C6/77/20, C8/241/13, C8/241/22, C8/247/7, C8/255/116, C8/269/79, C9/74/112, C10/128/17, C10/481/99.

46 PRO C10/481/99.

47 PRO C6/77/19.

48 PRO C6/77/19.

49 PRO C8/241/13.

50 PRO C8/269/79, C9/74/112.

51 PRO C7/316/37.

52 *Survey of London, St James, Westminster*, p. 139.

53 PRO C7/316/37; *Survey of London, St James, Westminster*, pp. 138-43.

54 PRO C7/316/37.

55 PRO C7/316/37.

56 *Survey of London, St Giles-in-the-Fields*, Pt II, Vol. V, 1914, p. 97.

57 PRO C8/427/84.

58 PRO C8/427/84.

59 I am grateful to Susie Barson of English Heritage for drawing this building to my attention.

60 PRO C8/420/53; Summerson, *Georgian London*, p. 43.

61 *DNB.*

62 PRO C7/126/93, C8/420/53, C9/294/7, C9/312/10, C9/457/109, C10/230/7.

63 PRO C8/404/37.

64 M. J. Power, 'Shadwell: The Development of a London Suburban Community in the Seventeenth Century', *London Journal*, Vol. 4, No. 1, 1978, pp. 29-46.

65 *DNB.*

66 Summerson, *Georgian London*, p. 43.

67 PRO C6/259/81, C7/137/63; *Survey of London, St Anne, Soho*, pp. 28-32.

68 PRO C6/259/81, C7/137/63, C10/262/37.

69 PRO C5/45/81, as quoted in *Survey of London, St Anne, Soho*, p. 30.

70 PRO C10/262/37.

71 PRO C7/543/52.

72 PRO C8/294/87, C7/225/4.

73 PRO C7/225/4.

74 Grassby, 'Social Mobility and Business Enterprise', p. 367.

75 *Survey of London, St Anne, Soho*, p. 30.

76 PRO C5/72/88, C10/336/74.

77 PRO C5/292/68.

78 PRO C8/263/91, C8/263/71.

79 *DNB*; D. C. Coleman, 'London Scriveners and the Estate Market in the Later 17th Century', *Economic History Review*, 2nd Series, No. 4, 1951, pp. 221-30; Frank T. Melton, 'Sir Robert Clayton's Building Projects in London, 1666-72', *Guildhall Studies in London History*, Vol. 3, No. 1, October 1977, pp. 37-41.

80 Richard Grassby, 'The Personal Wealth of the Business Community in Seventeeth-Century England', *Economic History Review*, 2nd Series, No. 23, 1970, p. 227.

81 Evelyn as quoted in Coleman, 'London Scriveners', p. 222; Coleman, 'London Scriveners', pp. 221-30.

82 PRO C5/614/105.

83 PRO C8/203/95, C8/241/22.

84 Melton, 'Clayton's Building Projects', p. 41.

85 Jessopp, *Roger North*, p. 56.

86 PRO C7/148/37.

87 PRO C6/326/51, C6/326/51, C7/148/37, C8/357/139, C10/236/48.

88 PRO C5/144/1.

89 PRO C9/321/10, C7/126/93.

90 PRO C8/357/139.

91 *Survey of London, St Anne, Soho,* p. 31.
92 PRO Prob. 11/449 fol. 19; C5/218/38, C5/203/51.
93 PRO C5/151/43, C6/342/50, C6/345/61.
94 PRO C8/353/231.
95 PRO C5/144/1.
96 PRO C10/236/6.
97 PRO C7/258/75.

3 Creating the city: the 'mad intemperance ... of building'

> I went to advise and give directions about the building of two streets in Berkley Gardens, reserving the house and as much of the garden as the breadth of the house. In the meantime I could not but deplore that sweete place (by far the most noble gardens, courts and accomodations, stately porticoes, etc., anywhere about the towne) should be so much straighten'd and turn'd into tenements. But that magnificent pile and gardens contiguous to it, built by the late Lord Chancellor Clarendon, being all demolish'd, and design'd for piazzas and buildings, was some excuse for my Lady Berkeley's resolution of letting out her ground also for so excessive a price as was offer'd, advancing neere £1,000 per ann. in mere ground-rents; to such a mad intemperance was the age come of building about a citty, by far too disproportionate already to nation: I having in my time seene it almost as large again as it was within my memory.
>
> (John Evelyn, *Diary*, 12 June 1664)

The system by which developers improved the value of their land through building is well known. The method adopted was that of dividing the ground up into plots and letting these out on what were called building leases.[1] According to Roger North, Barbon was 'the inventor of this new method of building by casting of ground into streets and small houses, and to augment their number with as little front as possible, and selling the ground to workmen by so much per foot front, and what he could not sell build himself'.[2]

Under this system the builder took a lease or leases from the developer for a number of years which was normally around sixty-six years, in this period, and became ninety-nine years by the nineteenth century. Usually there was only a nominal ground rent for the first year or so, so that there was an incentive to build quickly. It was agreed that the houses must be finished by a certain time and often the leases were not actually granted until the houses were complete. Once the houses were built their value was calculated by what was called the improved rent; that is the difference between the ground rent for the land payable to the freeholder and the rent on the house itself due to the leaseholder. When the leases on the properties expired they would revert to the ground landlord, who then had the possibility of rebuilding and raising the rents.

The advantages of the building lease system were many. For a start, as J. R. Ward has observed in a study of late eighteenth-century Bristol, it was a system which allowed finance to operate within a fragmented industrial structure.[3] It provided a way in which the capital of the investor could be combined with the skills of the builder, without the former being defrauded and with the latter maintaining his independent status. This was important, as Ward says, at a time when wage labour was considered a degrading servitude.[4] It devolved the supervision of labour and prevented the tying up of investment capital in wages. The landlord's objective above all was to increase income without committing capital. Furthermore, it allowed for the cost of development to be separated from the cost of construction, in theory at least, even if this did not always happen in practice. This meant that the overall costs of building did not fall solely on one group but were fairly widely spread. It permitted a number of levels of investment to operate, again facilitating the easy movement of capital and credit. It enabled a separation of long-term and short-term investment. The developer or freeholder had a longer term interest in the land which was sustained by the periodic falling in of the leases; the builder had a short-term interest. He could recoup his money very quickly by the sale or letting out of the property once it was completed. The developer was freed from the construction cost but received his return from the improved rents once the houses were completed. The role of the developer was to provide or attract the risk capital and business acumen necessary for speculative development. The building lease system was perfectly adapted to both the labour and the financial conditions of the period.

For the time being let us continue to consider the process from the lead developer's side. Having acquired the land either leasehold or freehold, the next task was to provide the infrastructure that would attract builders and make development possible. Of the two essential services for the house, water coming in and waste being taken out, only the latter was provided for. The building of sewage and drainage systems seems generally to have been undertaken by developers, while the matter of water supply was the responsibility of each individual household.[5] Water was piped to the house by private water companies, namely the New River Company at this time.

At Red Lion Fields Barbon agreed, in the building contract, to: 'make common sewers in the said respective streets for the conveniences of the houses agreed to be erected and built in and upon the said field, closes and premises before mentioned, and carrying the waste water of and from the said houses'.[6] As Neil Burton points out, sewers, or 'showers' as they were also called,[7] were not for carrying sewage in the modern sense (i.e. human waste), but for taking dirty water from the house. This expenditure on essential infrastructure was recovered from the lessees, as at Exeter Court where William Edge, one of the builders, had to pay the developer, Barbon, so much per foot towards the cost of building a drain for the two houses he had undertaken.[8]

Having secured and prepared his land the developer had to find builders to carry out the work. The art in attracting them lay in drawing up building leases which struck a balance between being at a low enough cost and of sufficient length to attract builders, and yet high enough to cover the developer's outlay and make a profit within a reasonable time-scale. The evidence from leases is scanty. However, some of the range and variety in types of leases can be gleaned from the examples that follow. The details of a large number of leases survive for the Wellclose development, they are nearly all dated 1683 with a few from 1696 as well.[9] These are all for 61 years. They are mainly in the £2-£12 bracket, with a few reaching £20. Most of the plots are small averaging around 25-50 ft by 20-100 ft. At Red Lion Fields leases made in the years 1686-88 were generally either for 40, 50, 60 or 61 years, with the average cost being £11-£20 p.a. Most of the frontages were around 20 ft by 100 ft deep, and there was an obvious correlation between frontage size and cost.[10] The final examples come from the 1690s and 1700s in Lamb's Conduit Fields.[11] The first set of leases form a group dating from 1689 to 1692. They are all either 44-47 years or 61 years in length and cost £6-£10. The next leases were made in 1701-02, they are for 61 years and average around £10. By 1703-04 the average price has dropped to around £6, and in 1707-08 they are selling mainly for £2-£6, albeit with seemingly smaller plots. This is an example of a developer dropping the price of the building leases and having obvious difficulty in disposing of them, as the cases surrounding this evidence make clear. (See figure 10 for a plan of the Ormond Street area built on Lamb's Conduit Fields which had a schedule of leases attached, dating from 1702-17 and 1719-20. These are transcribed in the Appendix.)

The necessity for the developer to dispose of the building leases as quickly as possible was not only so as to begin the building process, but also to provide a security against which to raise further capital. As Roger North said, Barbon's pioneering of the building lease system, 'has made ground rents high for the sake of mortgaging, and others following his steps have refined and improved upon it, and made a superfaetation [growth in the number] of houses about London'.[12] Not only could ground rents be

mortgaged, they were also sometimes sold off. This happened at
Red Lion Fields where in 1686 Barbon sold his ground rents to
Jeremiah Whichcott, a merchant. This seems to have been a
measure of last resort, with Barbon 'declaring his great want of
money, saying that he could not raise any elsewhere'.[13] Whichcott
paid £1,050 and Barbon agreed to convey to him ground rents of
either £100 p.a. freehold or £140 p.a. leasehold. In the event Barbon
did not make the conveyance, because according to Whichcott, he
realized that he had made a deal very disadvantageous to himself,
while Barbon claimed that Whichcott was, 'likely thereby to make
a greater profit of his money than by an East India voyage'.[14]

It is difficult to work out the overall finances and developer's
profit on most schemes as the improved ground rents and final
costings are hardly ever given. However, some idea of the sort of
return that could be expected can be gleaned from the calculations
made in connection with projected building at Smith Square, Westminster for the developer Bevis Lloyd.[15] Here the builder James
Friend estimated that, on the buildings then standing the current
owner was receiving a return of £160 p.a. If these were pulled down
and a new square was built this would cost £7,000–£7,400 to build,
and the rents would be improved to at least £900 p.a. Lloyd ran
into financial difficulties and only thirteen houses were completed
while he was directing operations. But it seems from later figures
for the development that Friends' estimate was probably credible.

At Essex House, Barbon was reported as making a profit of
£5,000–6,000 according to Samuel Vincent and £8,000 according
to various aggrieved builders and tenants.[16] The former is a more
reliable source as he bought Essex House from Barbon in 1676 for
£19,700 with ground rents amounting to £1,003 2s 7d. As Barbon
had paid somewhere between £13,000 and £15,000 for the freehold
Vincent's calculation would seem to be correct. Barbon only
bought the house in 1675, so this shows the remarkable speed with
which the ground was developed.

Barbon's attempts at building in Lamb's Conduit Fields were less
successful.[17] Here Barbon and his chief backer Richard Kent estimated that their scheme would bring in £2,000 p.a. in ground rents
but the development ran into trouble. Barbon seems to have had
considerable financial difficulties in the 1690s, and North thought
that by the time of his death in 1698 he had lost most of the fortune
he had made.[18] The schemes on the Bedford Ground and Rugby
estate in Lamb's Conduit Fields begun in this period remained
incomplete at his death. Kent and Barbon both died, and another
investor Sir Nathaniel Curzon took over the organization of the
building programmes. By 1699 he was despairing of the scheme
ever taking off and was ready to surrender his interest in the

ground for payment of his debt, because of the poor return that it had bought him. However, by 1709 he was very keen to maintain the properties, which nearly fifteen years after the land was acquired were at last beginning to be profitable. Curzon calculated that he was receiving a ground rent increase of 6 per cent p.a., and that in 1709 his profits from the Lamb's Conduit Field area were £1,726 7s 5d. This had not yet reached Barbon's £2,000 p.a. but it was beginning to approach it.

So far we have been considering the lead developers who took sites of land and initiated the development process. Now it is time to turn from them to consider the level below them, those who took building leases from the principal developer. Many of these people were developers too, but they were developers of houses rather than of land. They were essentially of two types: those who carried out the construction work themselves (i.e. builders and craftsmen), and those who employed someone else to undertake the construction for them. People from outside the construction industry might take a building lease or leases themselves, or they might lend money through a mortgage to a builder. Both these types of people, following Chalkin's definition, I shall refer to as building undertakers.[19]

There were then many tiers within the development process. Under the lead developer and his backers there would often be another level of developers. They would lease parts of the site supported by their own financial network. They might let off building leases in smaller parcels to lesser building undertakers, and they might let these again to those who would carry out the construction work. Summerson's model of developers letting building leases directly to craftsmen can hardly ever be found, and most developments operated through a complex web of financial and contractual arrangments with many intermediate levels and half levels.

J. R. Ward found that a significant amount of development in late eighteenth-century Bristol was financed by developers advancing money to builders in the form of mortgages. There was a great use made of mortgages as a way of organizing credit in late seventeenth- and early eighteenth-century London, but not usually in this manner. There were, of course, exceptions to this rule. In the building of Smith Square the developer Bevis Lloyd put all the work in the hands of one builder, James Friend, who was to receive leases of the ground, but who was financed by money lent on mortgage by Lloyd.[20] In effect Friend was employed by Lloyd, but the advantage of organizing the construction in this way, as opposed to Lloyd contracting directly with Friend, was that it placed the incentive for finishing the building with the building lessee. As Ward says of the developer, 'his builders might be not much better than employees, but they were employees who were paid by results'.[21]

It was more usual for the developer, if he was financing construction himself, to take building leases and then make contracts with the builders for the construction work. This is what Parsons and Barbon had to do on a large part of Wellclose, the Old Artillery Ground and Tower Hill, where they had trouble finding building undertakers for their plots. John Foltrop, for example, was employed by them to do the carpenter's work on nine houses at Wellclose Square, where he also built two others on his own account.[22]

It was much more likely that a mortgage to cover building costs would come from an intermediate investor arranged by the builder, rather than via the developer. At the Old Artillery Ground one building lease was taken by William Sabine. He turned to a professional financier to raise the money to build his house and borrowed £100 from William Bower a scrivener. This money belonged to Ann Miller who agreed to it being used for a mortgage to Sabine.[23] This is an example of what seems to be a fairly widespread phenomenon of people with small or lump sums of money to invest placing them in modest building projects. However, this was not necessarily a secure investment as can be seen in this instance, where Miller was likely to end up with only £50 as Sabine never finished the house. This also occurred at Great Essex Street where John Bland sold one of his leases to Thomas Alderman, a bricklayer. Alderman then mortgaged the lease to Thomas Manning, a gentleman of London, 'pretending that he would sell the house as soon as it was finished'. This he did not do nor did he repay his debt, so Manning tried to enter the house to let it himself. However, he was unable to do this as in law he was only a sublessee, and could not claim a legal title to the lease.[24] This was a common situation among those pursuing claims in Chancery.

There are several examples of mortgages being obtained either prior to building or during building,[25] but it seems it was more common to grant mortgages after building or once building was nearly completed. At Exeter House the builders asked Barbon for the leases on their houses before they had finished them, 'so that they could take up money on them in order to finish the building, which they could not then do for want of money'.[26] William Edge, a well-known bricklayer, but also described as a fletcher, had a lease on a house in Red Lion Fields on which he took a mortgage once he had 'nearly finished one messuage'.[27] He borrowed £200 from Samuel Newman, a painter, a loan that was arranged through a scrivener, Edward Bussey of Chancery Lane. House building and house ownership under the leasehold system provided a channel for the investment of small sums often from people in other trades, and also by women. Widows were among those providing capital for house builders, for example at Red Lion Fields where Abigail Eles, a widow, lent £280 to Peter King, a mason, plus a further £200 in trust for her son.[28] The investing of small legacies in property, often in trust for children, is also frequently found in the evidence.

There were many ways in which investors could lose out in the mortgaging system. Buildings could be double-mortgaged, as in the case of George Jackson, bricklayer, who mortgaged part of the Bedford Ground to William Robinson, gentleman, in 1689 for £600. When Robinson tried to reclaim the property because the debt was unpaid, he was informed by Jackson that part of the area was already mortgaged to Samuel Biscop for £200.[29] Mortgages might be reassigned leading to long lines of credit being established. James Groves, a painter stainer, had a title to a lease from Simeon Betts, a carpenter and builder; he then reassigned this mortgage to Joseph Hunt, a stationer and scrivener, from whom he borrowed £100.[30] Another way in which the security of a mortgage could be diminished, besides previous claims, was if it was deliberately allowed to decay so that its value was lessened. Matthew Allam, a stationer, claimed that he lent Robert Easton, a carpenter, £230 on a house in Arundel Street, Westminster. Easton then refused to pay the money and deliberately let the property decline.[31]

Mortgages could be used for either short-term or long-term credit and sometimes essentially as a form of payment. It is evident that Summerson's contention that most builders/craftsmen borrowed from each other is not correct,[32] rather they borrowed from other tradesmen and small investors on credit. Nor was it always building tradesmen borrowing from others. John Foltrop and John Warren, the former a master builder, the latter described as a carpenter, lent £600 to George Hudson, a gentleman of Lincoln's Inn, in the form of a mortgage.[33]

A good example of the chains of investors and lessees that were common in the development of houses can be found in part of Red Lion Fields.[34] Here it is possible to trace the long lines of credit and multiple lettings and sub-lettings which made the development process possible. To begin with the chain of leases on the ground. The land belonged to Trustees for the Poor of the Parish of St Clement Danes. They let it to Nicholas Barbon in 1687, and he assigned it to Richard Ingram, an ironmonger, almost certainly as a mortgage. Barbon and Ingram then jointly made building leases to John Prince, a bricklayer. Some of these leases Prince kept and built himself, and some he sub-let to William Gillingham, described as both gentleman and bricklayer, and some to William Keene, bricklayer. In other words there were at least three or four levels of leasing here before building even started. All of these people borrowed money to carry out their particular stage in the process. Barbon borrowed money from Richard Ingram to pay for his lease and for development costs. Ingram then assigned his leases once the buildings were underway, but unfinished, to George, Marquis of Halifax in return for £945. Prince meanwhile had assigned his interest to Robert Sympson, clerk of St Feltwell Mary's, Norfolk for £500, a rare example of an investor from outside London. William Keene the sub-lessee borrowed £300 on his three properties from John Burneby, a brewer. The other builder, William Gillingham, was lent the following amounts from the people listed, on the security of at least five houses in Dean Street, Holborn:

Robert Tym	scrivener	£240
Mary Goodwin		£100
Arthur Reeves	apothecary	£100
Thomas Avis	gentleman	£500

None of these people from Halifax to Avis had had their debts repaid, with the result that they all claimed the property which had been mortgaged several times over. Strype gives a wonderful description of the havoc that multiple mortgaging could wreak, in this instance in the redevelopment of Clarendon House:

> Which said house and garden being sold by the Duke of Albemarle was by the undertakers laid out into streets, who, not being in a condition to finish so great a work, made mortgages and so entangled the title, that it is not to this day finished and God knows when it will. So that it lieth like the ruins of Troy (some having foundations begun, others carried up to the roof and others covered, but none of the outside work done).[35]

It is very hard to estimate the sums involved in building houses. They vary greatly from place to place and the outlay of the building undertaker ranged from those building a single house to those developing quite significant tracts of land. But as a great generalization, whereas the lead developers were dealing in sums of thousands and tens of thousands of pounds, the building undertakers were generally dealing in hundreds and sometimes thousands of pounds.[36] This serves to underline the very considerable sums required for building and hence the massive dependency on credit to facilitate operations.

Some figures are available from the cases of how much a house cost to build. The prices given for houses in the City are very high. James Burkin's house, which was commissioned by him and described as a mansion house, cost the princely sum of £1,601.[37] This compares with a cost of not greatly over £100 for a West End speculatively built house. This might seem an abnormal figure, except that, for the only other City scheme for which figures are given, the number is also in the thousands. This is at Love Lane where three houses cost just over £3,000 to build (albeit that the original estimate was for around £1,500 for the three).[38] The highest West End figure was the estimate for Smith Square, where it was calculated in 1686 that twenty-eight houses would cost £7,000 (i.e. £250 per house). While at Drury Lane John Ragdall, a glazier, claimed to have erected eleven houses and a brick wall for only £1,100, i.e. £100 per house.[39] The average price was probably in the region of £100–£500. This would seem to be in line with the sums borrowed through mortgages by builders given above. The minimum cost for a building undertaker taking a lease on only one house was likely to be at least £150 and probably several hundred to a thousand pounds. It seems that it was not difficult to find small investors willing to lend such sums.

What the building undertaker's return for such an outlay would be is even more difficult to ascertain. Once the house was completed the lease would be either sold, or retained and the property let. Building undertakers who were builders were more likely to take the former route as this would provide them with the cash to pay off the debts they had incurred during building, while non-building trades lessees might be more likely to keep the property perhaps looking for a longer term investment or a regular income. Only a few figures can be found in the cases of the price that houses sold for once built. One of Barbon's houses in Mincing Lane was sold for £2,650,[40] and a house in Bedford Row for £880 in 1695.[41] Close by in Red Lion Square, or Fisher's Walks as it was also known, a house was sold by the builder Alexander Cutting to Sir Edward Dering for £800 in 1692.[42] Barbon sold a house in St James's Square in 1677 to the Earl of Kent for £6,400.[43] One reason that the price in this instance was so high is that the properties here were sold with their freeholds and not leasehold as was normal.[44] If the prices given previously for the cost of building are correct, these sales would represent a profit for the builder of at least several hundred pounds, and probably a great deal more in the case of the Mincing Lane house.

Ground rents in building leases were usually fairly low if calculated on an individual house basis. The problem is that they were not calculated in this way and so the figures given above relate to larger pieces of land on the whole. However, it is still worth considering examples of improved rents, where they occur, to see what kind of income they yielded for those who received them, bearing in mind that they had to cover the same construction cost of several hundred pounds for each house. A house in Bedford Walks was let for £76 p.a. in 1695. The ground rent was £5 p.a., so there was an increase in value of £71 p.a. since building. This was the same house that was bought for £880, so there was a choice between this sum immediately or £76 annually, which would take eleven and a half years to equal the £880.[45] At Drury Lane Robert Ragdall claimed to have improved the land on which he built his eleven houses to £154 p.a. over the ground rent, an increase of £14 p.a. per house.[46] The schedule of mortgages on properties in the possession of the developer Isaac Symball at the time of his death gives some idea about the ratio between ground rents and rents on houses in 1696.[47] Generally the ground rents are in the region of £3–£9 per house for properties in the Soho or Holborn areas, with a figure of £15 for a house in Arlington Street, Piccadilly. House rentals vary more widely. The range for Arlington Street was £7–£70. Most of the letting rents are around the £20 mark, although there are two other high ones in Red Lion Square of £40 and £60 with ground rents of £9 12s. The difference between the ground rent and the rent for a house then was substantial but not enormous.

While it is hard to trace those thousands of small investors who lent sums against finished properties or who bought the leases once the houses were built, it is much easier to form some idea about those involved earlier in the process, the building undertakers. Sometimes schedules of lessees giving occupations were included in the Chancery evidence. The following schedule of lessees was attached to a case about Essex House. All the following people took building leases from Barbon for sixty-one years from Lady Day 1675. The number of houses they built is given in another case.[48]

Non-trade		
Cornelius Battie	yeoman	1 house
William Taylor	gent	1 house
William Thompson	esq	1 house and a stable
Thomas Billing	blacksmith	3 houses
Edward Bradford	haberdasher	1 house and a wharf
William Howell	merchant	3 houses
Abraham Veere	coalmerchant	wharf
John Gascoigne	tailor	2 houses
John Bland	scrivener	7 houses (subsequently took more, probably totalling c.14)
Thomas Cox	merchant taylor	2 houses
Edward Gavill	mercer	2 houses
Leonard Hancock	coalmerchant	wharf
Thomas Price	goldsmith	2 vaults
Humphrey Hetherington	gent	1 house
William Edge	fletcher	2 houses

John Greene	carpenter	4 houses
Joseph Kithera	carpenter	3 houses
Thomas Alderman	bricklayer	3 houses
John Edge	bricklayer	7 houses
William Hughes	bricklayer	1 house
John Young sr	mason	N/A
Thomas Gammon	carpenter	4 houses
William Blackwell	carpenter	3 houses
George Cooke	bricklayer	2 houses
Thomas Staples	carpenter	N/A
George Curtis	bricklayer	3 houses

This list does not represent all the leases made at Essex House, but it seems to represent the majority made by February 1676. The list has been divided into two parts, in order to see the division between building undertakers from inside and outside the construction industry. Of these, fifteen come from outside the industry and eleven from inside. Those from outside fall into the categories of: gentlemen, one yeoman, a professional moneylender (Thomas Price), merchants, and those from other trades. Of these, three were gentlemen, three were merchants (of whom the two coal merchants had a direct interest in their buildings), and six were tradesmen. There was also John Bland, who was Barbon's agent. Most of these people were taking leases on one to three houses. William Edge is here described as a fletcher but elsewhere as a bricklayer, and therefore could be said to come into both categories. It was common to hold more than one job and so the terms by which people are described must be treated with some caution. There are eleven people from inside the building industry: five carpenters, five bricklayers and one mason. They built between one and seven houses each, but the majority built three or four, a higher number than the other group. Whether such a spread is typical there is no way of knowing. What it does show is the range of people who might act as building undertakers.

It is hard to find out about the smaller developers and investors in detail but we do have some information about Arnold Browne, who featured in the list of building lessees in Lamb's Conduit Fields. Arnold Browne, esquire of Mile End Green, is an interesting example of a building undertaker from outside the construction industry. We know a good deal about him because of a dispute in Chancery over his wife's jointure.[49] Browne was the son of Captain Arnold Browne, a mariner of Stepney. He married Hannah Blake in 1676 at All Hallows, London Wall. After his father died, which was some time around 1682, Browne's life changed dramatically.

In 1682 he had money, land and houses. He had estates in Mile End, Suffolk and Norfolk. He also held the office of Collector of Customs at Bristol, which brought him in £600 p.a. After his father died his mother discharged his father's interest in the £11,000 which he, his father and William Clough had paid for the office. This led to a falling out with his mother so that Browne left the post and came to London. Here, 'being of a very good estate he was prevailed upon to lend Dr Barbon money'.[50] He became joint promoter with Barbon in the development of Derby House in 1683, making the leases to the builders together with Barbon.[51] He also took leases of three pieces of ground in Lamb's Conduit Fields from Barbon in 1689.[52] However this association with Barbon brought him nothing but trouble. He said that he lent Barbon money, 'on security of grounds which proved far short in value than he promised to make them by building'.[53] By 1701 he was owed c. £11,000 as a result of his association with Barbon and he was also owed c. £6,000 by John Price. He said that if he had stayed in Bristol he would not have met with these 'many and great losses',[54] and that the debts are 'desperate and irrecoverable'.[55]

In conclusion we can say that the speculative building process that developed in this period was able to function primarily because of the separation of interests in land which the freehold/leasehold system allowed. The leasehold system permitted the easy movement of capital through the complicated layers of ownership and more importantly enabled the use of mortgages, which facilitated the extensive use of credit to fund operations. This dependency on credit was absolutely typical of late seventeenth- and eighteenth-century business operations, as Richard Grassby says: 'All men in active business had, moreover, a high proportion of their working capital in credit to clients and in debts owing.'[56] Above all we can see that far from adopting an amateur approach dependent on barter, this was a heavily financed major industry which drew on investment from a wide range of external sources and was one of the largest and most significant sectors of the metropolitan economy.

Notes

1 See: John Summerson, *Georgian London*, 1945 Harmondsworth, Penguin, 1978 edn, pp. 39–40; and for a more detailed account, Donald J. Olsen, *Town Planning in London: The Eighteenth and Nineteenth Centuries*, New Haven and London, Yale University Press, 1964.

2 Roger North, *The Autobiography of the Hon. Roger North*, ed. Augustus Jessopp, London, D. Nutt, 1887, pp. 54–5.

3 J. R. Ward, 'Speculative Building at Bristol and Clifton, 1783-1793', *Business History*, Vol. 20, No. 1, January 1978, pp. 3-18.

4   Ward, 'Speculative Building', p. 3.

5   The only account of servicing the house to date, although for the eighteenth century, is by Neil Burton in *Life in the Georgian City*, London, Viking, 1990, pp. 74-98.

6   PRO C9/294/7.

7   PRO C8/420/53.

8   PRO C8/263/91.

9   PRO C6/326/51, C7/148/37, C8/651/19, C9/245/3, C10/337/19.

10 PRO C5/153/95, C5/173/119, C5/251/11, C7/152/40, C7/165/5, C7/316/37, C8/353/231, C8/517/43, C8/535/71, C9/294/7, C9/457/109, C9/461/173, C10/244/50.

11 PRO C5/148/21, C5/155/66, C5/173/119, C5/178/4, C5/251/11, C8/614/9, C10/244/50, C10/324/5.

12 Jessopp, *Roger North*, p. 55.

13 PRO C10/336/74.

14 PRO C10/336/74.

15 PRO C7/210/8, C7/210/27, C6/351/22.

16 PRO C8/269/79.

17 PRO C5/151/43, C6/345/61, C5/251/11.

18 Jessopp, *Roger North*, p. 57; for more on the economic crisis in the 1690s see, D. W. Jones, *War and Economy in the Age of William III and Marlborough*, Oxford and New York, B. Blackwell, 1988.

19 C. W. Chalkin, *The Provincial Towns of Georgian England: A Study of the Building Process, 1740-1820*, London, Edward Arnold, 1974, p. 157.

20 PRO C7/210/8, C7/210/27.

21 Ward, 'Speculative Building', p. 10.

22 PRO C5/144/1.

23 PRO C5/299/53.

24 PRO C7/233/30.

25 For example, PRO C8/284/150.

26 PRO C6/280/107.

27 PRO C10/283/68.

28 PRO C8/517/43.

29 PRO C8/551/122.

30 PRO C10/322/17.

31 PRO C10/308/3.

32 Summerson, *Georgian London*, pp. 76-7.

33 PRO C10/321/9.

34 PRO C7/152/40.

35 Strype, *Survey of London*, as quoted in Norman Brett-James, *The Growth of Stuart London*, London, London and Middlesex Archaeological Society with George Allen & Unwin, 1935, p. 384.

36 Richard Grassby, 'The Personal Wealth of the Business Community in Seventeenth-Century England', *Economic History Review*, 2nd Series, No. 23, 1970, pp. 220-34. From his studies he gives the following as a rough guide to the wealth of businessmen in the 1670s: £20,000 upwards - super rich; £10-20,000 - very rich; £10,000 - rich; £5-10,000 - substantial; £1-5,000 - middling merchants; £500-1,000 - prosperous tradesmen; £500 or less - artisans.

37 PRO C10/181/4.

38 PRO C6/289/21.

39 PRO C5/65/41.

40 PRO C7/543/52.

41 PRO C7/258/75.

42 PRO C7/165/5.

43 PRO C8/231/11.

44 See, *Survey of London, St James, Westminster*, London, Athlone Press, Vol. XXIX, 1960, pp. 56–8.

45 PRO C7/258/75.

46 PRO C5/65/34.

47 PRO C7/316/37.

48 PRO C8/203/95, C8/241/22.

49 PRO C6/340/8, C7/169/26.

50 PRO C7/169/26.

51 PRO C7/365/27, C10/260/44, C10/272/96, C10/294/65, C10/503/187.

52 PRO C5/155/66, C9/440/94.

53 PRO C7/169/26.

54 PRO C6/340/8.

55 PRO C7/169/26.

56 Richard Grassby, 'English Merchant Capitalism in the Late Seventeenth Century: The Composition of Business Fortunes', *Past and Present*, No. 46, 1970, pp. 87–107.

4 Constructing the city: the standardization of production

> The greatest objection against London-houses (being for the most part Brick) is their slightness, occasioned by the Fines exacted by Landlords. So that few houses at the common rate of Building last longer than the Ground-lease, and that is about fifty or sixty years ... And this way of Building is wonderful beneficial to Trades relating to it, for they never want Work in so great a City, where Houses here and there are always Repairing, or Building up again.
>
> (Richard Neve, *The City and Countrey Purchaser and Builder's Dictionary*, 1703, p. 71)

The rapid development of London from the 1660s onwards led to unprecedented opportunities for the construction industry and those working within it. The building of new houses, as Neve wrote, was but the beginning of a cycle of growth, repair and renewal under the leasehold system which offered the prospect of a never-ending supply of work for builders and craftsmen. The building trades were still essentially medieval in structure through their organization into separate crafts.[1] This had been the major feature of the medieval guilds in which apprentices entered one of the crafts for life and each trade jealously guarded its independence and mysteries. The guild system had broken down well before the late seventeenth century and certainly in London any remaining vestiges of power that the Companies had were annihilated by the legislation following the Fire which allowed 'foreigners' from outside the City to work within its boundaries. The building industry might still be organized around separate trades, however the relationship between these different crafts and the methods for contracting them were undergoing a profound transformation.[2] The demands of the new market in housing forced changes in working practices and structures on to the traditional building sector, which struggled to accommodate new requirements for increased flexibility, rapidity and complexity.

The new house was essentially a brick and timber structure. This determined that in the London speculative building world it was the bricklayers and carpenters who dominated. Of all the different trades they are the ones most commonly found undertaking developments on their own account and it was their skills which were most in demand in the London building boom. R. Campbell in his *The London Tradesman* of 1747 wrote this of the bricklayer:

> He works by the yard ... and is a very profitable Business; especially if they confine themselves to work for others, and do not launch out into Building-Projects of their own, which frequently ruin them: It is no new thing in London for those Master-Builders to build themselves out of their own Houses, and fix themselves in Jail with their own materials ... But they are out of Business for five, if not six Months in the Year; and in and about London, drink more than one Third of the other Six.[3]

Joseph Moxon in his *Mechanick Exercises* of 1703 called the bricklayer the 'red mason' the hewer of brick, as opposed to the 'white mason' the hewer of stone.[4] Bricklayers were central to the construction of the house and therefore to the building process. The control of materials was a critical factor in these operations and it therefore makes sense to begin by examining the supply of bricks and the brickmaking process.[5]

There were two types of bricks used in the town house. These were place bricks and stock bricks. Place bricks were the cheaper, less well-burnt bricks which were used to build the skeleton of the house, the party walls and piers between the windows. Stock bricks were the facing bricks used for the external brick skin; they were better fired and therefore stronger. Isaac Ware in *A Complete Body of Architecture* of 1756 differentiated between the two as follows:

> Grey stocks are made of purer earth and better wrought and they are used in fronts of buildings being the strongest and handsomest of this kind; the place bricks are made of the same clay, with a mixture of dirt and other loam material and are more carelessly put in hand, they are therefore weaker and more brittle, and are used out of sight and where less stress is laid upon them: the red bricks of both kinds are made of a particular earth, well wrought and little injured by mixture and they are used in fine works, in ornament over windows and in paving.[6]

As Dan Cruickshank points out in *The Art of Georgian Building*, in fact, despite what Ware says, the place bricks were used where most strain was put on them in supporting the floor joists built into the inner brick skin.[7] In other words the strongest bricks were being used for the non-load bearing facade, while the weakest bricks were doing all the structural work on the inside. This paradoxical constructional concept would seem to suggest that it was the illusion that the facade presented to the world, rather than the inherent strength of the building, which was of primary concern.

In a case of 1679, which revolved around a dispute as to whether bricks ordered as stock bricks, on delivery only proved to be usable as place bricks, the place bricks are priced at 11*s* per 1,000 and the stock bricks at 20*s* per 1,000.[8] Analysis of the figures given in

Chancery cases provides a few firm figures for the cost of bricks to the builder or tradesman, given in the table below.

| | | *Brick prices* | | | |
Date	PRO no.	Cost per unit(s)	carriage inc.	unit	number
1667	C6/289/21	22s	yes	1,000	20,000
1668	C6/289/21	24s	yes	1,000	10,000
1681	C8/388/70	16s	yes	1,000	800,000

The lower price for the later date can probably be explained by the large number delivered. Carriage costs were normally included but one figure is given for the cost of transporting bricks, this is 3s per 1,000 in 1668.[9] This is a relatively high cost in proportion to the cost of the actual bricks. Alan Cox writes in his article 'Bricks to build a Capital' that although bricks sell relatively cheaply they are extremely heavy and so their transport costs are high. This would have been particularly so in the days of horse-drawn power.[10] To minimize costs it was important to obtain or make bricks as near to the place that they were required as possible. London was fortunate in having plentiful deposits of brick earth which were easily worked and after the Fire the exploitation of the land around the city for brickmaking began. Christopher Wren wrote, 'The Earth about London, rightly managed, will yield as good Brick as were the Roman bricks ... and will endure, in our Air, beyond any Stone our Island affords.'[11] Both the stocks and their inferior cousins, the place bricks, could be made from London clay, hence the name 'London stock' which developed at this time. Bricks were also imported along the Thames from such places as Kent and Sussex.

Brickmaking by its very nature results in a uniform product. Bricks were standardized by size and to some extent by type. Joseph Moxon described how to make mouldings for features such as brick cornices or fascias.[12] However, the use of ornamental brick-work on the facades of speculative houses would often only be confined to string courses and rubbed bricks for window and door surrounds. Wood was the normal material for more complex ex-ternal decoration at the time (see figures 33 and 34). The making of bricks was a hand process and it was not until the second half of the nineteenth century that brick production was mechanized. The main technological invention of the seventeenth century was the pug mill. This was a horse-powered mixing machine used to get the clay to the right consistency before making it into bricks, an operation which had previously been done by treading or by hand. As with the techniques for bricklaying those used to produce

bricks remained fundamentally the same, it was only the scale of
production that was greatly increased.

As the development boom took off, London became ringed with
brick fields around its outer edge. We find brickmaking going on
in the southern part of Shoreditch by one Thomas Barnes in Swan
Field, next to the obviously named Brick Lane.[13] What seems to
have happened is that areas were used for brickmaking until they
were exhausted and then built over. In Shoreditch a close is mentioned 'formerly digged for bricks', and Barnes is cited as having
'liberty to dig and carry away brick earth, to make cellars and build
houses'. Barnes was the manager of the operation: 'he contracted
with five men and one boy for their making bricks there in the
summer season; for their labour and pains he paid them £5 11s 0d
and was to give them 2s per 1,000 for the bricks'. Barnes then
assigned his lease to Barbon with, 'the benefit of the brickmaking
contract, the brick cart, the clay cart, the harness and 6 horses, 19
loads of sand, 6 loads of straw and 4 barrows'. The deal in fact never
came off and Barbon took possession of the land by force. Barbon
then threatened the new owner of the land Edward Proby, 'that
he will keep the said Proby in suit in Chancery about two years,
and in that time will make out and convert all the brick-earth on
the premises'. Brickmaking was going on in Red Lion Fields in the
1680s prior to building [14] and also in Lamb's Conduit Fields.[15]

Besides the clay, or 'malm' as it was known, the other vital
ingredient for London bricks was rubbish. The mixing in of
'Spanish', which was ashes or rubbish with ashes, was a practice
peculiar to the London industry. A comment from the Company
of Bricklayers and Tilers in 1714 explains how it came about:

> the practice of using ashes commonly called Spanish in making bricks
> begun about forty years since, occasioned by diging up several fields
> contiguous to the city after the great fire which fields having ben much
> dunged with ashes it was observed the bricks made with earth in those
> fields would be sufficiently burned with one half of the coles commonly
> used.[16]

Spanish therefore helped to reduce the amount of fuel needed
to burn bricks and it was used in vast quantities by brickmakers.
The best source was the city's rubbish which contained a large
amount of ash. There was a large market in waste and rubbish. Not
only was it used in brickmaking but also for making streets and
filling in and levelling off land, as the following extract from an
account for Lamb's Conduit Fields makes clear:

> Paid Parker, Ellarton and Smith at several payments the money
> which they expended for bringing in rubbish to fill and level
> the north side of Ormond Street for the conveniency of coaches

and carts passing and repassing, filling up and levelling Gloucester Street, filling up part of the square, levelling and gravelling £78 5s 0d.[17]

The use of large quantities of rubbish was one reason that the new developments were highly unpopular with those who adjoined them. It was reported to the Privy Council how at Red Lion Fields Dr Barbon, 'made several laystalls there out of garbage and offals from several markets, sufficient to endanger the bringing of a plague into the neighbourhood'.[18] A laystall was a burial place or rubbish heap. No wonder if Barbon was piling up rotting offal in the middle of Bloomsbury that the inhabitants objected so violently to his presence. Rubbish was also used to help level out land which had suffered the ravages of the brickmakers' operations.

Barbon's participation in brickmaking and therefore control over his own supplies was perhaps unusual. It seems that bricklaying and brickmaking were on the whole two separate activities, except perhaps in his unique case. Bricklayers generally did not have control over brick supplies or own brick fields. Between the brickmaker and the bricklayer came those such as Jeffrey and Isaac Wood, 'being partners and dealing in buying and selling bricks'.[19] While Campbell writes of the 'Brick Maker', whose 'business is by some not reckoned very reputable'.[20] He notes that he is paid by the master builder at so much per thousand, again implying that the two were generally separate activities.

Carpenters were the other key operators in the building of the speculative house. Traditionally there had been a distinction between the carpenter's and the joiner's functions. The carpenter was responsible for the structure of the building laying the joists, girders and rafters and sometimes putting on the roof. The joiner was responsible for the fine work such as making doors, laying floors, preparing ceilings and doing the partitioning and wainscotting.[21] With the relaxation of guild regulations following the Fire the boundary between the two began to blur and it became common to find both sorts of work being undertaken under the same contract. Hentie Louw, who has studied the division between the two areas, argues that by the latter part of the seventeenth century the power of the carpenters had waned, while that of the joiners was on the increase.[22] He writes that by the third quarter of the century there were three categories of carpenters in London. Firstly, a small group of master carpenters, 'whose organisational skills and business acumen enabled them to exploit the opportunities offered by an expanding economy to the full in order to become larger-scale building contractors, wholesale suppliers of building materials and "architects"'.[23] At the opposite end of the scale to the elite were an expanding number of non-affiliated craftsmen, who constituted a major challenge to institutional guild control. Sandwiched between these groups were the small master craftsmen and their apprentices who belonged to the Carpenters Company and continued to operate in the traditional manner.

The joiners by contrast, who were mainly small to medium operators, maintained a flexibility in their range of work and displayed a willingness to adapt to changing economic circumstances and markets which left them overall as a trade in a far better position. Louw sees their work by the end of the century as ranging over the entire spectrum of woodwork, 'from the delicate artistry of the master cabinetmaker and carver to the more mundane tasks of the building site'.[24] Campbell probably summed up the situation correctly for the mid-eighteenth century when he wrote: 'there are few Joiners but pretend to be Carpenters, so vice versa; but some hands excel more in the one than the other'.[25]

Unlike brick production the requirement for wood could not be met from native supplies. The huge amount of building activity in the late seventeenth and early eighteenth century created a demand for timber which could not be satisfied by the use of indigenous oak alone. Previously this had been the main building material, but there was competition from the Navy for homegrown oak. For the first time in the late seventeenth century imported softwoods began to be used in large quantities.[26] Softwood was easier to work and cheaper than hardwood but less durable. Fir and pine were imported from the Baltic and Norway, and it was said that the Norwegians warmed themselves while the Fire of London burned.[27] The ideal was to use softwood for the interior work, with oak being reserved for the showcase elements of the external windows and doors. In a specification for a square, for example, the doorcases and windows are to be oak but 'the roof, floors, mantletrees [a beam across the opening of a fireplace, an early version of mantlepiece], partitions and lintelling and all timber except the outward doorcases and windows, to be of good fir'.[28] The advantage of using oak on the exterior was both that it was more easily carved for decoration and that, unlike the softer fir, it did not need painting. But it was more common to find softwood being used throughout and fir became the standard constructional timber. This resulted in the painting of all the exterior wood with white lead to stop it rotting and the painting of the interior woodwork because of the fir's pale colour and uneven grain.[29]

Because oak was more expensive and had a prestige value, there was a demand for old oak as well as new. In Lamb's Conduit Fields while the buildings lay unattended and unfinished the majority of the timber was reported to have been stolen away.[30] The market in second-hand goods seems to have been greatest in timber but extended to all kinds of materials. When James Friend agreed to build the market building at Newport House he negotiated to have, 'all the stones, brick, timber, lead, glass, iron, tiles etc. (except wainscott) in that part of Newport House then standing' as part of the deal.[31] Later on in this case we hear of someone using old bricks, some purbeck stone and about fifteen or twenty old tiles in the supposedly brand-new houses of the West End.

As far as the supply and control of timber went the opposite situation seems to have prevailed from that which occurred with bricks. Campbell writes that:

> It requires no very inconsiderable Stock to set up a Timber-Merchant; he must always have a large Stock by him in his Yards, and give considerable Credit to the Master Builders ... Every man who keeps a Timber yard is not a Timber-Merchant, nor the Person I have been describing; most of the Timber-Yards, especially at the Court End of Town, are kept by Carpenters or Master-Builders. These buy their timber from the importer, and retail it to the Trade.[32]

This is possibly borne out by a comment in one of the cases, which describes how someone had, 'made a carpenter's shop and laid great quantities of timber there'.[33] Campbell described a timber merchant as one, 'who is either employed by or furnishes material to the carpenter'.[34] He said that the timber merchant would import wood from abroad: deal from Norway; oak and wainscot from Sweden and England; mahogany from Jamaica; and walnut from Spain.

It was not only in their procurement of materials that the brick and timber trades differed but also in the state in which they received them, particularly the degree to which they were finished or not. Bricks were a standardized product which were ordered from the brickmaker as recognized types. Once bought and delivered to the site no adaptation to the material needed to be made. Timber, however, was an entirely different matter and the different relationship of carpenters and joiners to their supplies may be partly a reflection of the product and its preparation. Any timber in a timber yard would have been cut into logs, at the very least, or planks. From that point on there was a huge range of specificity with which the timber may have been delivered to the site and indeed we find wood arriving on site in such a variety of guises and forms that it is impossible to speculate about prices, even in the most sketchy fashion. In examining the ways and extent to which timber might be finished and whether this would be done on- or off-site, this raises the issue of the extent to which the speculative town house itself may be said to be a standardized product.

It is quite obvious from contemporary building accounts that wood was delivered to the site by suppliers, already cut into different lengths and thicknesses. One set of accounts, for example, distinguishes between five different kinds of deals (i.e. types of fir and pine): 12 foot, 10 foot, flooring, slitt and Christiana.[35] Another includes timber pre-cut to perform different sorts of functions, for example, '67 girders, end and templets'.[36] Elsewhere in the same account we find '1713 feet of lintelling of yellow timber' and '850 feet of band timber and needling' (needling being a beam of wood used as a temporary support for a wall during underpinning), '22 mantletrees and tassells of oak, whereof 4 very large' and so on.[37] What is interesting here is the degree of specificity and finish with which materials were being produced off-site, making the construction of the house a matter of assembling various pre-ordered parts.

The same account shows that it was not just lengths of timber that were made up to order off-site. It includes orders for:

4 great doorcases 12 feet high and 5 feet wide with pilasters	£12 0s 0d
3 doorcases of oak at 15s a piece	£2 5s 0d
2 sash frames 9 feet high at 12s each	£1 4s 0d [38]

There is an order in another set of accounts for 'sashes'.[39] While at Smith Square the builder, James Friend, says that he had, 'sash windows brought sufficient' for the houses,[40] implying that he had them brought to the site ready-made.[41] This evidence shows that the whole structure of the building industry relied upon multiple sub-divisions of labour. Not just in the sub-contracting of work between the different trades, but within those trades, and between on- and off-site production as well.

It is clear that there was a considerable use of standardized elements in the construction of the house, and in the use of rationalized tools, moulds and cutting patterns to produce them. To take the case of the joiner, for example, we know that both doors and windows could be bought ready-made off-site. Summerson commented on the repeated use of regular patterns and parts in Barbon's houses.[42] Such features as the baluster, staircase string decoration and eaves cornice depended for their effect on the repetition of a single pattern. They were therefore ideally suited to large-scale production in standard types. It is noticeable that they were mainly made of wood, a material that was both cheap and familiar. The exception to this was the decorative brick string courses or dentil cornice on the exterior facade. However, this division of labour between the production off-site of building components and their assembly on-site does not mean that the production processes were in any way mechanized or the result of

concentrated factory style centres of production. As John Styles
has argued in his article 'Manufacturing, Consumption and Design
in Eighteenth-Century England', standardization and the large-
scale manufacture of products was a process that was established
long before the advent of mechanized factory production in the
nineteenth century.[43]

How these off-site joinery makers operated is not known. The
techniques they used to produce their standardized doors and windows would have been just the same as those for a custom-made
door. The difference would lie in the quantities produced, instead
of making one door to one pattern perhaps ten doors would be
made. The cutting plates and tracings used to produce such designs
did become more harmonized. What is far more uncertain is the
organization of labour behind these standard elements. It seems
likely that they were produced by teams working under a master
builder or carpenter. Whether some people specialized in working
off-site at the yard and others in working on-site assembling the
parts we do not know. Nor the extent to which individual joiners,
for example, produced only certain parts such as balusters or cornices, while others specialized in panelling and so on. Clive
Edwards in his study of the eighteenth-century furniture trade
details an extremely high degree of specialization, citing a group
of carvers who only did mirror frames and another who confined
themselves to traditional hardwood carving for items such as posts
and bed testers.[44] Edwards says that the extent to which individual
aspects of furniture production were sub-contracted is unclear but
that, 'It is more likely that specialists were developed within a
business, especially as the all-round training of apprentices began
to give way to the particular training associated with one part of
the making process.'[45]

Whether all speculative houses were standardized to this degree
is also open to question. All other speculators and builders were
operating on a smaller scale than Barbon, so that although they
may have used similar methods they would all have had their own
individual patterns and designs. In this way variety was introduced
within the basic model. There was a limited scope for wood carving on the London house, as can be seen at Laurence Pountney Hill
and Queen Anne's Gate (see figures 33–35 and 41). Dan Cruickshank
emphasizes the importance of the carver in the pre-Georgian
period.[46] He in fact makes his distinction in the woodworking
trades between the joiner, who he says carried out the structural
and interior work, and the carver who produced the detailing on
the facade. Carving eventually died out, not only because of the
increased use of repeatable patterns from books, but also because
of the change from oak to fir. Oak is very easy to carve whereas fir

lends itself more readily to regularized, cut shapes. The transfer from hardwoods to softwoods meant that although a traditional building material continued to be used, it was a very different type of timber. This must have led to some extent to a transfer in technology, towards pre-fabrication and off-site production. This might also explain why the joiners, who worked exclusively with the new softwoods, adapted more rapidly to changing conditions than the carpenters, many of whom had trained in the old hardwood, framed building tradition.

The central roles of the carpenter and bricklayer in the production of the London house were to the detriment of the stone masons, once the most powerful of the building trades, and the ones who have received most attention from historians.[47] Although much has been made of the critical role they played as mason contractors in some of the most complex building operations of the day, particularly at St Paul's and Blenheim, in the speculative building boom they were left far behind. While some of them prospered in London as mason contractors at St Paul's and the City churches, those without links to the stone quarries in the countryside were abandoning their trade and taking up other skills more in demand for the new housing market. The Court of Common Council of the Masons' Guild railed against this development but were, of course, powerless to prevent it. In 1694 the Court complained against: 'many persons who use and exercise the trade of masonry (but more especially since the late dreadful fire which happened in London) procured themselves to be made free of other companies by patrimony, redemption and otherwise, contrary to their known duty and to the great prejudice and hindrance of the Company of Masons'.[48]

In London housing the mason's work was confined to decoration and flooring. A list of the work performed by a stone mason is given in one case, it consisted of: paving yards, laying hearths of marble, stoning kitchens, making foot paces, making and placing necks and balls, and all other mason's work, and finding and providing all stone, marble both black and white, and other necessary materials.[49] As well as the masons, plumbers, smiths, plasterers, tilers, painters and general labourers all worked on the construction of the new terraces. However, very rarely do we find them playing a leading organizational or financial role in the way that a carpenter or bricklayer might do so. Besides timber and bricks the other materials required were tiles, stone, sand, lime and hair for the plaster, all of which could be supplied from native resources. Generally workmen provided their own materials, although sometimes they would be provided by the developer. There were specialist dealers in all the different sorts of materials, and traders such as the limeman or rubbish deliverer are mentioned in accounts. It seems that these traders normally provided carriage of goods to the site and there do not appear to have been specialist hauliers of materials as well.

In fact a clear-cut separation between the different trades, as with the carpenters and joiners, was breaking down. Many tradesmen not only came from other non-building trades, but some of them even had more than one trade within the building industry itself. This does not suggest a long apprenticeship system nor a bonding to one mystery or craft in the medieval sense. So we find for example: William Edge, fletcher and bricklayer;[50] Joseph Lem, tiler and bricklayer;[51] Joseph Girle of Marylebone, brewer and brickmaker;[52] William Gillingham, gentleman and bricklayer;[53] and Thomas Norfolk, tiler and bricklayer.[54] This pattern of double employment was not confined to those with some connection with building alone. Michael Power writing about Restoration London comments: 'It is assumed that a person's stated occupation defines his economic role, but in fact it was common for individuals to pursue more than one avocation'.[55]

Building agreements and methods of contracting

The organizational systems within which building took place were also undergoing change at this time, particularly in the areas of contracting and the negotiation of the construction programme. A key part of this process was the building agreement, which was a legally binding document detailing the terms of building and the specification for the structure to be undertaken. It was drawn up between a client or developer and a builder. A very full account survives in Chancery of a building agreement, which is worth giving at some length to show the kinds of conditions that they imposed and the aspects which they covered.

Articles of agreement for building were made on 1 June 1674 between James Burkin Esq. of London, and Thomas Norfolk, tiler and bricklayer, of London and Thomas Denning, carpenter, of London.[56] This is a rare example of a bricklayer and a carpenter contracting jointly together. They agreed to build a mansion house for Burkin on the west side of Mincing Lane in the City, adjacent to a house where Burkin was already living. The house was to be three storeys with vaults below and an attic storey or 'garretts' above. The heights of the different storeys were given and for all the work Norfolk and Denning were to follow the directions of Burkin or 'his supervisor of the said building'. Directions were given for the dimensions and layout of the gardens at both the front and the back with their attendant yards and house of office or privy. Norfolk and Denning covenanted to do all carpenter's work, tiler's, bricklayer's, mason's, plasterer's, plumber's, painter's, smith's, glazier's and other artificers' work. They were to find all timber, boards, bricks, tiles, lime, glass, lead, ironwork, nails and other materials. Directions were given as to the interior sub-division of the house and the exterior ornament. They were directed to follow the third rate of the Act for the Rebuilding of the City for thickness of walls and timber scantlings or exceed it. (The Act is discussed in Chapter 8, below.) They were to use what were called 'good materials', such as spire oak, with some yellow fir, best deals and oak laths. The work was to be finished by the following Christmas, if the weather allowed; or by the latest it should be finished by 25 March 1675, ready to 'turnkey and go'. This was a phrase commonly used to describe fitness for occupa-tion. It was normal to specify a set completion date, often with a financial penalty clause if the building was not finished on time, and most of these houses were erected very speedily.

Norfolk and Denning agreed to remove all rubbish and to pay the workmen and labourers. They were to have all bricks and materials remaining for free when the work was finished. Burkin agreed to pay them at the rate of £40 per square. They would receive this in instalments: £100 after the sealing of the agreement, £100 when the vaults were crowned, £100 when the first-storey walls were built and the floor laid, £100 when the third-storey walls were built and the floor laid, £200 when the roof should be set up and tiled and the chimneys done, £100 when the stairs were set up, £100 when the plasterer's work was laid and lathed, and the rest when the house was finished. Payment for building in stages as work was completed was the normal method outlined in build-ing agreements, where the tradesman was working for someone else. Burkin was permitted to add to or diminish from the building as he wished. Any dispute over work done or payment due was to be arbitrated by two workmen. Burkin gave Norfolk and Denning a bond of £2,000 for performing his covenants. Referral to arbitra-tion with one arbiter being chosen from each side was the usual means of settling disputes, only when this failed was a judgment then sought in the courts.[57]

This agreement covered most of the areas normally detailed and contained the standard conditions. It was common for building agreements to specify that leases would not be granted until build-ing had reached some stated point, often the top floor. This was to ensure that building took place. When Richard Frith and his part-ner Cadogan Thomas were building in St James's, they received their building lease for forty-one years once they had reached the fourth floor as laid down in the building agreement.[58] Sometimes it was stated that a lease would be granted when the house was tiled. At Exeter House the Earl of Exeter convenanted to grant leases to the builders as soon as the houses should be tiled, leaded, or otherwise covered in.[59] This was in order to prevent the scenario which occurred at Lamb's Conduit Fields where many builders abandoned their houses before completion: 'they were forced to run away and leave them when only the foundations of some of them were laid, and some others of them carried higher, but for want of covering the timber rotted and became useless'.[60]

The building operation contractually seems to have been tightly controlled and building agreements were fairly comprehensive and sophisticated. The building agreement specified the number, type and location of houses to be built. The dimensions and materials were given, the work was paid by an agreed rate and within a fixed time-scale, after which financial penalties might be incurred. In practice, of course, things did not always run so smoothly. Firstly, legal arrangements were by no means strictly adhered to in this period and because of the slowness of the courts the penalties of the law were hardly a deterrent. Secondly, the contracts covered most aspects of the construction process, but what they could not adequately cover was the area of quality control. The nearest contracts came to setting a standard for work was by the use of phrases such as to be done in 'good workmanlike manner'[61] or to be 'well made'. Disputes over the quality of the work were therefore common. Thirdly, building is a notoriously difficult activity to regulate comprehensively and an extremely aggravating one for neighbouring parties. There were no building nuisance clauses in contracts in this period and this was another cause of complaint. There were also no conditions covering site safety or good building practice. The speculative building site must have been a relatively safe place to work on account of the low heights involved, compared to places like St Paul's or the royal palaces. However, there was at least one death at Crane Court, where a mason was 'unfortunately killed by a fall of a pole or piece of timber from an house'.[62]

Building agreements, of course, did not prevent building disputes. In the agreement outlined above, Burkin claimed that Norfolk and Denning did not finish the work. He said that they had not paved the yard, laid the steps going into the house, finished the vaults and other things. Neither had they finished within the agreed time. He offered them the money he thought due to them or arbitration. Norfolk and Denning were not satisfied with this and they brought a court action against him charging for work and materials unpaid. They claimed that they did carry out the work properly but that Burkin did not pay them at the agreed times and that he owed money for extra work to them.

In another dispute the architect Sir John Vanbrugh owned an old house and buildings in Palace Yard at Westminster Abbey which he redeveloped.[63] He employed workmen but did not fix any particular sum or rate in advance. When the bills for the work were presented to him he disputed the amount charged and the quality of work carried out. The pantiling he said was not done 'in workmanlike manner' and Henry Doogood, the plasterer, carried out his work but 'not so well as he ought to have done'.[64] It is interesting that no contract appears to have been made between Vanbrugh and the tradesmen here, for at Blenheim Vanbrugh pioneered a form of competitive tendering of which he was extremely proud.[65] In this instance where he was his own developer, he dispensed with a contract altogether. This was probably because to a large extent the building world of the time operated on a system of personal contacts and knowledge of individuals. Contracts were increasingly used but first-hand experience also counted for a great deal.

The importance of personal credibility is borne out by an incident in which a joiner was imprisoned at the suit of Barbon following a fire in a house, where the joiner and his men were working for Barbon. The joiner then brought a case of malicious prosecution against Barbon primarily on the grounds that his long imprisonment, which he held was unjust, had 'lost his credit and reputation'.[66] The word 'credit' had a dual meaning encompassing both the notion of personal credibility and the concept of credit-worthiness.[67] In this period the two went hand in hand, and reputation was the most important asset of all. Elsewhere Barbon employed one Richard Hutchinson, a mason 'having received a very good character of the honesty and fair dealing of the said Hutchinson and of his abilities and skilfulness in his said trade'.[68] Barbon was therefore he said, 'less curious in making such strict and precise bargains with the said Hutchinson as otherwise he should and in prudence ought to have insisted upon'.[69] This theory is refuted by the example of Barbon himself, who undercut everybody who came into contact with him but who continued to operate on a massive scale.

The problem of quality control was not just an issue for those employing workmen but also for those who bought houses and found that they had been shoddily built and were sometimes unfinished. The following is a description by two people who bought houses from Barbon. This is what they found when they took over their properties. The houses:

> were very incomplete, imperfect and unfinished, and such works as were
> done were so ill and artificially done that the same were found to be

new done and amended and repaired, several of the piers being cracked,
the floors shrunk, and the house in some places in danger of falling ...
the vaults thereof are not tight but are so built whereby the rain comes
in to them whereby the defendants cannot lay any goods in them.[70]

As this example shows, although building activity was highly regu-
lated on paper, in reality this did not prevent poor and insufficient
workmanship. Roger North related the low-grade construction at
the Earl of Arlington's ground:

> particularly the high buildings in Arlington Street, which were scarce
> covered in before all the window were wry-mouthed, fascias turned SS,
> and divers stacks of chimneys sunk right down drawing roof and florrs
> with them; and the point was to find out whence all this decay pro-
> ceeded ... We had conversed so much with new houses that we were
> almost turned rope-dancers and walked as familiarly upon joists in gar-
> rets, having a view through all the floors, down to the cellar, as if it had
> been plain ground.[71]

Unlike later eighteenth-century estate development, which was
tightly controlled by the ground landlord, the chain of short-term
interests in the earlier period ensured, despite the strict building
agreements, that few houses were built to last. The nature of the
houses produced under this system was essentially transitory, as
Richard Neve pointed out in the opening quotation of this chapter.[72] The new London house was both more solid and yet at the
same time more impermanent than the traditional timber-framed
buildings that it replaced. A timber-frame construction is far more
flexible; it can be added to, altered and repaired with ease. A brick
building is a shell construction and therefore, although seemingly
more complete, is less flexible and ultimately more impermanent.
The terraced house with its built-in obsolescence was perfectly
suited to the new market conditions. Besides periodic renewal it
also required more maintenance, particularly as regards external
paintwork, and this again made it more profitable in the workings
of a market economy. We might get nearer to the spirit in which
these houses were conceived if we consider them as temporary or
short-life housing for an unstable and uncertain market.

Methods of contracting in the late seventeenth century were
based in part on medieval systems, but were also undergoing a
period of change. The early medieval system had been for the
person commissioning the building to buy the materials and then
hire labour by the day to work it. Later in the Middle Ages there
was scope, for masons especially, to provide their own materials
and there were opportunities for entrepreneurial initiative within
the building trades. This was particularly so for the master craftsmen. However, labour tended to be employed directly by the

patron or body organizing the construction process. Sometime around 1550, according to Malcolm Airs, the direct labour system began to be abandoned and a system in which builders contracted by a predetermined measure and value system started to be introduced.[73]

The contracting system for the late seventeenth and early eighteenth century has generally been considered in terms of the three categories that Wren outlined, 'by the great, by measure, by the day'.[74] 'By the day' was the old direct labour system, in which work was paid for on a daily basis. 'By measure' took various forms but essentially involved a piece-work system which was valued on completion by measurement. 'By the great' meant the undertaking of the whole building operation by a single contractor, who would then sub-contract the work he was unable to carry out himself. Wren elaborated:

> if by the Day it tells me when they are Lazy. If by measure it gives me light on every particular, and tells me what I am to provide. If by the Great I can make a sure bargain neither to be overreached nor to hurt the undertaker: for in things they are not every day used to, they doe often injure themselves, and when they begin to find it, they shuffle and slight the worke to save themselves. I think the best way in this business is to worke by measure.[75]

Wren preferred the measuring option because it gave him the greatest combined supervisory and financial control. In fact what became the most common procedure was one in which patrons made separate contracts with different trades. This was a form of contracting by the great, but it spread the risk among several different operators. This was the system used at St Paul's, for example. None of these alternatives was essentially new, but it is in the seventeenth century that we see a major shift towards the use of contract labour almost exclusively and the use of the measuring system as a basis for determining building costs. The contracting process therefore was an increasingly capitalistic one.

But these were arrangements which evolved for directly commissioned buildings. In the speculative building world a distinction can be made between circumstances in which the tradesman is employed by somebody else and those instances where the tradesman is the holder of a building lease and is working for himself. Payment by the day was the normal method for journeymen workmen who were paid by the masters. The usual way of evaluating work and drawing up contracts in London was by measure. In doing this a tradesman was agreeing to carry out a set amount of work for a particular job at a set price per unit of measurement. When he had finished the work would be measured and he would be paid according to the amount of work done. For example, Nicholas Barbon and John Foltrop made an agreement on 22 September 1687 by which Foltrop agreed to build several houses at Westminster at £5 5s 0d or £5 5s 10d per rod for brickwork and £18 per square for carpenter's work.[76] It was primarily when disputes over measuring arose that they would be submitted to arbitration by two measurers or surveyors, one appointed from each side.[77]

Brickwork was measured in two ways, by the square and by the rod. There were two prices, the 'price between craftsmen' and the 'higher rate' that they charged to others.[78] The rate, of course, would vary with the kind of brickwork being carried out but the rate for the standard constructional brickwork for the 1690s and 1700s is quoted as being £5 5s per rod.[79] This is called the 'usual rate' while the higher rate charged was £5 10s.[80] Other brickwork would be charged differently, brick paving at 14d a yard and brick drain at 14d per foot in this account.[81] Unfortunately schedules of work carried out and the rates at which they were paid are not that common and therefore no complete set of figures for the period can even be hazarded from the prices I have analysed. The other way of charging for brickwork was by the square. This is priced at £32 10s per square in 1686[82] and £40 per square in 1674.[83] The latter price is given as being the same for party walls, front walls and flats within the walls (the latter would unusually suggest some kind of internal brickwork).

Prices for joinery and carpentry work are even harder to ascertain as they occur more rarely in accounts or building schedules. In 1689 the rate for undertaking carpenter's work in building a house is given as £18 per square;[84] this would be for the basic constructional carpentry. Again different jobs were paid at different rates and even within the same job there could be great variations in the way it was paid for and assessed. In an agreement of 1686 sawing old timber was to be paid at a rate of 5s per day, while sawing new timber would be paid by piece-work at 6s per load.[85] Other examples of rates given are plain tiling at 20s per square as the 'price between craftsmen' and 26s per square as the 'higher rate'.[86] In another case the figure given is much lower at 3s 6d per square, although the kind of tiling is not specified here.[87] Lathing and plastering was paid at 9d per yard in c. 1700 and digging at 6d per yard, while whiting (i.e. whitewashing or lime-washing) came in at 1d per yard.[88] These figures although interesting cannot provide a complete economic picture and are perhaps more useful in indicating the range of activities involved in construction and the complexity of the measuring and building operations. Different commodities were evaluated in entirely

different ways and units, and sometimes even minor variations on
taskwork were assessed in an inconsistent manner. Measuring was
indeed, as Wren said, a skilled and complex job.

So far these categories tally with Wren's comments. It is when
we investigate how these established rates might be paid for, that
the picture becomes more complicated and a rather different pattern of contracting begins to emerge. In the case of Barbon and
Foltrop already mentioned, the latter agreed to build several houses
at Westminster at £5 5s 0d or £5 5s 10d per rod for brickwork and
£18 per square for carpenter's work.[89] There are two important
points to be made here. Firstly, it will be noticed that Foltrop is
contracting for more than one trade at the same time. I will return
to this point presently. Secondly, this would seem to imply a
straightforward arrangement whereby Barbon is employing Foltrop and paying him money to carry out work. But on examining
how this work was being paid for it turns out to be a completely
different kind of arrangement altogether. Foltrop was to receive no
money at all for his pains. Instead he would receive leases at the
Middle Temple where he was involved in Barbon's rebuilding of
the chambers.[90] So in fact Foltrop was undertaking to build these
houses himself using his own finances, at the end of which he
would obtain property elsewhere. He received no actual cash during the building operation, which he organized and sustained
himself. This contract therefore uses the concept of 'by measure'
to evaluate and determine costs; it is not a contract between a
payer and a payee but rather between a head developer and an
underdeveloper, each remaining financially autonomous. The
other thing which is significant in this case is that Foltrop was
contracting for both the bricklayer's and the carpenter's work. In
fact he was undertaking to build the entire houses covering all the
work of the different trades. The overall cost was evaluated on
these two contracts alone because, as we have seen, they formed
the major part of the work both structurally and decoratively.
What Foltrop was doing in effect was contracting by the great.

Contracting by the great in the speculative market occurred
when a tradesman undertook to build either a whole house or a
number of houses on a piece of land. It was shown in previous
chapters how it was common among those working in the building trades to take on a number of building leases for a section of
land from the lead developer. Or they would come in at the stage
after that when an intermediate developer (not from the building
trades) bought or leased a part of the development and then sold
his building leases on to the traders. Alternatively, instead of taking
a building lease themselves, builders would sometimes enter into
contracts to build whole houses with the person who owned the

lease. Both these methods, either taking a building lease or carrying out a building operation for someone owning one, were in effect a form of contracting by the great. The lease essentially was a building contract between developer and builder. The lease would contain the building agreement with its covenants stating how many houses were to be built, their type, their location within the overall development and the ground rent cost. In 1688 John Foltrop undertook to build eleven houses on the Artillery Ground development of Nicholas Barbon and Sir John Parsons. The houses were to front Stuart Street and Gun Street and the ground rents would be levied at a cost of 5*s* per foot in Stuart Street and 3*s* per foot in Gun Street.[91] It is in this sense that we can think of a building lease as a contract even when a tradesman was working for himself, in that he was entering into an agreement to build with the lead developer. As we have seen, leases were often not granted until the houses were substantially complete. In these cases the building agreement acted as the legal contract. The taking on of building contracts covering all the different trades, by those from one particular trade, led in the speculative building market to great changes in labour organization and the structure of the industry. Not all craftsman dealt only in one trade and worked by a process of sub-contracting, some were major contractors and master builders. They will be considered in more detail in the following chapter.

We see here a picture of a building industry in a state of flux. On the one hand the technology and labour skills required were different only in the quantity and speed of output which were demanded. On the other hand employment patterns and operating procedures were changing rapidly. For some the changes were bewildering and threatening and they hung on desperately to the business and craft ethos, as embodied in the guilds, with which they were familiar. For others it was a period of liberation, which provided them with once undreamt of business horizons and opportunities. For all it was a period of profound transformation as the separateness of the crafts disintegrated and new organizational structures for managing the building process developed.

Notes

1 For the medieval system see: D. Knoop and G. P. Jones, *The Medieval Mason*, Manchester, Manchester University Press, 1933; G. P. Jones, 'Building in Stone in Medieval Western Europe', in *Cambridge Economic History of Europe*, Vol. II, Cambridge, Cambridge University Press, 1952.

2 For information on contracting and the organization of the building trades see: Howard Colvin, *A Biographical Dictionary of British Architects, 1600-1840*, London,

John Murray, 1978, pp. 18-25; D. Knoop and G. P. Jones, *The London Mason in the Seventeenth Century*, Manchester, Manchester University Press, 1935.

3   R. Campbell, *The London Tradesman*, London, 1747, pp. 159-60.

4   Joseph Moxon, *Mechanick Exercises, Or the Doctrine of Handy-Works*, London, 1703, p. 237.

5   Information on brickmaking is largely drawn from the following: Alan Cox, 'Bricks to Build a Capital', in Hermione Hobhouse and Ann Saunders, eds, *Good and Proper Materials: The Fabric of London since the Great Fire*, London, London Topographical Society Publication No. 140, 1989, pp. 3-17; Dan Cruickshank and Peter Wyld, *London: The Art of Georgian Building*, London, Architectural Press, 1975, pp. 178-91; Linda Clarke, *Building Capitalism: Historical Change and the Labour Process in the Production of the Built Environment*, London and New York, Routledge, 1992, pp. 47-8, 95-101.

6   As quoted in Cruickshank and Wyld, *The Art of Georgian Building*, p. 181.

7   Cruickshank and Wyld, *The Art of Georgian Building*, p. 181.

8   PRO C8/230/72.

9   PRO C6/289/34.

10 Cox, 'Bricks to Build A Capital', pp. 10-11.

11 *Wren Society*, Vol. IX, Oxford, 1932, p. 16.

12 Moxon, *Mechanick Exercises*, p. 268.

13 PRO C8/260/63, all subsequent quotes relating to this case from the same source.

14 PRO C9/457/109, C10/230/7.

15 PRO C5/148/21.

16 As quoted in Cox, 'Bricks to Build A Capital', p. 4.

17 PRO C5/251/11.

18 PRO PC2/70.

19 PRO C8/320/72.

20 Campbell, *The London Tradesman*, p. 169.

21 For more on this see, Paul Drury, '18thC Construction: Joinery', *Architects' Journal*, 14 August 1991, pp. 36-41.

22 H. J. Louw, 'Demarcation Disputes between the English Carpenters and Joiners from the Sixteenth to the Eighteenth Century', *Construction History*, Vol. 5, 1989, pp. 3-20.

23 Louw, 'Demarcation Disputes', p. 15.

24 Louw, 'Demarcation Disputes', p. 13.

25 Campbell, *The London Tradesman*, p. 161.

26 For a more detailed account see: David Yeomans, 'Structural Carpentry in London Building', in Hobhouse and Saunders, *Good and Proper Materials*, pp. 38-47; David Yeomans, '18thC Timber Construction: 1. Trade and Materials', *Architects' Journal*, 10 July 1991, pp. 51-6.

27 Yeomans, 'Structural Carpentry', p. 42.

28 PRO C7/210/27.

29 Cruickshank and Wyld, *The Art of Georgian Building*, p. 204.

30 PRO C5/251/11.

31 PRO C8/388/32.

32 Campbell, *The London Tradesman*, p. 168.

33 PRO C6/223/34.

34 Campbell, *The London Tradesman*, p. 167.

35 PRO C7/120/1.

36 PRO C5/144/1.

37 PRO C5/144/1.

38 PRO C5/144/1.

39 PRO C7/120/1.

40 PRO C7/210/8.

41 For more on this see, H. J. Louw, 'The Origin of the Sash-Window', *Architectural History*, No. 26, 1983, pp. 49-72. He suggests that the sash-window was an English invention in use from the late 1660s onwards.

42 John Summerson, *Georgian London*, 1945, Harmondsworth, Pengun, 1978 edn, p. 45.

43 John Styles, 'Manufacturing, Consumption and Design in Eighteenth-Century England', in J. Brewer and R. Porter, eds, *Consumption and the World of Goods*, London and New York, Routledge, 1993, pp. 527-54.

44 Clive D. Edwards, *Eighteenth-Century Furniture*, Manchester, Manchester University Press, 1996, p. 39.

45 Edwards, *Eighteenth-Century Furniture*, p. 25.

46 Cruickshank & Wyld, *The Art of Georgian Building*, pp. 204-9.

47 For more on this see, Knoop and Jones, *The London Mason*.

48 Act of Common Council of Masons' Company, II, September 1694.

49 PRO C8/219/41.

50 PRO C10/283/68.

51 PRO C5/617/93.

52 PRO C6/86/78, C6/259/81, C7/137/63, C9/457/109, C10/230/7.

53 PRO C7/152/40, C7/595/93.

54 PRO C10/181/4.

55 M. J. Power, 'The Social Topography of Restoration London', in A. L. Beier and Roger Finlay, eds, *London 1500-1700: The Making of the Metropolis*, London and New York, Longman, 1986, p. 213.

56 PRO C10/181/4.

57 For example, PRO C7/163/60.

58 PRO C8/388/70.

59 PRO C8/263/91.

60 PRO C5/251/11.

61 PRO C8/309/23.

62 PRO C8/219/41.

63 PRO C5/314/25.

64 PRO C5/314/25.

65 See, G. F. Webb, ed., *The Complete Works of Sir John Vanbrugh, Vol. IV, The Letters*, London, Nonesuch Press, 1928, Nos 55-8 inc.

66 PRO C8/309/23.

67 *OED*, 'credit': 1. The estimate in which the character of a person (or thing) is held; reputation, repute (1576) 2. Reputation of solvency and probity in business, entitling a person or body to be trusted (1573).

68 PRO C8/219/41.

69 PRO C8/219/41.

70 PRO C7/543/52.

71 Roger North, *Lives of the Norths*, Vol. III, p. 210, London, Henry Colhern, 1826.

72 Richard Neve, *The City and Countrey Purchaser, and Builder's Dictionary: Or, The Compleat Builders Guide*, London, 1703, p. 72.

73 Malcolm Airs, *The Making of the English Country House, 1500-1640*, London, Architectural Press, 1975, p. 57.

74 *Wren Society*, Vol. V, 1928, p. 20, Letter No. 3 to the Bishop of Oxford, 25 June 1681.

75 *Wren Society*, Vol. V, p. 20.

76 PRO C5/144/1.

77 For example, C6/289/21.

78 PRO C6/351/22.

79 PRO C6/351/22, C5/144/1.

80 PRO C6/351/22.

81 PRO C6/351/22.

82 PRO C7/210/27.

83 PRO C10/181/4.

84 PRO C5/144/1.

85 PRO C5/153/95.

86 PRO C6/351/22.

87 PRO C10/248/3.

88 PRO C6/351/22.

89 PRO C5/144/1.

90 PRO C5/144/1.

91 PRO C8/553/97.

5 The builders: honest artisans and crafty contractors

craftily - cunningly; artfully; with more art than honesty
craftsman - an artificer; a manufacturer; a mechanick
craftsmaster - a man skilled in his trade
crafty - cunning; artful; full of artifices; fraudulent; sly
  (Dr Johnson, *Dictionary*, 1755, derivations from the word 'craft')

The construction process, as we saw in the last chapter, was evolving in the late seventeenth and early eighteenth century from a locally organized craft activity centred around the guilds into a national industry. The impact of these changes upon labour divisions and functions has largely been discussed in the secondary literature in terms of the rise of the architect and the development of the 'profession' (something which is of relatively recent origin).[1] The role of the craftsman, still the predominant force in the building and design worlds at the time, has remained little explored.[2] I use the term 'craftsman' here rather than the modern term 'craftsperson' as the workforce was overwhelmingly male. This chapter will investigate who the craftsman was and the ways in which he operated in speculative development, an area in which architects were not involved as designers, although sometimes as developers and investors. Did the craftsman inevitably suffer from the rise of the architect and the impact of commercialization in this period as has generally been assumed? Or did the context and conditions of late seventeenth- and early eighteenth-century London offer previously undreamt of possibilities for the making (and breaking) of fortunes? It is important to begin by establishing the identities and definitions attached to the label 'the craftsman', a figure who has been reinvented and mythologized by subsequent generations.

It was in the Middle Ages that the craftsman reached his apogee as the designer and maker of architecture, and it is this period which has become the touchstone against which subsequent developments have been measured. As Andrew Saint has written in his essay 'Myth and the Mediaeval Architect', 'mediaeval architecture and the mediaeval architect became the proverbial mirror in which each culture caught an idealized glimpse of its own aspirations'.[3] Saint outlines three dominant interpretations of the

medieval craftsman which have held sway from the nineteenth
century up until the end of the twentieth century. In the early
nineteenth century the myth of the pious, monkish craftsman was
propounded by writers such as the French critic Charles, Comte de
Montalembert. In England this interpretation was superseded by
the mid-nineteenth-century Gothic Revivalists. Led by Ruskin, and
later elaborated by Morris and the Arts and Crafts Movement, they
held that the key characteristic of medieval architecture was its
anonymous, collective nature and its joy in handiwork. In the
twentieth century a different picture has been presented by some
medieval historians, notably John Harvey, who presented the
craftsman as an autonomous designer, rather similar in fact to his
present-day counterpart the architect.

Under the modern system a new figure, the architect, enters the
equation, a person responsible for the design of the building and
often the making as well, but in a supervisory rather than a direct
capacity. This change has provoked a recurrent debate about
whether this has been to the impoverishment or the enrichment
of the art. The nineteenth-century revivalists and some medieval
historians have seen the development of 'architecture' separate
from building in the Renaissance as the beginning of the decline
of Western civilization. The Marxist Italian historians such as
Giulio Argan and Bruno Zevi have taken a similar stance from a
not altogether different direction. They argue that architecture was
once a popular activity which under classicism was appropriated
by the ruling class and became elitist.[4] Prince Charles and the recent classical revivalists have advanced a similar line in relation to
the modern movement arguing that it resulted in an excessive
specialization and politicization of architecture which removed it
both from its roots and from society.[5] In this instance the solution
is seen as a return to classicism, this time proposed as a populist
and inclusive alternative tradition to modernism.

Two unshakeable assumptions have arisen from these ideological legacies. The first is that the craftsman was indissolubly
linked to his craft and his handiwork. His talents and activities
have been held to lie entirely within the realms of the making and
design of buildings. Secondly, he has been perceived as an economic virgin, disinterested in and disconnected from matters of
finance and monetary accumulation. The joy in handiwork has
been considered as his prime interest and motivation. Although
these myths and traditions have developed around the medieval
craftsman, they have equally coloured thinking about his early
modern counterpart. Furthermore the craftsman has been
presented as being almost instantly subservient to the architect in
both economic and design terms once the latter begins to emerge.

This, however, is something of a red herring. The critical issue is not the role of the architect, but the separation of design and production.[6] Adrian Forty in *Objects of Desire* identified the separation of design and production as taking place in the eighteenth century. Prior to this there had been what he called craft production in which the same person was responsible for the form and the making of an object.[7] Although Forty has illuminated one of the key issues in design history his model is not so applicable in the architectural sphere, where buildings have always been produced by more than one person and where a number of different working practices can often be found employed within a single building. Within the medieval building industry there was extensive sub-division of labour, not just between the different crafts but within each craft.[8] To take masons, for example, at the bottom of the ladder would be the hewers and stone-cutters who would cut the stone into blocks. Then there would be the more skilled masons, the carvers, who would carry out the fine work on the stone. At the top of the hierarchy there would be the master mason who, depending on the size of his group, might carry out the carving, but who would also oversee the works, organize the ordering of stone and might to some extent provide specifications for the kind of work to be produced. Evidence of off-site standardization of parts such as windows has been discovered in the medieval period by Frank Woodman.[9] Clearly there is no single craftsman at work here.

Forty's placing of the watershed in the eighteenth century has also been criticized by John Styles, in his piece 'Manufacturing, Consumption and Design in Eighteenth-Century England'. He says that it is well known to economic historians that there was no absolute separation of design and production even before this date.[10] Styles shows that prior to the eighteenth century, large-scale production to fixed specifications involving extensive division of labour was common in some industries. In other words, even before 1700, the notion of the craftsman responsible for every facet of the design and production of an item is, in many trades, a false one.

Little research has been carried out into the workings of the craftsman involved in the building trades in the post-medieval period. Dan Cruickshank has characterized the constructor of the Georgian speculative house as a builder rather than a craftsman.[11] However, when the evolution of a 'craftsman' into a 'builder' occurred is not known, nor what the differences were in the craftsman's role between the late medieval and early modern periods. Both Summerson and Colvin in their accounts of those engaged in speculative building in the period stress the independence of the separate crafts and a training in craft skills as being the essential foundation and expertise of such workers.[12] Summerson's account of the building of the late seventeenth- and eighteenth-century speculative house by sub-contracting craftsmen bolsters the assumptions outlined above.[13] It presents a picture of the new house erected by a craftsman little removed from his medieval counterpart, a pre-capitalist figure reliant on his craft training and knowledge alone to survive in the frenetic world of speculative development. Linda Clarke has offered evidence to challenge this view in her book *Building Capitalism: Historical Change and the Labour Process in the Production of the Built Environment* of 1992.[14] She argues that in the seventeenth century the remnants of feudal social relations were replaced in the building industry by capitalist modes of production. However, despite this she insists – as the result of a rigidly deterministic Marxist mode of analysis – that the building tradesman remained an artisan; full capitalism, based in her view on wage labour, not being 'reached' until the nineteenth century.

A very different picture of 'the craftsman' emerges from the Chancery evidence. Indeed the use of such terminology in the speculative building context may be anachronistic, and the use of the word 'craft' was problematic at the time. Dr Johnson defined the term in his dictionary of 1755 as having two meanings: firstly that of a manual art or trade, and secondly fraud, cunning or artifice.[15] To this list the *Oxford English Dictionary* adds one further later meaning of 'craftsman' – 'one who cultivates one of the Fine Arts 1876'. Our modern understanding of the word embraces both this nineteenth-century addition and the original medieval meaning of one who practises a manual trade or handicraft. We have abandoned the pejorative associations so forcefully outlined by Johnson, but these had a powerful resonance for contemporaries.

The word 'craft' or 'craftsman' is rarely found and it may have been that its derogatory overtones inhibited its use among those involved in building. Joseph Moxon discussed the problem in the Preface to his *Mechanick Exercises, Or, the Doctrine of Handy-Works* of 1683:

> I thought to have given these Exercises the Title of The Doctrine of Handy-Crafts; But when I better considered the true meaning of the word Handy-Crafts I found the Doctrine would not bear it: because Handy-Craft signifies cunning, or sleight, or craft of the hand, which cannot be taught by words but is only gain'd by practice and exercise.[16]

'Craft' was also associated with the notion of the guild and its 'mysteries'. This may be another reason for its lack of use in the speculative building world, where guild regulation was of little consequence.

What then were the words that building workers used to describe themselves at the time? In a case surrounding the Newport House redevelopment a group of 'builders and tenants' bring a complaint against the developers. This is how they describe themselves: 'The complainants are mainly artificers, joiners, carpenters, bricklayers, plasterers, plumbers, painters, masons and other such like traders.'[17] The words most commonly used seem to have been 'artificers' and 'traders'. The word 'mechanick' is less used. It too had derogatory implications; Dr Johnson's definition is a 'manufacturer' or 'low workman'. The term 'artificer', by contrast, stressed the skill aspect rather than the labouring aspect of the work; it meant 'one who makes by art or skill'.[18] However, Johnson again gives it a parallel less flattering meaning of, 'a forger, a contriver'. The term 'trader' or 'tradesman' was a more neutral term meaning anyone employed in a manual or commercial occupation. This was a common contemporary term and the one which is used in this book. The term 'craftsman', although also used in the period, has acquired too much subsequent anachronistic and misleading ideological baggage to convey an accurate impression of building practice at this time.

There were of course different kinds of workers operating at different levels, as the earlier example of the operations of the masons and Johnson's distinction between 'the craftsman' and 'the craftsmaster' demonstrates. However, neither the surviving evidence nor the contemporary secondary literature provide much information about the journeymen, or their relative position *vis-à-vis* the master craftsmen. This chapter therefore necessarily concentrates upon practice among the higher ranks of the building trades, although more information about the divisions and structures within those trades is needed for a fuller picture.

The structure of the house, as we have already seen, ensured that it was bricklayers and carpenters who were most heavily involved in London housing. A high proportion of bricklayers can be found among those tradesmen taking leases in speculative developments. Some of these would have been people new to the building trades as well as existing craftsmen switching their skills to a new material. Many of the master builders were bricklayers and it seems likely that among the more well-off or entrepreneurial of those who went into the building trades from the 1660s onwards bricklaying was often their chosen point of entry. One of the bricklayers who made it into the first rank of developers was Richard Frith. He went on to become one of the greatest builders of his day with his development of Soho Square and the surrounding area. He also built in the St James's vicinity[19] and at Milford Lane next to Essex House.[20] He was responsible for part of the building at Leicester House and he was involved in the redevelopment of Clarendon House in 1683 into Dover, Albemarle and Old Bond Streets. He built in Holborn, Hampden Garden and probably Bow Street.[21] He was described after his death as: 'in his lifetime a great builder of houses or a great undertaker in or for the finishing of many dwelling houses with their outhouses and appurtenances in or near the City of London or the suburbs thereof, as well upon his own proper account as for others his customers, who from time to time employed him therein'.[22] Frith was so successful that, 'for sundry years before his death he had left off his trade of a bricklayer and was generally taken or reputed to be a man of a very considerable estate'.[23]

James Friend was another successful bricklayer who was also a clothier.[24] He was a Quaker and rather bitterly described by one of his aggrieved clients as, 'a man pretending to more than ordinary sanctity'.[25] Friend undertook the building of twenty-eight houses in Westminster with his own materials and at his own cost. For this he was to be paid half in leases and half in money.[26] He also contracted with Barbon to build the new Market House in the grounds of Newport House and the evidence surrounding this scheme refers to Friend's labourers on several occasions, indicating that he was a employer of a substantial number of people. Like Barbon's men they seem to have been ill-disciplined and violent. Friend was described at one point as participating in 'former dishonest dealings'.[27]

This picture of the most successful bricklayers as substantial operators is borne out by Anthony Quiney's researches into Thomas Lucas, a bricklayer in the Deptford area in the early eighteenth century.[28] He employed other craftsmen to carry out the building work on his development of Union Street and, as Quiney remarks, was as much a businessman as a local craftsman. 'On one side he had marked architectural sensibility, on the other he was an entrepreneur and as such the prototype of the speculative builder who dominated the rest of the century and much of the next.'[29]

Moving on to the woodworking trades we have a short account of the activities of George Pawley, joiner of London. He had a shop and yard by London Wall. He made his living buying and selling deal and other boards and timber and also made chests of drawers, tables, bedsteads and other things.[30] This is interesting as it shows that he was engaged in both dealing in timber and making household objects, and possibly architectural features. It does seem then that, unlike bricklayers who generally bought their bricks from

brickmakers, many carpenters and joiners were dealers and impor-
ters of timber as well as workers of the material. The provision by
the carpenters of the scaffolding on-site gave them another fundamental role in the building process. This plus control of their
own supplies enabled some of the most commercially astute to
become master builders or developers. Typical of these might be
John Foltrop, carpenter and citizen of London, whose name crops
up in many of the major developments of the day and whose
activities as a master builder are discussed later in this chapter.

Joseph Collins of St Martin-in-the-Fields was another carpenter
active in property development. He is known about because a
claim was made against his estate in Chancery after his death. John
Foltrop, John Warren and Charles Hopson claimed that Collins
owed them £226 for deal boards, fir timber, oak boards, sawn fir
and fir baulks with which they had supplied him. They claimed
that Collins died intestate in January 1708 leaving an estate worth
over £20,000.[31] In answer to this his widow Lydia Collins produced
a schedule of Collins' assets and debts.[32] Collins held leases or had
interests in the following properties:

Property details	Value of Collins' share
1 unfinished house in Great Marlborough Street half share with John Rokeby, grocer lease from John Steele, gent mortgage to Timothy Emerson for £200	£360
1 house and back buildings in Great Marlborough Street let to Lord Pawlett at £110 p.a. half share with John Rokeby lease from John Steele joint mortgage to Timothy Emerson for £500	£650
1 house and back buildings in Great Marlborough Street unlet part share in lease from John Steele joint mortgage to Timothy Emerson for £400	£420
1 house in James Street, Covent Garden let to Butler at £40 p.a. part share with Thomas Hughes, bricklayer lease from the Duke of Bedford	£60
Collins' dwelling house and 2 front houses in St Martin's Lane lease from Robert and Christian Cecil	£25
6 acres of Coleman Hedge Field ¼ share with James Pollet and Robert Walkton lease from Mr Wardour and Mr Hare mortgage to Timothy Emerson for £800	£1,200

6 acres of Coleman Hedge Field improved rent £199 p.a. ¼ share	£450
The Tunn, Pulteney Street and 2 houses improved rents £47 p.a. part share with James Pollett joint mortgage to Susanna Rudsby for £250	£150
Part of Millfield half share with John Rokeby lease from John Steele Collins let 'underleases to encourage building' at rents = £200 p.a. mortgage £1,000 to Mrs Mary Hodges	£1,094 12s 9d
an estate improved rent £1 18s 0d over ground rent lease from Gilbert Herring part share	£13
plus: money in house at time of intestate's death	£19 3s 11½d
contents of the house	£64 6s 3d
assorted timber	£56 10s 0d
Total: [The actual total is £4,562 12s 11½d]	£4,454 10s 8d

This shows us the number of people who could be involved even in a single house. The schedule indicates that Collins rarely worked on his own but carried out his developments with partners such as John Rokeby the grocer, or Thomas Hughes the bricklayer. It is noticeable that nearly all the premises are mortgaged, often to nearly their full value. Most of the premises listed are in roughly the same area. This must be either because this is where he carried out most of his work or because it was in this vicinity that he had most trouble disposing of the properties he had built. He is also listed in the *Survey of London* working as a carpenter at No. 30 Soho Square.[33] Besides building, he also took parcels of land which he then sub-let to others to build on, as he did at Millfield from 1704.[34] After the list given above there follows a schedule of moneys received and paid by Lydia Collins since her husband's death. Among the latter are included payments for 'workmens wages' and specific payments for bricks, sashes, and to a glazier, a smith and an ironmonger. This shows Collins to be a master carpenter of the new type, taking on contracts for all trades and not just those for carpentry alone.

Summerson's model of the sub-contracting craftsman stressed the individual skills of each trade. Colvin commented that, 'the training and equipment of an eighteenth-century master workman were confined to his own craft'.[35] However, this model of the craftsmen tends to reduce all tradesmen to one type. It takes insufficient account of the different levels within the trades and the varying points at which tradesmen engaged in the development process. Summerson did allow for this when he wrote about the master builder:

> In the building trade, as in almost every other, there was, at the beginning of the eighteenth century, a strong capitalist element. The capitalist in the building trade was the 'master-builder'. Usually either a carpenter or bricklayer by training, he would undertake the construction of entire houses and build for the speculative market. He was not necessarily (for reasons which we shall see in a moment) a great employer of labour but he was of the greatest importance because he took the initiative in building; as his point of view - the point of view of the businessman rather than the craftsman - became dominant, skill and orginality became of secondary account. The constructional trades - bricklaying and carpentering - became businesses, and the trades requiring taste and good workmanship - joiners and carvers, for instance - became largely dependent on these.[36]

Summerson's analysis in this instance was absolutely accurate. But he was mistaken in the date at which he placed the beginning of this process, and hence also perhaps in its impact on what he calls 'originality'. There is plenty of evidence of master builders operating in the late seventeenth century, among them John Foltrop. Foltrop was a London carpenter typical of those involved at the middle level of development. Besides taking land at the Old Artillery Ground in the 1680s from Barbon and Parsons he was also active at their parallel development at Wellclose Square. He acted as a developer at Great Russell Street and it seems that he had some involvement in building the Compter Prison, Southwark. He built houses in Lamb's Conduit Fields, at the Middle Temple and in Westminster at Channel Row and Charles Street in the 1680s and 1690s.[37] Sometimes he undertook work by the great and sometimes he only contracted for the carpenter's work which he could carry out himself. At Wellclose, for example, he agreed to do the carpenter's work on nine houses and build two others 'on his own account'.[38] For this he would receive the leases of the two houses for which he was wholly responsible plus payment for the carpenter's work in stages. At Westminster he agreed to build houses for which he would be paid by measured work. It was Foltrop's ability to sustain credit which allowed him to operate on this large scale. It made him an attractive proposition for the larger developers, especially when he was carrying out work for them rather than on his own account. When Foltrop worked for Barbon at the Middle Temple the building agreement of 1687 allowed him a higher than normal rate for the work, 'which was above the usual

price because he was to be paid when they were sold'.[39] Unusually
here Foltrop was employed, 'for the making and finishing some
inward works' as well. In houses the interior wainscotting was
normally arranged by the tenant, but with legal chambers possibly
the responsibility lay with the Inns of Court.

What is clear from Foltrop's activities is that even where he is
not acting as his own undertaker, he is usually contracting for the
whole work and not just for the contract in his own trade of
carpentry. At Westminster he agreed to work for £5 5s 0d for brickwork and £18 per square for carpenter's work.[40] An account is
included in the same case of the amount he was owed for work at
the Middle Temple. This lists individually: the carpenter's bill, the
bricklayer's bill, the plasterer's bill, the plumber's bill, the smith's
bill, the painter's bill, the mason's bill, the joiner's bill and the
ironmonger's bill. It then goes on to list entries for mending slates,
for locks, for paying the bricklayers, for building the chimney
blown down, and 'paid the carpenters for mending the roof and
cornice in the same building'.[41] Besides this there is evidence that
he acted as a timber merchant as well. He made a claim in
Chancery, along with two others, against the estate of Joseph Collins, as discussed previously. They claimed that between 1
December 1704 and 30 September 1707 they delivered to Collins:
8,300 deal boards, 220 loads of fir timber, 20 oak boards, 20 other
pieces of timber, 40 pieces of sawn fir and 300 fir baulks.[42]

The multi-tiered development system meant in practice that
there were tradesmen acting as master builders. The master builder
took on contracts for whole houses from other developers. He then
employed workmen in the different trades to carry out the work,
sometimes paying them himself and sometimes letting out contracts to the separate trades. He later received either payment or
building leases for the whole work from the developer. His role was
as a building organizer, manager and supervisor. He undertook this
work not in the manner of a clerk of works employed by
somebody else, but at his own risk and with his own money.

As a master builder Foltrop's principal asset was his credit and
capital resources and not his trade. These must have been considerable, since the work at the Middle Temple for which he was to
be paid when the chambers were sold came to £2,266 14s 2d.[43] The
building agreement was entered into on 22 September 1687 and by
16 December 1689 he claimed still not to have received any money
for them. This figure is part of complex interrelated sets of accounts
for different developments, including payment in leases and
finished properties, so it is hard to know how accurate a statement
this is. However, what is abundantly clear is that this is an operation on a large scale involving substantial amounts of money,

even though in none of these cases is Foltrop the lead initiator in the development process.

Although Foltrop called himself a carpenter I think it is quite probable that he only came into the building world following the Fire and the start of the building boom in the West End. The term 'master builder' is used quite regularly by Campbell in his *The London Tradesman* of 1747. He writes that carpenters and joiners 'are esteemed according as the Master-Builder wants them'.[44] However, although the old master craftsmen were people of substance, it does not necessarily follow that the development of the master builder should be seen as coming in a direct line from the master craftsman. Summerson says that the master builders were usually carpenters or bricklayers, and we have seen that when they came from the crafts this was likely to be true.[45] However, master builders might also have been people new to the building industry who called themselves bricklayers or carpenters or such like, but who we would call builders/developers or small businessmen.

Foltrop was a typical master builder. Above him were the big speculators like Barbon and the myriad business investors. Below Foltrop were those with less business acumen or money who plied their trades and undertook their own projects, if they could, but otherwise worked for others. Other examples of tradesmen who built widely, took on building leases on a large scale and employed a workforce are: Alexander Cutting who is described as a plasterer and a gentleman;[46] George Jackson, bricklayer, who will be discussed in more detail below;[47] and John Slater, more unusually a plumber.[48] There were also people from the non-building trades such as Thomas Lownes, a haberdasher of London.[49] These people are surely more accurately described as builders, master builders and building undertakers than craftsmen. Where they differed from the large numbers of gentry and merchants who also took on building leases as a matter of speculation was that they actually participated in or supervised the construction process, whereas the former would employ a builder such as themselves to do this for them.

David Yeomans supports this interpretation in relation to the eighteenth-century carpenter. He writes that the increase in the scale of operations after the Fire led to changes in the structure of the building industry.

> At that time payment for work was notoriously slow, so the tradesman would be providing the initial funding for the work in the anticipation of payment at a later date. Works of this kind needed large firms with sufficient capital to cope with such major undertakings. Because of this and the importance of carpentry in building, many carpenters acted as general contractors. And with their ability to manage building

operations and their financial standing, some also became speculative builders.[50]

Although both Campbell and Summerson wrote about the master builder, this capitalist builder has largely been ignored from the late seventeenth century until the nineteenth-century, when he once more becomes a figure for discussion. The master builder or building contractor is usually seen as a nineteenth century phenomenon, with Thomas Cubbitt in the early nineteenth century being seen as the first of a new breed. E. W. Cooney in his definitive article on the subject gave four classifications for those contracting for building work in the eighteenth and nineteenth centuries:[51]

1 Master Craftsman – who undertook work only in his own trade and employed a small number of journeymen and apprentices.

2 Master Craftsman – contracting by the great, but employing directly only workers in his own trade, contracting with other master craftsmen for the rest of the work.

3 Builders – not a craftsman but often an architect or merchant, erecting complete buildings on the basis of contracts with master craftsmen in the various trades.

4 Master Builders – contracting by the great and employing a more or less permanent and a relatively large body of labourers and workmen in all the principal building crafts.

Cooney saw the development of No. 4 as an early nineteenth-century development pioneered by Thomas Cubbitt around 1815. Cooney's assessment of the change from a building industry organized around individual trades to one organized in general building firms is on the whole correct, although I would use the contemporary term of 'master builder' to describe what he calls a 'master craftsman' in No. 2. However, there is an implicit assumption in this article and other writing on the subject, that the advent of the large-scale general contractor and the related phenomenon of competitive tendering, ushered in a newly capitalistic building industry. Howard Colvin writes that the early nineteenth century, 'brought opportunities for a new type of builder who was more of an entrepreneur than a craftsman',[52] while Cooney implies that because the building industry was previously organized along the lines of the separate crafts it was therefore somehow not capitalist and not industrial. This book, I hope, has dispelled any such notions and highlighted the anachronistic and confusing connotations that the persistent use of the word 'craft' has in relation to the late seventeenth- and eighteenth-century building industry.

Contracting by the great was very common therefore before the nineteenth century as was the master builder who undertook the responsibility. The workforce he employed, although it may have been large, as Campbell relates, probably did not cover all the trades. Other work that could not be covered by the master builder would be sub-contracted out. All work would be undertaken on a measure and value system where the final cost would not be known, unlike the competitive tender system of the nineteenth century where fixed-sum contracts became normal.

The credentials for the master builder in the late seventeenth and eighteenth century have been firmly established. The question is why has this figure been ignored, and considered only in his nineteenth-century form to date? The answer must lie in nineteenth-century romantic notions of the craft world and in twentieth-century romantic notions of the Georgian city. His neglect is also part of a tendency in industrial and economic studies to focus on the nineteenth-century. It is only relatively recently that more attention has been given to the non-mechanized, small-scale workshop production of the eighteenth century. It has now been shown that although these industries were not factory based they were still highly productive and competitive.[53] In other words pre-nineteenth century 'craft production' was neither productively insignificant nor of marginal economic importance. These were the major industries of their times, none more so than building. There is another reason why the master builder has been ignored in this period, and that is because he is primarily seen as a production figure and not as a design figure, and therefore of limited interest to architectural history.

Is there any evidence at all then for the sort of system that Summerson envisaged? He was certainly right in identifying sub-contracting as the key to the whole process. However, there is little evidence for the barter economy that he and more strongly Colvin advocated.[54] Instead it is more usual to find money for building construction being raised through mortgages and journeymen being paid in cash. All those concerned in property development – the master builders, leading tradesmen and developers – used cash, land and houses as their three forms of currency. The chapters on development have shown that tradesmen were more capable of raising capital or operating on credit than has previously been imagined. Sometimes, as with the example of Foltrop, payment was made in leases as well as money. However, this trading of leases or houses in lieu of cash was, as we have seen, common at all levels of the development process and should by no means be seen as something which was confined to the building tradesmen alone.

The only evidence of any kind of barter system occurs in two cases where beer appears to be used as a substitute for cash payment. In one case it appears beer was used to pay off the sums due to brick carters for their deliveries of bricks to the site.[55] In another case part of the sum due to a tradesman from a developer was paid in beer.[56] Whether this was for his own use or for distribution to other workmen is not clear. Such a practice may spring from an older tradition of supplying beer and victuals to labourers on-site. This is suggested by a case in which it is implied that the chief builder should provide meat and drink for the workmen although in fact the developer, the owner of the building lease, had been doing this himself.[57]

The master builder was not the only new figure in the construction industry at this time. The introduction of the measure and value system as the basis for contracts and the means of costing work brought a new supervisory role into the building process, the surveyor. Unlike the master builder the surveyor has received a great deal more attention in the history books, primarily because he was to some extent the forerunner of the architect. This discussion will focus not on the surveyor's design functions, but rather on his work as a measurer of buildings and from this a role which developed as an overseer of the building operation. Richard Frith, it was reported, worked 'as well upon his own proper account as for others his customers, who from time to time employed him therein'.[58] In a case involving George Jackson we gain a greater insight into what precisely this might mean.[59] Jackson says that he has for many years past been, 'concerned in the building of houses and surveying the workmanship of them in and about the city of London and elsewhere, has been employed by several persons in viewing, surveying and ordering the ground and work of great numbers of houses, and by that means your orator became acquainted with diverse bricklayers and other tradesmen'.[60] He was asked by Sir John Parsons 'to undertake the surveying and managing and ordering the building of certain houses in Wellclose', where he should employ workmen as he thought fit. Jackson was employed 'as agent or surveyor' with Parsons paying the bills.[61] This practice of developers and investors handing over the supervision of the building operation created another kind of employment for the building tradesman, acting in effect as a clerk of works or site operations manager. At Gloucester Street, near Red Lion Square, John Knight employed Robert Kely, carpenter, to oversee the workmen employed on building on his sites and to buy in materials for him, because of his great age, being over eighty.[62]

One result of the measure and value system was that it required a worker who was sufficiently literate and numerate to understand and administer the sophisticated techniques of quantity surveying. Wren considered this to be a problem when he recommended contracting by measure as his preferred method. He wrote, 'But you must have an understanding trusty Measurer, there are few that are skilled in measuring stone worke, I have bred up 2 or 3.'[63] Accurate measuring was necessary not only for measuring the building when it was completed but also as a means of fixing prices on which to base contracts. Richard Neve in his *The City and Countery Purchaser* laid great stress on the importance of accurate measuring for determining costs. The title page makes specific the primary concern with valuation in the book:

> The Customs and Methods of Measuring of all Artificers Work, concern'd in Building; together with the City and Countery Prices, not only of Workmanship, but of Materials also: The which will be extraordinarily useful in making of Bargains or contracts betwixt the Workmaster and Workman; and likwise in computing the Value (or Charge of Erecting) of any Fabrick, great or small.[64]

Despite Wren and Neve's concern, the skill of numeracy was one that was already required of the masters of several trades such as masons, carpenters and bricklayers. Campbell, for example, commented on the joiner's facility in this direction: 'his Business requires that he should be acquainted with Geometry and Mensuration; and in these respects an accurate accomptant'.[65] This was another reason why bricklayers and carpenters/joiners dominated the building trades. Their measuring and mathematical skills were superior to those of trades such as plumbing, painting or plastering.

Surveying, that is measuring of work, was carried out by building professionals such as George Jackson, John Oliver, the City Surveyor,[66] and William Biggs described as a 'measurer' and 'valuer'.[67] People from outside the building world also operated as surveyors, such as John Bland, Barbon's agent and for a while his right-hand man, who is described in various places as a 'measurer' as well as a 'scrivener' or 'gent'. Edward Tasker was recommended as a 'skilful surveyor and contriver of buildings', although he was 'not an artificer but pretending great skill and judgement in building, and an advantage over others in buying materials at reasonable prices and getting workmen at reasonable rates because of some place he had in the City'.[68] He was in fact the keeper of the City Storeyard and Collector of the duties out of Leadenhall Market.[69] He undertook the 'surveying, ordering and contrivance' of three houses in the City, burnt down in the Fire.[70] Tasker may have been related to John Tasker who crops up as a surveyor in a few places.[71] Edward Tasker operated as a master builder, and in rebuilding a house in the City we find him making contracts with the bricklayer, the carpenter, the plasterer, the glazier and the mason.[72] Despite what Wren thought, there seem to have been plenty in the building world who could carry out this task, even if judging by the number of disputes over measuring, the highest standards of accuracy did not always prevail and quantity surveying was a far less precise activity than it is today.

Knoop and Jones in the only previous piece to consider the impact of the new contracting systems on building tradesman in this period, argued that it was the increasing use of contract, as opposed to direct labour, in which materials would be provided by the contractor that gave power to those able to control their own supplies.[73] They pointed to the rise of the mason contractor, people such as the Strongs and the Kempsters, who were able to take on large contracts because of their links with the countryside where they owned stone quarries. In this way they could raise the necessary capital to carry out big projects. In the speculative area, however, control of materials was not a vital factor. Bricklayers and carpenters had a differing control over their supplies, yet each appears to have been equally active as entrepreneurs in the speculative market.

Knoop and Jones placed great emphasis on the importance of capital. They were writing in the days before the central role of credit in the eighteenth-century economy had been established. It was the ability to sustain credit which was the essential feature for a master builder or tradesman taking on leases for speculative houses. Significant numbers of them seem to have had no problem in doing this.[74] Many of them, however, went bankrupt in the process and contemporary tracts are full of dire warnings about builders overreaching themselves to their own ruin and that of their clients.

The contracting system did make other demands and it is these which must ultimately have separated out those tradesmen who could act as master undertakers and those whose dependence on their one skill would enforce their position as employees. The two skills that the new contracts required were numeracy and literacy. Numeracy of a particular kind, the ability to measure and survey, was needed in order to estimate costs and therefore to make profitable contracts.[75] However, in the rush of the property boom techniques which once would have been learnt over years, were presumably having to be picked up very quickly by those new to the trades or those who had not been in them for long. The apprentice system must have collapsed to a considerable extent in these years although again we know lamentably little about this.[76]

Neve's *The City and Countrey Purchaser* provided a crash course in surveying techniques. The reason he gave as his motivation for writing the book is extremely illuminating:

I have been in great measure excited to it of late [to write this book] out of pity to some poor workmen; for I have been informed of several, that for want of skill, and foresight have undertaken buildings by guess, by which they have been almost ruined, or at least kept very low in the World: tho' they have been very industrious in their callings, and that purely by the means of unadvised Contracts. And then again on the other hand, it hath been an Observation made by others as well as myself; that some honest well-meaning Gentlemen, (and others) that have had occasion to Build etc. They have been strangely over-reach'd by some Fradulent Crafty Workmen.[77]

Levels of skill and craft knowledge no longer determined who succeeded and who failed in the building trades. It was not enough to be a good craftsman, it was also essential to be a good business-man, and this required a different set of techniques and aptitudes. The ability to read was common among the masters; Campbell commented that the carpenter, 'must read English [and] write a tolerable Hand',[78] While Lorna Weatherill has shown that owner-ship of books and literacy rates among London tradesmen were exceptionally high.[79]

The consequences of illiteracy in an industry which was increas-ingly operating within an established legal framework are revealed in the case of Thomas Slaymaker, a bricklayer of Stepney, and Anglebert Volering for whom he erected a house.[80] Slaymaker stressed that he was 'a builder and undertaker of building of houses who had money to purchase ground and materials, and whose bonds and engagements were good security'. Financing and credit were not therefore a problem. Volering assigned his building agree-ment from Nicholas Barbon to Slaymaker for £65. This was an agreement to lease ground for forty-seven years with a provision for a lease to be made when the first floor was laid. However, as so often happened, when Slaymaker came to claim his lease there was already a prior claim on the property, so that Slaymaker could not sell the house with an undisputed title. This was a very common occurrence and one of the main reasons why many of these cases came to court. However, the reason Slaymaker gives for this happening is that Volering had defrauded him by giving him a lease made out in someone else's name, 'knowing him to be an illiterate person'.[81]

The contracting system even in the speculative world helped maintain labour relations and an organization of manpower seem-ingly not that different from the old guild system. Those with the requisite financial, measuring and literacy skills could operate suc-cessfully as master builders and tradesmen. They would take on building contracts from other people or building leases of their own and then employ a team to carry out the work. In this way

the old system of a master and his men was maintained in a different economic environment. Although these teams had less
permanency and rigidity than under the guilds, the hierarchy of
master, tradesman and journeyman survived. The team system
continued because it was a productive and economically viable
structure. Building is necessarily a collaborative activity requiring
a high labour input and a variety of skills. The individual trades
were organized separately, although perhaps not as exclusively as
has been thought to be the case. Within each of those trades there
were men performing a wide variety of tasks, working both off-
and on-site and sometimes operating a supplies yard as well. On
the one hand the building trades were still group based as many
of the jobs they performed necessitated this. On the other hand
because of the nature of the speculative system in which small
units, that is houses, were being produced on a large scale but using
identical techniques, there was scope for tradesmen to operate in
a more autonomous manner as their skills were directly transfer-
able from site to site and team to team. This created mobility both
within trades and sometimes between trades as well, which, in
combination with the use of sub-contracting, made the organization of the building industry far more individualistic than it had
been previously.

The building lease system offered building tradesmen far greater
financial opportunities and economic flexibility than ever before.
In the long run and in commissioned buildings it is probably true
that contracting by the great worked against the small contractor.
This was not true in the speculative market in this period, where
the greater barrier lay in the literacy and numeracy skills that
contracts required. This ensured that only the educated could engage in contracting and increasingly it was these skills that were
needed for success. It was not just the financial need for capital that
ultimately forced the tradesman or craftsman from his central role
in the building process but also the necessity for paper-based
skills in an industry increasingly organized around contractual
requirements.

Notes

1 See: Barrington Kaye, *The Development of the Architectural Profession in England:
A Sociological Study*, London, Allen & Unwin, 1960; J. Wilton Ely, 'The Rise of the
Professional Architect in England', in Spiro Kostof, ed., *The Architect: Chapters in
the History of the Profession*, Oxford, Oxford University Press, 1977, pp. 180–208;
H. M. Colvin, 'The Architectural Profession', in his *A Biographical Dictionary of
British Architects, 1600-1840*, London, John Murrary, 1978, pp. 26–41.

2 Notable exceptions include, for London buildings: D. Knoop and G. P. Jones, *The
London Mason in the Seventeenth Century*, Manchester, Manchester University

Press, 1935; John Summerson, *Georgian London*, 1945, Harmondsworth, Penguin edn, 1978, pp. 69-83; for country houses: G. W. Beard, *Georgian Craftsmen and their Work*, London, Country Life, 1966; G. W. Beard, *Decorative Plasterwork in Great Britain*, London, Phaidon, 1975; G. W. Beard, *Craftsmen and Interior Decoration in England, 1660-1820*, Edinburgh, J. Bartholomew, 1981; and for an overview, H. M. Colvin, 'The Building Trades', in his *Biographical Dictionary*, pp. 18-25.

3   Andrew Saint, 'Myth and the Mediaeval Architect', in his *The Image of the Architect*, New Haven and London, Yale University Press, 1983, pp. 19-50. Also see, Mark Swenarton, *Artisans and Architects: The Ruskinian Tradition in Architectural Thought*, Basingstoke, Macmillan Press, 1989.

4   See for example, Bruno Zevi, 'Il linguaggio moderno dell'architecttura: guida al codice anticlassico', 1973, translated as 'Part One' of Bruno Zevi, *The Modern Language of Architecture*, Seattle and London, University of Washington Press, 1978. He writes that in the fifteenth century 'Architects stopped working concretely on architecture and limited themselves to designing it. The damages were enormous; they have increased through the following centuries; and they continue to proliferate with industrialized building techniques. There is probably nothing comparable in other areas of human activity. An almost unbridgeable chasm has opened up between architects and architecture' (p. 23).

5   See for example, Mark Crinson and Jules Lubbock, *Architecture - Art or Profession?: Three Hundred Years of Architectural Education*, Manchester and New York, Manchester University Press, 1994, which was published in association with the Prince of Wales's Institute of Architecture.

6   I am heavily indebted to Adrian Forty and Mark Swenarton for this insight (and many others in this book) which arose from their 'History of Practice' course which I took in 1984-85 as part of the M.Sc. in 'History of Modern Architecture' at the Bartlett School of Architecture, University College, London.

7   Adrian Forty, *Objects of Desire: Design and Society, 1750-1980*, London, Thames & Hudson, 1986, p. 29.

8   For information on masons and building practice in the Middle Ages see: Spiro Kostof, 'The Architect in the Middle Ages, East and West', in Kostof, *The Architect*, pp. 59-95; D. Knoop and G. P. Jones, *The Medieval Mason*, Manchester, Manchester University Press, 1933; B. W. E. Alford and T. C. Barker, *A History of the Carpenters Company*, London, Allen & Unwin, 1968; J. Harvey, *The Medieval Architect*, London, Wayland, 1972; J. Harvey, *The Master Builders: Architecture in the Middle Ages*, London, Thames & Hudson, 1971.

9   Frank Woodman, in lectures at the Bartlett and the University of North London Schools of Architecture, 1984, 1989.

10 John Styles, 'Manufacturing, Consumption and Design in Eighteenth-Century England', in J. Brewer and R. Porter eds, *Consumption and the World of Goods in the Seventeenth and Eighteenth Centuries*, London and New York, Routledge, 1993, pp. 527-54.

11 Dan Cruickshank and Neil Burton, *Life in the Georgian City*, London, Viking, 1990, pp. 115-16.

12 Summerson, *Georgian London*, pp. 69-72; Colvin, *Biographical Dictionary*, pp. 18-20.

13 Summerson, *Georgian London*, p. 43.

14 Linda Clarke, *Building Capitalism: Historical Change and the Labour Process in the Production of the Built Environment*, London and New York, Routledge, 1992.

15 Samuel Johnson, *A Dictionary of the English Language*, London, 1755.

16 Joseph Moxon, *Mechanick Exercises, Or, the Doctrine of Handy-Works*, London, 1683, Preface.

17 PRO C10/270/21.

18 *OED.*

19 PRO C8/388/70, C8/570/15.

20 PRO C5/475/56.

21 *Survey of London, St Anne, Soho*, Vol. XXXIII, London, Athlone Press, 1966, p. 29.

22 PRO C10/454/86.

23 PRO C10/454/86.

24 PRO C7/210/27, C7/210/8, C8/388/32, C8/427/100.

25 PRO C7/210/27.

26 PRO C7/210/27.

27 PRO C8/388/32.

28 Anthony Quiney, 'Thomas Lucas, Bricklayer, 1662-1736', *Post-Medieval Archaeology*, No. 136, 1979, pp. 269-80.

29 Quiney, 'Thomas Lucas', p. 277.

30 PRO C5/290/59.

31 PRO C7/118/26.

32 PRO C7/120/1.

33 *Survey of London, St Anne, Soho*, p. 114.

34 *Survey of London, St James, Westminster*, Vol. XXXI, 1960, pp. 250-2.

35 Colvin, *Biographical Dictionary*, p. 20.

36 Summerson, *Georgian London*, p. 70.

37 PRO C8/553/97, C10/273/42, C5/144/1, C10/422/30, C8/615/27, C5/155/41, C5/295/49, C6/318/30.

38 PRO C5/144/1.

39 PRO C5/144/1.

40 PRO C5/144/1.

41 PRO C5/144/1.

42 PRO C7/118/26.

43 PRO C5/144/1.

44 R. Campbell, *The London Tradesman*, London, 1747, p. 161.

45 Summerson, *Georgian London*, p. 70.

46 PRO C7/126/93, C7/163/60, C7/165/5/, C8/342/7, C8/446/24, C8/446/35, C8/591/67, C10/258/20.

47 PRO C8/553/97, C10/236/48, C8/651/194, C10/248/3, C10/270/21, C8/551/122.

48 PRO C5/295/49, C8/553/97, C8/651/19, C10/230/54, C10/236/48, C10/260/44, C10/273/42, C10/294/65.

49 PRO C6/280/107, C8/263/91, C8/263/71, C8/263/81, C8/281/55.

50 David Yeomans, '18thC Timber Construction: Trade and Materials', *Architects' Journal*, 10 July 1991, p. 52.

51 See: E. W. Cooney, 'The Origins of the Victorian Master Builders', *Economic History Review*, 2nd Series, No. 8, 1955, pp. 167-76; M. H. Port, 'The Office of Works and Building Contracts in Nineteenth-Century England', *Economic History Review*, 2nd Series, No. 20, 1967, pp. 94-110; H. Hobhouse, *Thomas Cubbitt*, London, Macmillan, 1971.

52 Colvin, *Biographical Dictionary*, p. 24.

53 Maxine Berg, *The Age of Manufacture,1700-1820*, London, Fontana Press, 1982; Maxine Berg, Pat Hudson and Michael Sonenscher, eds, *Manufacture in Town and*

Country Before the Factory, Cambridge and New York, Cambridge University Press, 1983.

54   Colvin, *Biographical Dictionary*, p. 20.

55   PRO C6/289/34.

56   PRO C10/248/3.

57   PRO C8/326/124.

58   PRO C10/454/86.

59   PRO C10/248/3.

60   PRO C10/248/3.

61   PRO C10/248/3.

62   PRO C8/614/9.

63   *Wren Society*, Vol. V, Oxford, 1928, p. 20.

64   Richard Neve, *The City and Countrey Purchaser, and Builder's Dictionary: Or, The Compleat Builders Guide*, London, 1703, title page.

65   Campbell, *The London Tradesman*, p. 161.

66   PRO C10/181/4.

67   PRO C5/144/1, C10/248/3.

68   PRO C6/289/21.

69   PRO C6/289/34.

70   PRO C6/289/21.

71   PRO C5/251/11, C7/258/75.

72   PRO C6/289/34.

73   Knoop and Jones, *The London Mason*.

74   For more on the role of credit and attitudes to business see, Julian Hoppit, *Risk and Failure in English Business, 1700-1800*, Cambridge, Cambridge University Press, 1987.

75   For a discussion of the subject of numeracy in general see, Keith Thomas, 'Numeracy in Early Modern England', *Transactions of the Royal Historical Society*, 5th Series, No. 38, 1987, pp. 103-32.

76   M. D. George, *London Life in the Eighteenth Century*, Harmondsworth, Penguin, 1965 provides some information on the apprentice system.

77   Neve, *The City and Countrey Purchaser*, 'Prelude'.

78   Campbell, *The London Tradesman*, p. 160.

79   Lorna Weatherill, *Consumer Behaviour and Material Culture 1600-1760*, London and New York, Routledge, 1988, p. 88 Table 4.4 shows that from her sample in London 18 per cent of gentry and tradesmen recorded books in 1675, 41 per cent in 1705 and 56 per cent in 1725.

80   PRO C10/497/191.

81   PRO C10/497/191.

II   The design of the city

Conceiving the city I: design through drawing

6

> Now forasmuch as the sufficiency of no quantity can be discovered, of which there is no determinate measure, it is evident that some certain measure must first be found out, and afterwards the quantity applied to it, and that in this case will be either the exact designs, or model, of the intended building; which being thoroughly understood, we may then thus go on to our designed calculation.
>
> (Sir Roger Pratt, 'Memoranda Concerning Buildings', c. 1672, in his 'Notebooks', pp. 49-50)

The following two chapters explore how the city was designed. It is important to begin by outlining what is meant by the term 'design'. The word is open to a variety of meanings and interpretations. On the whole these refer to the same subject, but they relate to different and distinctive activities within that arena. As a noun 'design' can refer to a whole industry, or a particular kind of activity concerned with the ordering of form and matter in either two or three dimensions. For example, the term 'the design' can mean: the general look or style of an object, building or work of art; or the process by which this was brought into being; or more specifically the drawings utilized in that process. It is therefore necessary to use a more clearly defined term, that of 'design practice', in order to convey what these chapters are about. They will examine the processes by which a definition of form was arrived at and the methods used to achieve this. The word 'design' in this chapter will generally mean the way in which the form of the building was determined; not the actual physical shape of the building itself, for which the word 'form' will generally be employed.

The central question for design practice in early modern England, as for building practice, is the extent to which there was a separation of design and production. How was design determined? How were instructions passed on and how was an idea of form arrived at? This issue is critical because it helps us to explain the way in which the forms themselves were originated and then perceived. The historiography on the topic has concentrated on the introduction of the use of drawings in this period as a means of specifying design, implying a separation of the design and production processes. This interest has arisen because the introduction of drawings has been seen as a crucial benchmark for the arrival of 'the Renaissance' in England and the attendant rise of the architect. The result of such interpretations has been to skew perceptions about the role of drawings and to assign to them the sole design function. The problem is not only the emphasis which has been given to drawings hitherto, but that far too much attention has been given to one sort only, that is, drawings by famous architects of important buildings. The second problem is that the role of drawings has been seen almost exclusively as evidence of a Renaissance approach to design and hence used as a means of establishing the architectural canon, which is generally presented in terms of a later eighteenth- or nineteenth-century understanding of classicism. Very little attempt has been made to understand drawings in terms of the contemporary approach to design, or to consider in a broader sense what their purpose might have been.

In the absence of many surviving buildings from this period and with the great emphasis placed on trying to trace previously unattributable buildings to their designers, drawings have become a subject in their own right. It might not be going too far to say that drawings as opposed to buildings had at one time become *the* subject area for late seventeenth- and eighteenth-century English architectural history. Such an approach is exemplified in the work emanating from the RIBA Drawings Collection, particularly during the curatorship of John Harris, 1956-86.[1] He utilized the techniques of the drawings specialist to catalogue the collection there and established architectural drawing studies as a unique subject area. As David Watkin wrote in 1980, 'the Drawings Collection now became the true centre of research into English post-mediaeval architecture'.[2] Several exhibitions at the Royal Academy exemplified this approach: *Inigo Jones: Complete Architectural Drawings*, 1989-90; *Sir Christopher Wren and the Making of St Paul's*, 1991; *The Palladian Revival: Lord Burlington, His Villa and Garden at Chiswick*, 1994.[3]

John Harris's Introduction to the Inigo Jones catalogue contains some interesting and perceptive notes on the direction that drawing studies have taken. Harris writes that he sees drawings studies as central to the growing academic respectability of architectural history: 'This growing study of architectural drawings can be seen as a corollary to the recognition of architectural history as a professional discipline.'[4] He says that in the past architectural drawings had been studied in three ways: 'for aesthetic merit (the Old Master syndrome of colour and prettiness), for the building for which it was drawn, or as a representation of the drafting style of the architect'. Today, however, what he calls 'old-fashioned connoisseurship' is being transformed through a more technical approach to the subject which concentrates on the paper, watermarks, handwriting, and the scientific study of the effect of drawing instruments on paper.

There is much which is of great value in this work; as Harris says these studies are contributing to an understanding of office practice through the discovery that several hands may often be involved in one drawing. But its drawbacks are that by its very nature it exacerbates the concentration on great names. It presents drawings as an end in themselves rather than as a means to an end, which is what any type of architectural drawing, even a presentational one, must be. It focuses on the drawings as the sum of an architect's *oeuvre* rather than the buildings, or the drawings and the buildings together. The result of all this is to present architecture as a self-contained activity unrelated to other areas of life. The Jones exhibition was remarkable for the consistency it achieved in presenting an entirely solipsistic understanding of Jones's work.[5]

The Inigo Jones catalogue demonstrates the second less acknowledged role that drawings have been given by historians of this period. This is the use of drawings as part of a legitimizing process for defining what are and what are not acceptable areas for study in the architecture of the period. Harris's final chapter is on 'The Courtier or Subordinate Style, 1615-50'.[6] In this are included all those who inexplicably chose not to follow the example of Inigo Jones, in other words the majority of superior buildings put up at the time. He wrote, 'The "Dutch House" at Kew may be a virtuoso performance in cut brick, but for 1631 it can only be described as "Artisan", and is an accurate measure of the type of country-house favoured by the merchant classes and the gentry.' Summerson dubbed the architecture of this period 'artisan mannerism',[7] but Harris say he prefers the term 'Subordinate Style'. In this style he says 'the rules are broken in ignorance of what was proper'. But rules can only be broken if one agrees to abide by them in the first place, and propriety is equally a subjective criterion.

Perceptions of the type of drawings produced and the use made of drawings in this period have been skewed, I would suggest, by the Public Works drawings and by *Vitruvius Britannicus*.[8] The first is an atypical collection by perhaps the two outstanding draughtsmen of their day, Wren and Hawksmoor, whose interest in the design process was as an intellectual and artistic activity in its own right. The second utilizes a graphic approach quite inimical to the feel of the original buildings, which has immortalized them in a style other than their own and has therefore conveyed a rather misleading impression of their design genesis. Its author Colen

Campbell 'palladianized' even those Baroque buildings he felt com-
pelled to include, so that they give the impression of being the
product of a more coherent and drawings-based design process
than was in fact the case.[9] *Vitruvius Britannicus* is a key source for
many late seventeenth- and early eighteenth-century buildings
that have been demolished, but its influence has ultimately
become pernicious. Historians have swallowed Campbell's propa-
ganda and confused the image with the reality. We have allowed
ourselves to imagine that the draughtsmanship through which
these buildings were presented to the public directly correlates
with the drawing style and method in which they were originally
conceived. It is my contention that it did not.

Even at the highest levels of architecture it is possible that drawing skills were neither necessary nor common.[10] Vanbrugh, as is
well known, could not draw and he has received much criticism
from architectural historians as a result. Colvin comments:
'Though Vanbrugh could communicate architectural ideas by
means of eloquent freehand sketches, there is no evidence that he
ever troubled to learn the tedious discipline of formal architectural
draughtsmanship.'[11] But he was perhaps more typical of his age in
this than either a Wren or a Hawksmoor. There was no notion of
fidelity to a drawn design at the time. Two of the greatest buildings
of the age – St Paul's and Blenheim Palace – were altered extensively
and redesigned throughout the building operation. Kerry Downes
in his *Sir Christopher Wren: The Design of St Paul's Cathedral* provides a fascinating account of the role of drawings in the design
process for the building. He says that the use of drawings in architecture was relatively new at this time and we should be careful
therefore in our interpretations of them. He points out that the
drawings are often in several hands: 'Moreover, most if not all of
the surviving drawings are ones that were superseded, some were
discarded, some never finished. In this lies part of their value, for
they tell us more about the process of design than about its final
realisation.'[12] Downes then goes on to make a case for drawings
being used as a medium for working out ideas and for experimentation. The use of drawings for research and development purposes
was itself relatively new in Europe, having been pioneered by such
architects as Bernini and François Mansart, both of whom Wren
had met in Paris. But the Cathedral was not in any way determined
in a final drawn design prior to construction. Drawings were
utilized inside the Office of Works for circulation within the architectural team. They were not, however, a means of communicating
information to the builders and craftsmen.

Design to a large extent took place on-site and evolved alongside
the building operation. The drawings that survive it seems were

more for presentation to the client than a blueprint upon which
to proceed and hence the production of large numbers of drawings
for state buildings. That is not to say that there were not other
drawings, working drawings used for on-site construction. Indeed
there were and they are mentioned in some contemporary sources
such as the Blenheim correspondence.[13] They, however, do not
survive for the most part and nor has any consideration been given
to them in the literature.[14]

If design was incremental, empirical, and not solely paper based
in the upper echelons of English architecture, it was even less likely
to rely on a consistent use of drawn designs in the speculative
housing market. There is some evidence in Chancery of drawings
being used in connection with speculative developments.[15] From
this and other published contemporary sources there is sufficient
documentation for the London developments to suggest the kinds
of drawings that were made, the purposes for which they were
intended and the ways in which they were utilized in the design
process.

Drawings were made on paper or vellum, a fine kind of parchment. The kind of material used would depend on whether the
drawing was expendable or not, and whether it formed an official
document or not. Paper was presumably enough of a rarity for
Joseph Moxon in *Mechanick Exercises* to inform his readers that, 'a
small sheet of paper is not above fifteen or sixteen inches long'.[16]
When mention of drawn designs does occur the contemporary
word was not 'drawing' but nearly always the terms 'scheme',
'model', 'plan', 'platt', 'plattform' or 'plot'. For example, when
Thomas Neale was planning his Seven Dials development he
agreed to build, 'according to the scheme or model annexed to the
agreement'.[17] Or when Bevis Lloyd was working at Channel Row,
Westminster he referred to, 'a plan attached to the lease'.[18] These
terms do not seem to have fixed meanings as is suggested by the
common habit of using several terms together in a very imprecise
way. At the Middle Temple Barbon was recorded as building,
'according to the model, draught, map or ground plot thereto
annexed'.[19] It is hard to know exactly what sort of drawing is being
referred to, but most of these terms seem to relate to the ground
plan for either an individual house or a whole scheme. Moxon
distinguished the ground plot, 'the peece of ground a building is
to be erected upon',[20] from drawn representations such as the draft
and the profile. However, in the Chancery evidence 'plot' is certainly used to indicate a drawn plan as well as an actual plot of
land. Richard Neve following Moxon states in *The City and
Countrey Purchaser* that the 'ground-plat or plot' refers to the land
itself and the word 'platform' to its graphic representation: 'This

word in Architecture is sometimes us'd to signifie the Ichnography, or Draught of the Ground-plot of a House; but more commonly for a broad smooth, and open Walk upon the top of any Building.'[21] The *OED* gives the terms plan, platt, plot and platform as being interchangeable at this date, as does Chambers in his *Cyclopaedia* of 1728.[22] The words, elevation, upright, ichnography and orthography are to be found in the dictionaries and treatises of the period but are rarely encountered in other contemporary writing.

The noun a 'model' had three meanings relating to design at this time. The usage that is common today was just beginning to be found in the seventeenth-century, that is as a three dimensional representation of a projected or existing structure. The *OED* gives the first architectural usage of the word as being in Moxon's 1665 translation of Vignola. The use of a three-dimensional model to provide an overall idea for the scheme before building work started was being encouraged by writers such as Roger Pratt.

> As to a Model, the use of it hath been very ancient ... and is thought at this day to be so necessary by the Italians, the best architects of all others, that they will hardly ever undertake to build anything considerable, or of expense, without it ... Whereas all the other drafts aforesaid do only superficially and disjointedly represent unto us the several parts of a building, a model does it jointly, and according to all its dimensions.[23]

However, in normal usage the term 'model' meant something far less precise. More often it meant a design or a drawing of any type be it plan, section or elevation.[24] The terms 'schemes', 'model' and 'plan' seem to have been interchangeable, and the fact that models are often detailed as being annexed or attached to the building agreement or lease, suggests that these were paper rather than material designs.

The word 'modellizeing' is used in one place, referring to the staking out of the ground for building plots.[25] This brings us on to the third meaning of 'model' which was a mould, or as a verb to mould. In Dr Johnson's *Dictionary* the words 'model' and 'mould' are given as being interchangeable.[26] The architectural use of the word 'mould' was a much earlier one, meaning a pattern by which something is shaped. At this date the term 'model' was beginning to separate from the older term denoting a physical shaping of form, to take on another meaning whereby the representation of form through drawings or three-dimensional structures became separate from the form itself.

The word 'drawing' was not used although the verb 'to draw' was common. The contemporary word for a drawing was a 'draught' or 'draft'. Joseph Moxon described a 'draft' as being: 'The picture of an intended Building described on paper, whereon is laid

down the devised Divisions and Partitions of Every Room in its
due proportion to the whole building.'[27] When Henry Serle and
Robert Clerke, the developers of Little Lincoln's Inn Field, were
planning their scheme they engaged a person to make 'a draft' for
building in the field,[28] while Sir Nathaniel Curzon's accounts for
Brookfield Market include the following entry:

22 December 1702

Paid the surveyor for two new draughts of Brookfield	£8 12s 0d
for putting them into frames	8s
Spent and gave for the old draught	£1 18s 0d[29]

What is possibly more surprising is the remarkable coincidence
in the way in which the word 'design' parallels modern usage. The
specifically artistic meaning of the word 'design' as opposed to its
general usage of 'to plan, to intend', came into English in the seventeenth century from Italy. The Italian verb 'disegnare' and the
noun 'disegno' developed a specifically artistic sense in the sixteenth century.[30] According to the sixteenth-century writer John
Florio the Italian meant, 'to design, contrive, plot, purpose, intend,
also draw, paint, embroider, model, portray'.[31] This artistic sense
got taken into French and English. But whereas the French differentiated the two meanings of the word, so that in modern French
'dessein' is 'purpose, plan' and 'dessin' is 'design in art', in English
both meanings were contained within the one word 'design'.

In its more specific sense 'design' then and now incorporates a
number of meanings. Chambers in his short definition managed
to encapsulate most of them: 'Design, or Draught, with regard to
the Arts and Sciences, signifies the thought, Plan, Geometrical Representation, Distribution, and Construction of a Painting, Poem,
Book or Building.'[32] Sometimes it is to be found being used as a
verb with the specific meaning of the planning, drawing or working out of a form prior to execution; for example, one case
regarding Essex House refers to a 'plot or draft whereby a street of
four and twenty feet in front was laid out or designed from the
Strand to the cross street' (figure 9).[33] 'Design' is also used as a noun
signifying preliminary drawn details or an outline of a scheme or
building prior to construction. The OED gives this meaning of the
word as dating from 1638. Nicholas Barbon at Essex House says that
he drew 'a plotform or design' to show how the ground should be
laid out.[34] Elsewhere he refers in several places to 'his design and
model'.[35] This could refer specifically to the drawn details, or he
could be using the word in the wider sense of the overall form and
the combination of elements that contribute to the totality of that

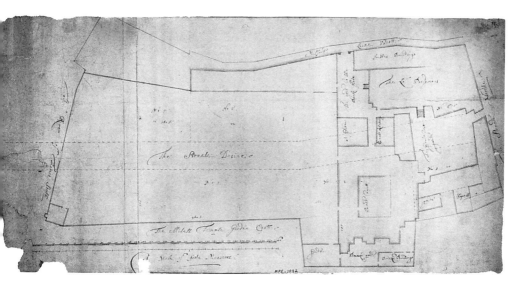

] Plan of the *Street Desine* from the River to the trand on the site of Essex louse and Garden, *c.* 1675. his is a rare example of a surviving layout for a proposed development. The division of the site nto six plots can be seen, five of them give the rontages from which the estimated ground rents could be calculated. The sixth plot, Lady ridgeman's house, at the op right did not form part of the scheme and remained unaltered.

particular form, a usage which is found from 1644 onwards.[36] The term 'designer' became current from the mid-eighteenth century onwards.[37]

The term 'design' had a variety of meanings by this date which had extended considerably the common non-technical usage of 'to plan or intend'. Through the various terms relating to drawings and the design process a vocabulary was beginning to develop to describe different kinds of drawings and their functions. However, as we have seen, the new terms were not clearly differentiated at this date nor were they entirely separated from an older vocabulary, and this is matched by a blurring of the processes themselves in practice.

Let us begin with the ground plan and its use for speculative housing developments. It seems that drawings alone were only of limited help in the construction process.

> The foundation being all made firm, and levelled, the Master-Bricklayer, or his Foreman, must take care to see all the Foundation set truly out, according to the design of the Ground-plat, or cellar-floor, and that all his Walls be made of the same thickness as they are in the design; which is very difficult to do to wit, to take the true thickness of the Walls from a Design that is drawn to a small scale, because the breadth of the points of the Compasses will vary somewhat; therefore 'tis advisable for him that draws the draught to set the Dimensions in figures to each wall, chimney, window etc and then the Workman cannot so easily make a mistake.[38]

This was written by Joseph Moxon, an advocate of the use of drawings, but one aware of their limitations. Other evidence shows that older established ways of laying out plots continued alongside the new drawn system. In a case concerning the development of

Soho Fields we hear how Richard Frith: 'marked and trenched out what part of the said fields was in his present possession into streets for building'.[39] In the evidence given surrounding the case it is quite clear that the drawn designs played only a minor part in determining the scheme. It would probably be fair to surmise that although plans could provide general guidelines for a development's layout, they were by no means hard and fast fixed documents and could be altered as and when necessary.

Such an approach would be in keeping with what is known already about late seventeenth- and early eighteenth-century attitudes to the design process. But if design was such an empirical and flexible process it might be asked, why did they bother to produce ground plans at all? The answer to this must surely lie in the new leasing and financial arrangements that the speculative building system required. It is evident that where ground layouts are mentioned, their primary purpose was to establish the division of plots and building leases within a development. It was therefore not the division between design and production which made these plot layouts necessary but rather the sub-divisions of labour and capital within the production process itself. The building lease system operated by means of a series of tiers, sometimes distinct and sometimes overlapping, forming a complex matrix through which capital and credit were filtered. It was the division between the speculators who bought the land and sustained the financial risk for the whole development, and the people who took on an individual plot or plots, that necessitated the creation of a document that determined both the individual and collective responsibilities. It was the ground plan which gave physical shape in a very immediate way to the often complex and sometimes uneasy relationship between the desire of the speculator to achieve a workable whole, and the concerns of the small-scale developers within their individual plots.

A description of a ground plan is given in connection with building at Lamb's Conduit Fields:

> which said scheme or model did contain the extent and dimensions of the whole ground and premises, and the several streets, places, number of houses and divisions in which the whole was intended to be divided, and the number of feet of the front of the houses and buildings intended to be erected on each side of every such street, place and division, or at least a scale of feet was drawn in the said scheme or model where by the number of feet in the front might be computed.[40]

The first purpose of the model was to specify the extent of the scheme and to give it overall shape and definition. Given that all these developments took place in open fields, this was to some extent a marking of territorial rights on paper which would by no

10] A plan of houses in part of Lamb's Conduit Fields, 1752. The tenants of each plot and their annual rents are written on the drawing. The plan was drawn up using the information from two earlier schedules of building leases which were attached to the document. (See the Appendix for a transcription of the leases and their inscriptions.)

means be obvious on the bare ground. Within the general layout the description tells us were marked the streets, the individual houses and the dimensions of each plot. This information provided the basis on which individual building leases could then be drawn up. It also gave a clear indication to those taking on such leases what the extent of their individual commitment was, and the relationship of their plot in proportion to the whole. In the Lamb's Conduit Fields case it is told how there were articles of agreement between Kent and Barbon by which it was agreed that the ground should be let for building and that those who undertook to build 'should have all reasonable encouragement for so doing, and for that purpose there was a scheme or model drawn out and annexed to the said articles'.[41] (Figure 10 shows a similar plan in the same vicinity.)

Here we have the reason for the adoption of the technique of a regularized ground plan layout drawn out on paper by the speculative building market in the late seventeenth century. The use of a regular plan layout and drawings is usually seen as evidence of the principles of Renaissance design. However, although the use of such a drawing is a technique derived from classical architecture, its adoption in this area was not primarily to do with design factors but rather as a result of the economic organization of the speculative building market. Barbon and Kent in the quote already given

on Lamb's Conduit Fields said that they needed the model to attract people to take on building leases.[42] In other words it was the
unique capacity that the drawn plan had for crystallizing in
graphic form a complex set of legal, financial and environmental
relationships which ensured its use. By being able to show potential building lessees exactly what they would be taking on in terms
of the size of the plot, the scale of the development and the level
of the market aimed at - discernible primarily through the size of
the frontage of the houses and the spatiality of the layout (the
more complex and the more space, the greater the development)
- Barbon and Kent hoped to entice smaller speculators to take on
building leases, at a time in the late 1680s when the building market was less buoyant. But builders and investors were not the only
people at whom the drawings might be targeted. They could also
be used to entice a prospective client into building. At the Middle
Temple which burnt down in 1679 the evidence records that,
Barbon 'taking notice and being a great undertaker of buildings'
contacted the Society and produced before them 'several models,
draughts, maps or ground plots', with proposals for rebuilding
there.[43]

It is interesting to note that no mention is made in the Lamb's
Conduit description of the 'model' that the ground plans of the
individual houses themselves were shown. This was because the
internal planning of the houses did not form part of this initial
negotiating stage between developer and building lessee. The
dimensions of houses were fixed both for the frontage and
the depth, but the internal planning was presumably a matter
for the individual builders themselves. Joseph Moxon recommended the use of ground plans for each floor of the building:

> and also to have a Draught of the Ground-Plat or Ichnography of every
> story in a Paper by it self: because many times the Conveniences, or
> Contrivances in one Story, differ from those in another, either in bigness
> of Chimneys, or division of the Rooms, some being larger in one Storey
> than another, and sometimes having more Chimnies in one Story than
> in another.[44]

The information given in these books, being of an advisory and
ideal nature, has to be treated with care. Probably some builders
did make a draft before carrying out the work, but equally some
did not. In a case concerning the building of a mansion house in
Mincing Lane there is a reference to the vault or privy being
marked on the drawing, suggesting a fairly high level of detail on
the plan.[45] Generally these would be working drawings which have
not survived because there was no client involved and they were
not needed for display purposes.

However, the plan also had more specific purposes, first of all as a form of legal documentation. Most of the references to drawings in the cases occur in connection with a building agreement or lease. In the Lamb's Conduit case quoted in the previous paragraph it is stated that the model was annexed to articles of agreement.[46] The same terminology is used with reference to the Seven Dials development,[47] while at Channel Row, Westminster there is mention of 'a plan attached to the lease'.[48] The use of drawn plans with land and property documents demonstrating a title to ownership was nothing new and goes back to the Middle Ages. It was helpful to have a plan attached to a lease to show the exact area that the lease covered, and this is still the system used today. There is a document in the Royal Institute of British Architects which explicitly demonstrates the legal function of the ground plan (figure 11). It is part of a contract (indenture of articles of agreement) between Joseph Titcombe, armourer of the City of London, and Thomas Steane, a wax chandler, for Titcombe to build a house and shop in Cheapside for Steane. Attached to the indenture which is on parchment is a drawing on paper with a plan of the house. On the outside of the contract is written:

30 October 1668
Articles of Agreement for Building the house in Cheapside together with a seale or modell of the ground with its Boundings necessary to be kept in case of dispute.

The drawing is labelled 'Mr Stains Draught', which would suggest

11] *Mr Staines Draught*. A plan attached to a contract for building a house in the City between Joseph Titcombe, armourer, and Thomas Steane, wax chandler, 1668.

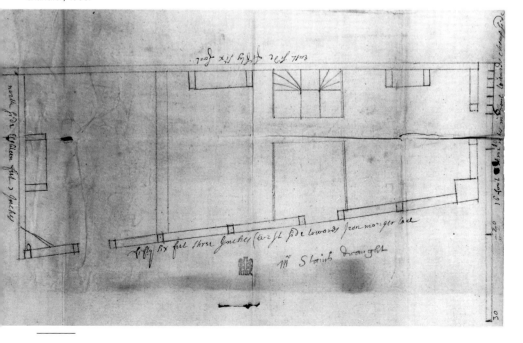

that they had one each. What is curious is that although the drawing forms part of the legal contract it should be both so insubstantial and so imprecise. Compared to the beautifully drawn-up indenture in black ink on parchment, the drawing in pencil on flimsy paper is distinctly scrappy. This reinforces the idea that although drawings were beginning to be used as a form of legal documentation they were considered inferior to the written word. The drawing is also extremely vague, giving little more information than the boundaries of the site and a suggestion as to the area within this that the building should occupy. In no way could this plan be seen as a generator of form. Plans of completed houses might also be attached to leases, as we see in figure 12, which shows newly built houses in Westminster attached to a lease of 1702.

Ground plans were also required in order to gain royal approval for new developments. A licence to build would be given in accordance with the model or plan. The Earl of Bridgewater petitioned for permission to build in 1673, which was granted after Wren had drawn up a plan.

> It was ordered by their Lordships That Christopher Wren Esq Surveyor Generall of his Majesties Workes do view the severall Places aforesaid, where ye Petitioner desires to build, and that he frame a Draft to ye proportions observed in the Buildings of London, and the Pet. is hereby Ordered to conforme himself in his said Buildings to such Plat or Draft as the said Surveyor General shall settle and fix upon herein.[49]

Wren also drew up plans for the redevelopment of Drury House and Craven House by the Earl of Craven [50] and for some houses in Mile End Green to be built by Lady Philadelphia Wentworth

12] Plan attached to a lease of 'five new built messuages situate in Tothill Street and six messuages with appurtenances in Carteret Street', 1702. These buildings were erected on the Christ's Hospital estate in Westminster. The internal planning of the premises is clearly shown. Those along the Broadway have shops at the front and the establishment on the corner with Cartwright Street has a 'Bake House' and oven to the rear. Those along Carteret or Cartwright Street are purely residential, with rear staircases attached to one wall, while those on Broadway are centrally placed. Notice the closet wings to the rear of some of the houses and the privies and sheds at the end of the relatively large gardens.

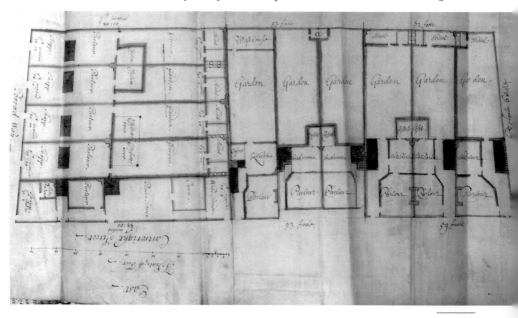

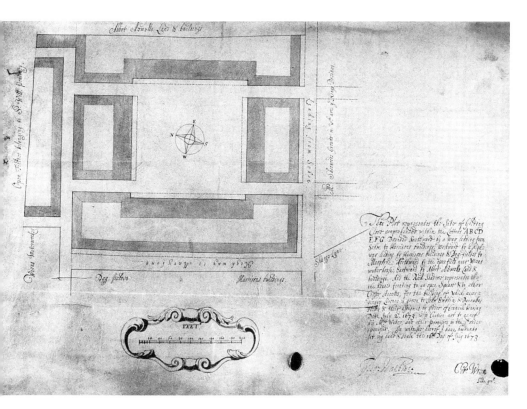

13] Plan for Golden Square, 16 July 1673, for a licence to build for John Emblin and Barnaby Holly, signed by Christopher Wren. The plan conforms with the square as built 1684–98 and was probably drawn up in the Office of Works. The darker shading indicating the terraces to be built is in red ink on the original.

which were given a licence to build, 'according to a Designe or Modell thereof to be prepared by the said Surveyor General'.[51] At Golden Square, the petitioners to the King were granted permission to build in 1673, firstly 'according to a Designe to be approved by the said Surveyor [General]' [52] and secondly 'according to the modell and forme … designe draught mapp or Chart' annexed to the patent (figure 13).[53] *The Survey of London* considers it unclear as to whether the plan was drawn up and submitted by the petitioners to Wren or whether it originated in the Surveyor General's office.[54] The plan is drawn in black and red ink on parchment; 'the Red Shadows representes the houses fronting to an open Square & to other Cross streetes'.[55] It is signed and sealed by Wren. A few similar plans exist using the same red shading to indicate new building, also signed by Wren: one for the Earl of Bridgewater for rebuilding in the Barbican area,[56] and another for the Earl of Salisbury for the redevelopment of Salisbury House, both in the Public Record Office.[57] A further plan in the same style and hand for the new buildings on the site of Exeter House, showing the proposed access to the river and to Covent Garden, survives at All Souls.[58]

It seems clear that Wren's office did draw up plans for some developments and that the Golden Square and other plans listed above came from this source. The Privy Council minutes show that Wren's involvement in processing applications was extremely detailed. Besides reporting on major new projects he was also called upon to consider 'how the Ditches and Sewers will be kept cleansed and sweet' for five new houses in Stepney [59] or whether Edward Billings, 'a late brewer', should be allowed to build a street in Westminster leading to the horse ferry. This was opposed by his neighbours as it meant filling in a mill stream on which they and several other breweries depended for water.[60] Permission was granted and the standard clause inserted provided he, 'do build regularly according to direction & ye Designe to which his Patent may refer'. The Privy Council also asked for an extra clause to be inserted: 'That ye Designe of the Building be enrolled in the Chancery, and the Petitioner obliged to cause two exact copies to be made of his said Designe, one whereof is to be left in ye Chancery & ye other with his Majesties Surveyor General.' Sometimes therefore it was the petitioner who submitted the plan and a surviving example is the plan for Barbon's development at Essex House. He was threatened with prosecution over his unlicensed building there in 1675 and ordered to stop work forthwith.[61] This may have resulted in the submission of the development plan for the site now in the Public Record Office, which is not signed by Wren and is obviously from a different source (see figure 9).[62]

The ground plan was an essential document not just for establishing legal ownership but also for calculating the economic basis for a scheme. The reason that the precise frontage of each house was given on the plan or a scale of feet was included was that development costs were worked out on a square footage basis. The street frontage determined the size of the houses and hence their position on the social scale and the level at which subsequent rents could be pitched. Most developments for which the details survive seem to have shied away from having houses of a uniform size. Thus in the plans for Smith Square in Westminster, twenty-four of the houses were to be 20 ft in front and 36 ft deep, while the other four were to be 22 ft in front and 38 ft deep.[63] At Lamb's Conduit Fields the frontages varied between 20 ft and 40 ft in front.[64] The ground plan was then a precise economic document from which the cost of the development could be determined and on the basis of which the necessary return would be calculated.

This method of calculating cost by the square or the foot was likely to lead to repetitive, geometric design. The use of regularized layouts and ground plans was due as much to methods of cost computation and the requirements of the new building contracts, as it was to the adoption of a new style. Or, to put it another way, the speculative market was able to utilize classical design because it fitted in so well with its developmental and constructional processes. The failure of the Lamb's Conduit scheme to come to fruition was blamed by the Kent family on Sir Nathaniel Curzon's failure to adhere to the plan, and this failure is depicted very much in economic terms:

> and if such designs had been pursued by the said Sir Nathaniel Curzon and the said premises had been built and carried up in the form and method prescribed and intended by such schemes, model and ground platt aforesaid the ground rents to be reserved thereon would in all likelihood have answered and raised the yearly sum which was then computed to amount to £2,000 p.a. as aforesaid.[65]

The new contracting system in which work was paid for by measurement relied on the use of detailed specifications to produce costings and contract documents, which at the same time established a precise form for the house. Roger Pratt grasped the implications of this as his comments demonstrate in the opening quotation of this chapter.[66] He realized that a contracting system which necessitated a fully worked-out design prior to construction, inevitably led to the use of drawings to achieve this precise vision of shape and form. In the long term Pratt was correct. The need for accurate specifications on which to base building contracts must have been critical in the adoption of drawings as the primary means of determining form in the architectural design process. It was for this purpose primarily that ground plans were initially adopted, rather than for aesthetic or rational planning reasons.

What is more surprising is possibly how little they were used. And when they were used, like all documentation, they were immediately discarded or ignored if this proved to be more expedient. There seems to have been some ambiguity about their precise legal status and the extent to which they were binding. A dispute about the building of a passageway between the Strand and the new Essex House development reinforces the implication that the written word was considered superior legally to a drawn plan. Samuel Vincent, one of Barbon's agents, did not dispute the existence of the passage on the plan, but implied that because the existence of the passage was not confirmed in words the drawing was not contractually binding.[67] It may also be that plans were used more than we know, but that they do not survive or were not mentioned, because they were seen very much as working calculations which would be thrown out once their original purpose had been served.

To turn now from the generalized ground plan to the means of specifying the exact characteristics of each individual house, including its elevations and detailing. The quote given previously concerning Sir Nathaniel Curzon's failure to conform to the model and the subsequent short-fall in the estimated ground rents hints at a determination of outline which went beyond the ground plot alone: 'and [if] the said premises had been built and carried up in the form and method prescribed and intended by such schemes, model and ground platt aforesaid the ground rents ...'.[68] 'Form and method', these are the critical factors and, as with the ground plan, I will argue that the general form of the house, its shape, style and decoration, can only be seen to exist within the constructional and developmental requirements of speculative building.

There is no mention of any drawings being used in the cases for elevations or sections, except in the rather vague way suggested in the quote above. Certainly the contemporary term for an elevational drawing, an 'upright', is never encountered. Moxon advocated the use of elevations as well as ground plans prior to building:

> in which designs and Model, the Ground plat or Ichnography of each floor of Story is delineated and represented: As also the fashion and form of each front, together with the Windows, Doors, and Ornaments, if they intend any, to wit, Facias, Rustick Quines, Architraves, Friezes and Cornices, are to be shewn in the Draughts or Designs of the Uprights or Orthographyes.[69]

There is far less evidence that uprights as opposed to plans were used for speculative building, and it is almost impossible to know to what extent they were employed. Hardly any drawings survive of this type. One exception is an elevation attached to a building agreement for Nos 6-10 Frith Street which exists in the Northamptonshire Record Office.[70] This part of Frith Street was not developed until 1718 as a block by Sir James Bateman who made the agreement with William Thomas of Soho. The small scale of the development, the relatively late date, and above all the very direct involvement of the lead developer here may all explain the use of an elevation for the site.

But even if elevations and designs of details were little used, this does not mean there was not a prior realization of form or a common consensus and understanding as to what form should be. Bevis and Ann Lloyd's proposed building of a square in Westminster, later Smith Square, shows the use which might be made of drawings in the planning of a development.[71] Having contacted the builder James Friend he then produced calculations for the scheme, and approached Isaac Rowe 'a surveyor' to draw up a plan for the square.[72] This is one of three cases in which we hear of a person being specifically employed to produce drawings.[73] Rowe was an architect who worked chiefly in Northamptonshire, according to Colvin,[74] however he features several times as a surveyor for Christ's Hospital in London.[75]

The evidence relates how Friend and Rowe measured the ground on which the square was to be built and then Rowe drew 'a platform thereof of thirty houses'.[76] Friend and Rowe 'staked out the ground': this would suggest that the earlier example of trenching in Soho Fields was possibly common practice. When they did this they found there was not enough room for thirty houses and they asked Lloyd to surrender two of his houses. This he did, and then a new platform or model for twenty-eight houses was drawn. The lack of accuracy in the drawing would lend credence to the idea that the plan was less a precise design tool than a legal and commercial document. It is conceivable that the model included other drawings besides a ground plan, and the involvement of Isaac Rowe makes this more likely. But it is also possible that it did not for several reasons. Firstly, because the use of elevations or general perspectives has not been specifically mentioned anywhere else in the evidence. Secondly, because the drawing is referred to first of all as a 'platform' and then as a 'platform or model', which implies a ground plan. Thirdly, because elsewhere in the case we are given a very precise written description of exactly what the buildings were to look like, in other words, a building specification.

Many of the references to drawings in the cases mention them as being annexed to the articles of agreement, which would include the building specification. It is worth quoting from this building specification at some length before going back to consider what the relationship might be between such specifications and the use of drawn designs.[77] The articles of agreement were made between Bevis Lloyd and James Friend on 13 September 1686. They open by stating that Friend had agreed to build twenty-eight houses in a square by Michaelmas 1687. A description is then given of the dimensions of the houses, twenty-four of the houses were to be 20 ft in front and 36 ft deep, the other four to be 22 ft in front and 38 ft deep, according to the agreed plan. Information given in the plan is therefore written out in the specification as well. This could also be true for the elevations. There then follows a description of the overall layout including the central square. Every part of the house is then detailed in terms of its materials, the specifications for the materials, and design details or styling where relevant.

The fronts of the houses were to be two and a half bricks thick in the cellar, two bricks in the next storey, then one and a half bricks to the raising plate, with no brickwork above the raising plate except the topping of the chimneys. An oak doorcase was to be made in front of each house, with two lights over, the scantling (measurements) to be 7 inches by 5 inches, with a good deal door, lined and battened, fixed to the same. Two sash-windows to the front on the same floor. An oak doorcase to the rear with two lights over, the scantling to be 6 inches by 5 inches, with two oaken windows 5 ft 6 inches high and 4 ft wide. The roof, floors, mantle-trees, partitions and lintelling, and all timber except the outward doorcases and windows, to be of good fir; the front side of the roofs to be slated and the back part tiled, with a leaden gutter in the middle between the double roofs 25 ft long to carry the water backwards. Render and plaster all walls in the upper storey, the next storey below it and the kitchen, 'and no more plastering in the houses'. There are only two descriptive directions in the specification, one is for 'a plain cornice in the front' and the other is 'to make an escollop shell over each front door'. The final comment in the building specification is that all this work is to be done 'necessary to turn key and go' except wainscotting and painting. The rest of the articles of agreement quoted in the evidence form a building agreement detailing the rates of pay, which were to be £32 10s 0d per square of brickwork, the estimated cost of the houses, the way they were to be paid for and the building lease arrangements. The work was to be finished by Michaelmas 1687. The house does not conform exactly to the specifications laid down in the 1667 Rebuilding Act but would fall somewhere between the second and third sorts of houses in terms of the brick thickness of its walls and the number of storeys, which are four.

There is no mention of any drawings being attached to the building articles other than the ground plan. It must be assumed that speculative houses in this period were sometimes put up with ground plans, but whether other drawings were used is very difficult to assess. Even then I would conclude that the use of ground plans was by no means universal nor critical in the design formulation of a development. The pattern of drawing use we see in speculative developments is therefore to some extent the reverse of that which we know about for commissioned buildings. In speculative building, drawings were used to attract investors and builders and they were therefore particularly utilized in the very early stages. As the main concern was with land values there was a concentration on the ground plan. Drawing is a means of communicating information, but it was not primarily information about form that was being given in the drawings produced for this market, and to interpret them as such is fundamentally to misunderstand them. These drawings were passing on other sorts of information. They may have included information about form as well; but the lack of attention given to elevations and details would suggest that communication about form and the determination of form proceeded by other channels. The drawings for speculative buildings were produced for specific purposes which they soon outlived. They have not therefore survived. We find the reverse situation with regard to commissioned buildings where some drawings survive which were working drawings, but where many of the drawings that we know about seem to have been presentational drawings intended for the client to keep as a record of the design and where the emphasis was on form and style.

Notes

1 See David Watkin, *The Rise of Architectural History*, London, Architectural Press, 1980, pp. 163-4.

2 Watkin, *Architectural History*, p. 164.

3 Catalogues: John Harris and Gordon Higgot, *Inigo Jones: Complete Architectural Drawings*, London, Royal Academy of Arts, 1989-90; Royal Academy of Arts, *Sir Christopher Wren and the Making of St Paul's*, London, Royal Academy of Arts, 1991; John Harris, *The Palladian Revival: Lord Burlington, His Villa and Garden at Chiswick*, London, Royal Academy of Arts and Yale University Press, 1994.

4 Harris and Higgot, *Inigo Jones*, pp. 9-10, from which all subsequent quotations in this paragraph are drawn.

5 For a more comprehensive approach to Jones see the catalogue of another exhibition in which Harris was involved: J. Harris, S. Orgel and R. Strong, *The King's Arcadia: Inigo Jones and the Stuart Court*, London, Arts Council of Great Britain, 1973.

6 Harris and Higgot, *Inigo Jones*, pp. 298-302.

7 John Summerson, *Architecture in Britain, 1530-1830*, Harmondsworth, Penguin, 1983, p. 157.

8 In published form many of these are to be found in the *Wren Society*, Vols I–XX, Oxford, 1924-43 and Kerry Downes, *Sir Christopher Wren: The Design of St Paul's Cathedral*, London, Trefoil, 1988; H. M. Colvin, *Catalogue of Architectural Drawings of the 18th and 19th Centuries in the Library of Worcester College, Oxford*, Oxford, Clarendon Press, 1964; Colen Campbell, *Vitruvius Britannicus*, Vols I, II, III, London, 1715, 1717, 1725.

9 John Bold in *John Webb: Architectural Theory and Practice in the Seventeenth Century*, Oxford, Clarendon Press, 1989, argues that the English neo-Palladians' dependence on drawn sources had an impact on the style they developed themselves. 'In the Campbell/Kent engravings, the divorcing of the object from its context, framed by plain, white paper rather than by its landscape, imparted an iconic quality which was translated, perhaps unconsciously, into neo-Palladian architecture itself, which, unlike the work of Jones and Webb is essentially two-dimensional and static' (p. 148).

10 Kerry Downes' books on Vanbrugh and Hawksmoor demonstrate the paucity of surviving drawings for large country house commissions such as Blenheim and Castle Howard.

11 Howard Colvin, *A Biographical Dictionary of British Architects, 1600–1840*, London, John Murray, 1978, p. 851.

12 Downes, *The Design of St Paul's Cathedral*, p. 27.

13 Reproduced in: Kerry Downes, *Hawksmoor*, London, Zwemmer, 1979, Appendix A; G. F. Webb, ed., *The Complete Works of Sir John Vanbrugh, Vol. IV, The Letters*, London, Nonesuch Press, 1928; L. Whistler, *The Imagination of Vanbrugh and His Fellow Artists*, London, Batsford, 1954, Appendix I.

14 This uncritical acceptance of the use of drawings as proof of a classical ideology in architecture in England is particularly ironic when studies on early Renaissance Italy have uncovered a far more complex picture. It is not until the sixteenth century that a consistent relationship between Renaissance theory and practice and a systematic use of drawings is observable in the work of designers such as Raphael, Peruzzi and Michelangelo. See: L. D. Ettlinger, 'The Emergence of the Italian Architect During the Fifteenth Century', in S. Kostof, ed., *The Architect: Chapters in the History of the Profession*, Oxford, Oxford University Press, 1977, pp. 96-123; H. Saalman, 'Early Renaissance Architectural Theory and Practice in Antonio Filarete's Trattato di Architettura', *Art Bulletin*, Vol. 41, 1959, pp. 89-106; James S. Ackerman, 'Architectural Practice in the Italian Renaissance', *Journal of the Society of Architectural Historians*, Vol. 13, 1954, pp. 3-11; Christoph Luitpold Frommel, 'Reflections on the Early Architectural Drawings', in Henry A. Millon, ed., *The Renaissance from Brunelleschi to Michaelangelo: The Representation of Architecture*, London, Thames & Hudson, 1994, pp. 101-23.

15 Mention of drawings occurs in a very small number of cases, in 22 out of a total of 221 Chancery cases looked at: PRO C5/251/11, C5/295/49, C5/614/105, C6/259/81, C6/351/22, C7/152/40, C7/210/8, C7/210/27, C8/203/95, C8/230/72, C8/269/79, C8/388/7, C8/420/53, C8/553/97, C9/74/112, C9/294/7, C9/457/109, C10/181/4, C10/224/3, C10/225/12, C10/227/5, C10/230/7.

16 Joseph Moxon, *Mechanick Exercises, Or, the Doctrine of Handy-Works*, London, 1703, p. 129.

17 PRO C5/614/105.

18 PRO C5/295/49.

19 PRO C8/230/72.

20 Moxon, *Mechanick Exercises*, p. 168.

21 Richard Neve, *The City and Countrey Purchaser, and Builder's Dictionary: Or, The Compleat Builders Guide*, London, 1726, p. 225.

22 Ephraim Chambers, *Cyclopaedia: Or An Universal Dictionary of Arts and Sciences*, London, 1728.

23 R. T. Gunther, ed., *The Architecture of Sir Roger Pratt*, Oxford, 1928, pp. 22-3.

24 The *OED* gives as an example of the use of the word in this sense: 1597 Shakespeare, Henry IV, I. iii. 142. 'When we meane to build, we first suruey [sic] the Plot, then draw the Modell'.

25 PRO C10/214/19.

26 Samuel Johnson, *A Dictionary of the English Language*, London, 1755.

27 Moxon, *Mechanick Exercises*, p. 166.

28 PRO C10/224/3.

29 PRO C5/251/11.

30 For more on the use of the word in this period see, Michael Baxandall, 'English *Disegno*', in Edward Chaney and Peter Mack, eds, *England and the Continental Renaissance: Essays in Honour of J. B. Trapp*, Woodbridge, Boydell, 1990, pp. 203-14.

31 John Florio, 'Firste fruites. Also a perfect induction to the Italian, and English tongues', 1578, as quoted in the *OED*.

32 Chambers, *Cyclopaedia*.

33 PRO C9/74/112.

34 PRO C8/269/79.

35 PRO C9/457/109, C10/230/7.

36 *OED*.

37 Charles Saumarez Smith, 'Eighteenth-Century Man', *Designer*, March 1987, pp. 19-21.

38 Moxon, *Mechanick Exercises*, p. 257.

39 PRO C6/86/78.

40 PRO C5/251/11.

41 PRO C5/251/11.

42 PRO C5/251/11.

43 PRO C8/230/72.

44 Moxon, *Mechanick Exercises*, p. 252.

45 PRO C10/181/4.

46 PRO C5/251/11.

47 PRO C5/614/105.

48 PRO C5/295/49.

49 PRO PC/2/63 p. 400.

50 PRO PC/2/63 p. 404.

51 PRO PC/2/63 p. 402.

52 PRO PC/2/64 p. 51.

53 PRO C66/3151/No. 13.

54 *Survey of London, St James, Westminster*, Pt II, Vol. XXI, London, Athlone Press, 1960, p. 139.

55 PRO MPA/69.

56 PRO MPA/22.

57 PRO MPA/40.

58 PRO PC/2/63 p. 341; All Souls Wren Drawings Vol. IV No. 67, reproduced in *Wren Society*, Vol. XVIII, 1941, Pl. I.

59 PRO PC/2/63 p. 27.

60 PRO PC/2/63 pp. 23, 33, 38.

61 PRO PC/2/64 pp. 383, 394, 398, 404.

62 PRO MPE/1092.

63 PRO C7/210/8.

64 PRO C5/251/11.

65 PRO C5/251/11.

66 Gunther, *Pratt*, pp. 49-50.

67 PRO C8/269/79.

68 PRO C5/251/11.

69 Moxon, *Mechanick Exercises*, p. 252.

70 *Survey of London, St Anne, Soho*, Vol. XXXIII, 1966, pp. 154-8; *Survey of London, St Anne, Soho*, Vol. XXXIV, Pls 118, 119, 121a.

71 PRO C7/210/8, C7/210/28.

72 PRO C7/210/8.

73 The other two are PRO C5/251/11 and PRO C10/224/3.

74 Colvin, *Biographical Dictionary*, pp. 864-7.

75 For example, Guildhall Library, Records of Christ's Hospital, MS 22635/21 is part of a group of survey plans by Rowe of houses in the Woolstaple and Westminster Market in 1683.

76 PRO C7/210/8.

77 All subsequent quotes from the building specification detailed in PRO C7/210/27.

Conceiving the city II: books and alternative design methods

7

> Model, is particularly used in Building for an Artificial Pattern, made of Wood, Stone, Plaister, or other Matter, with all its Parts and Proportions; in order for the better Conducting and Executing of some great Work, and to give an Idea of the Effect it will have in Large. In all large buildings, it is much the surest way to make a Model in Relievo; and not to trust to a bare Design or Draught.
>
> ('Model', Chambers, *Cyclopaedia*, 1728)

If drawings were not widely used prior to construction for the London house and yet there was obviously an accepted notion and consensus about the form that the house should take, then other means of transmitting information must have been available. How else might ideas about form have been communicated and where might these concepts have originated?

The other medium, besides drawing, that has been seen as crucial in the transmission of the classical style is the written word. This may appear to be particularly so in Britain where the succeeding phase of speculative building was accompanied by a 'unique publishing boom in this country in the eighteenth century',[1] to such an extent that the buildings produced under this system are commonly referred to as 'pattern-book' architecture.[2] From about 1725 onwards builders and craftsmen used an ever-increasing range of literature as both their technical and stylistic guides. Foremost among these were works such as Batty Langley's *The City and Country Workman's Treasury of Design*, 1740, Isaac Ware's *A Complete Body of Architecture*, 1756, and William Halfpenny's publications such as the *Builder's Pocket Companion*, 1728, or *The Modern Builder's Assistant*, 1757. These books, besides providing practical information, propounded a particular kind of Palladian classicism which their users seem to have adopted without hesitation, judging by the surviving evidence and comparisons between pattern-book plates and built examples.[3] This is an observable and well-documented phenomenon, although one which has not been explored sufficiently with regard to the issues it raises about notions of skill and the transmission of techniques and knowledge within the labour force.

The situation in the late seventeenth and early eighteenth century was entirely different. The building boom of the time produced a crop of publications aimed at an expanding market of builders and tradesmen adapting to new building techniques and practices. In Eileen Harris's *British Architectural Books and Writers, 1556-1785* the 'Chronological Index of Titles' shows a marked increase in the numbers of books being published from the 1660s onwards compared with the preceding one hundred years.[4] The literature is wide-ranging in type and has its genesis in a variety of activities. However, it differs from the later eighteenth-century output in generally making a distinction between aesthetic and practical concerns and in being less prescriptive in terms of style.

There were several categories of literature relating to architecture, the first and best known of which was that of the architectural treatise. As Rudolf Wittkower pointed out in his pioneering article on the subject there were no homegrown theoretical works in England in the seventeenth century.[5] On the whole the treatises published consisted of translations or retranslations of what were coming to be seen as the Italian masters. Thus in 1655 Joseph Moxon produced an English edition of Vignola, and in 1669 the sixth book of Scamozzi came out in a translation from the Dutch edition of 1662. French writers were also influential with translations of Le Muet, Perrault and Fréart de Chambray all appearing in the late seventeenth and early eighteenth century. The greatest attention was given to the orders and their deployment in these translations. However, it is unlikely that they were used in any meaningful way by speculative builders before they set about their work. Joseph Moxon in his *Mechanick Exercises* (which was primarily a practical guide to building), gives his readers a list of some books of architecture that he considers might be helpful:

Sebastion Serlio in folio
Hans Bloom's Five Collumns, folio
Vignola, in folio
Vignola, Or the Compleat Architect, in Octavo
Scamotzi, Quarto
Palladio, Quarto
Sir Henry Wotton's Elements of Architecture, Quarto[6]

As a bookseller and as a publisher of Vignola himself, Moxon had a vested interest in trying to increase demand for such literature among the public. He was also at pains to stress to his readers that, 'These books are all printed in English: But there are many others extant in several other languages, of which Vitruvius is the chief.'[7] In the introductory remarks to his translation of Vignola, Moxon said that the purpose of the book was to make the use of the orders comprehensible so that, 'any that can but read and understand English, may Readily learn the Proportion that all Members in a Building have one unto an other'.[8] Moxon considered that there was a market for architectural treatises for those who could read English but not foreign languages. This would suggest that the reading of architectural treatises was not confined only to the intellectual and aristocratic elite among whom the comprehension of other languages might be taken for granted. In other words treatises in English at this time were generally populist rather than elitist or academic.

This does not mean, however, that the architectural treatise was of direct significance in the design of the speculative house. The distinction Eileen Harris makes between books on the orders, and books of designs and pattern books, is of use in this context. Books on the orders such as Vignola or Scamozzi were not of much interest to the speculative builder putting up his terraced house, for the simple reason that the majority of these houses were astylar, that is they did not use columns at all (See Chapter 8). But Eileen Harris claims the opposite was the case for pattern books: 'The rebuilding of the City after the Great Fire of 1666 created a sudden and unexpected demand from builders and craftsmen for helpful ideas and patterns, which could not satisfactorily be answered by native talent or quickly drawn from English books of designs.'[9]

Harris cites Robert Pricke as the pioneer producer of architectural pattern books in this country. Pricke was a printseller who used his contacts to put together a collection of European material, mainly French, which he copied and engraved himself. Harris lists his books of designs as being English editions of: Alessandre Francini, *New Book of Architecture wherein is Represented Fourty Figures of Gates and Arches Triumphant*, 1669; J. Barbet, *New Book of Architecture*, 1670; Pierre Le Muet, *The Art of Fair Building*, 1670, 1675; *The Architect's Store House*, 1674; and *The Ornaments of Architecture*, 1674.[10] Harris states that, 'No English publisher contributed as much to the rebuilding of London after the Fire as Robert Pricke' on the basis of his pattern books and other publications.[11] However, an analysis of the works listed above makes one question this judgement. Nearly all of them contain designs for 'eminent buildings', which are of a scale and complexity completely inappropriate to the normal London town house. The exception to this is Le Muet's book which illustrates houses, 'fitting for persons of several qualities'.[12] His first house is three storeys high and only 12 ft wide by 21½ ft deep. Certainly this example could be used to demonstrate how to achieve the uniform house type on a small site and with appropriate elevational details. But how much influence the book had is questionable for two reasons. Firstly, it is a folio production and therefore it could not have been used on-site in the same way as an eighteenth-century pocket-book. Secondly, apart from the very smallest houses, Le Muet's plans all follow the French system of incorporating a central courtyard with stabling entered through an arch from the street. This kind of planning is not relevant to the English terrace layout with mews behind. The courtyard arrangement was only used in London for new buildings for town palaces and exceptionally grand houses.

These books of designs may have been used in an indirect, but not in a direct, way in the expansion of the city. This does not mean that tradesmen might not own such books. The Royal Institute of British Architects' copy of Alexandre Francine's *A New Book of Architecture*, which was a book of triumphal arches and gateways composed in each of the different orders, has written in the back: 'Bought of Mr Will. Emmett['s] widow, 1706'. Emmett was a carver and engraver who came from a well-known family of bricklayers who took contracts on most of the major public buildings at the time.[13] It is worth refering to Lorna Weatherill's work again here which suggests that the wealthier London tradesman in this period had a very high level of ownership of new or decorative goods including books.[14]

What Wittkower essentially objected to in the English editions and what is abundantly clear from looking at the works themselves, is the extent to which the treatises and publications on architecture must be seen as a product of the publishing trade. The commodification of knowledge which resulted from the invention of printing has been well documented.[15] John McKean has convincingly shown the explicitly commercial nature of the publishing programme behind Serlio's treatise of 1537 onwards.[16] As Eileen Harris says in the Preface to her book, 'It has become patently clear that what was published, when, and in what form, was, in the last analysis, determined by market forces.'[17]

If we move on to another category, that of publications on measuring and surveying, the influence of the book trade is easily discernible. According to Wittkower a spate of surveyors' books first appeared after the dissolution of the monasteries, which then continued throughout the seventeenth and eighteenth centuries. Books on quantity surveying increased considerably in the later part of the seventeenth century. This was a by-product of the widespread use of contract by measure, and also of an improvement in mathematical techniques and instruments which were filtering through from the navigational field into the building industry by the 1650s.[18]

William Leybourn (1626–1716) was one of the most prolific publishers of this type of material. As the information in the

frontispieces to his books tells us, Leybourn was both the producer
and the retailer of his works and sometimes the author as well. This
was not uncommon at the time.[19] He styled himself a 'philo-
mathematicus',[20] and as advertisements contained in his books
proclaim he was a teacher of 'arts and sciences mathematical' as
well.[21] The advertisement tells his readers that he lives in Southall,
'where he instructs young gentlemen, whom may also board upon
reasonable terms'.[22] His first book was on astronomy, published in
1649, which he followed up with *The Compleat Surveyor* of 1653.
Leybourn's publications on surveying, architecture and building
were the product of his mathematical and scientific knowledge.
This interest in mathematics led Leybourn into the world of surveying, which was primarily concerned with measurement and
geometry. The list of contents at the beginning of *The Compleat
Surveyor* demonstrates the close relationship between the two: 1
Geometrical Problems, 2 A Description of Instruments, 3 Trigono-
metry, 4 Application and Use of Instruments in Practice of
Surveying.

It was probably on the strength of this work that he was appointed one of the official surveyors of the ruins of London after
the Fire, a post which he paraded as practical proof of the success
of his surveying methods in his books thereafter. From measuring
land, Leybourn went on to develop a range of titles all of which
utilized essentially the same techniques but applied to the mensuration of different things. After the Fire Leybourn reacted with
remarkable speed gaining a licence only sixty days or so later to
publish his *Line of Proportion*, a manual detailing the use of Gunter's
Lines, one of the measuring scales for evaluating building work.[23]
This was the first of a series of relatively cheap, portable books
published by Leybourn explaining in simple terms the various
methods used for measuring building materials. The *Architectonice,
or A Compendium of the Art of Building*, for example, which was
attached as an appendix to his edition of Scamozzi's *The Mirror of
Architecture*, is no such thing, but instead an account of how to
measure and make valuations and contracts and how to use a five-
or ten-foot rod.[24] Information on how to use new instruments is
given more specifically in *The Art of Measuring: Or the Carpenters
New Rule Described and Explained*. This publication also included a
'logarithmical table' for use in quantity surveying.[25] Leybourn was
just one of a number of people involved in a publishing competition to provide easy explanations for the uses of the rulers and
tables necessary for measuring the solids and surfaces of a variety
of materials that the new contracting system required.

In 1668 he brought out *A Platform, Guide, Mate, for Purchasers,
Builders, Measurers which is concerned with the measurement of land,*

materials and the works rates for artificers. 'Whereby', he wrote, 'estimates, valuations and contracts may be made, without damage either to builder or workmen.'[26] This is the only one of his books which includes building matters other than measuring, such as: the making and selling of materials, labour rates and how to draw a perfect draught upon paper. It was the second of two books giving the prices of materials and labour after the Fire. The first was by Stephen Primatt, a lawyer who published *The City and Country Purchaser and Builder* in 1667, which included the cost of different sizes of houses in various locations. He published the book he said because of the building conditions of the time in which craftsmen and surveyors were, 'observed to make Harvest in the City Ruines and combine together for excessive Rates'.[27] Leybourn produced a similar pricing book for the commercial field called *Panarithmologia*, in which he gave tables for comparing the gold standard, currency rates, bills of exchange and customs procedures worldwide.[28]

Leybourn's publications reveal several things. Firstly, surveying was a highly specialized and distinct activity. The use of the term 'surveyor' for architects at this time is therefore in some ways misleading. Secondly, both architecture and surveying were seen as sciences, and the introduction of contracting by measure increased the mathematical and technical skills required from all those working in the building industry. It was undoubtedly the change in contracting procedures, rather than solely the impact of the Fire, as Harris argues, which was responsible for the dramatic increase in publications of this type. Reading Leybourn's books it is obvious that they assume no previous knowledge. They must have been targeted either at those seeking to move into construction from other trades, or at those already working in the building sector who needed to learn the new mensuration and surveying skills in order to survive.

Another prolific publisher of the period was Joseph Moxon (1627–91) who concentrated on a different sort of work, namely building and trade manuals. Moxon came from similarly learned circles to those of William Leybourn. He began as a printer but later took up globe- and map-making and hydrography, becoming Hydrographer to the King in 1662 and a fellow of the Royal Society in 1678.[29] Like Leybourn he published on a variety of subjects, but he particularly concentrated on the different building trades, printing, the drawing of sundials and hydrography. Moxon's books are less mathematical and scientific than those of Leybourn. He says in his Preface to the *Mechanick Exercises, Or, the Doctrine of Handy-Works* that geometry, astronomy, perspective, music, navigation, architecture etc. are excellent sciences but of no use without manual work to produce them. Moxon's motivation for producing the work is made clear in his opening sentences:

> I see no more reason why the sordidness of some workmen should be the cause of contempt upon Manual Operations, than that the excellent invention of a mill should be despised, because a blind horse draws in it. And though the Mechanicks be by some accounted ignoble and scandalous; yet it is very well known, that many Gentlemen in this nation of good rank and high quality are conversant in handy-works. And other Nations exceed us in numbers of such. How pleasant and healthy this their Divertion is, their Minds and Bodyes find and how harmeless and honest all sober men may judge? [30]

As Benno M. Forman writes in his Introduction to a 1970 reprint of *Mechanick Exercises*, Moxon's output was unique and iconoclastic in laying bare the workings of the crafts at a time when the guilds still retained some of their powers.[31] The text contains information on the tools and equipment necessary for each trade, the main tasks to be undertaken and sometimes a description of how to carry them out. *Mechanick Exercises* was the first English number book or serial publication. The work came out at irregular monthly intervals in parts between 1678 and 1680.[32] The advantage of this method, as opposed to the alternative which was publishing by subscription – in which part payment was provided by readers in advance of publication – was that it spread costs for both publisher and reader. It also allowed the author or publisher to gauge reader reaction in a new market which was ill-defined and experimental to a large extent. At the end of each monthly section a key illustration for the following month's topic would be placed, thus ensuring that no part was entirely self-sufficient. In 1683 the series was first collected together and reproduced as a book, and in 1700 a new edition was brought out in which a section on bricklaying was included for the first time. The other aspects covered were smithing, joinery, carpentery, turning, printing and 'mechanick dyalling'. *Mechanick Exercises* in fact did not sell particularly well, according to Eileen Harris. One might suppose therefore that the kind of practical information contained in the work was more usefully gleaned in the traditional manner through experience on the building site or in the workshop. Harris assumes that this is the case in relation to another category of publications: carpenters' manuals. Only one work in English on carpentry was published before 1733. Therefore Harris concludes: 'The fact that no other work on structural carpentry was published during that time suggests that the information which was passed in the traditional manner from master to apprentice sufficed, and no other book was wanted.'[33] There were, however, plenty of other books published on matters essential to carpenters at this time, namely books on measuring timber and the use of the carpenter's rule. In other words, where aspects of building practice had changed, such as in contracting procedures, new books were quickly published to supply the necessary information. But where practice remained unchanged, such as in the methods used to create a timber structure, there was no market for explanatory literature and little was produced. This would explain the lack of books detailing working practices and methods of construction, with the exception of Moxon and one or two others.

Such books, although possibly atypical of the majority of publications relating to building, are interesting to the architectural historian precisely because they provide information unavailable elsewhere. It is instructive to note their comments on the role of the craftsman *vis-à-vis* the architect or surveyor. Most of the publications suggest that on non-superior buildings craftsmen would normally work without the involvement of an architect and produce their own designs, albeit that they present the design process largely in terms of the production of drawings, as Moxon does here:

> The drawing of Draughts is most commonly the work of a Surveyor, although there be many Master Workmen that will contrive a Building, and draw the Designs thereof, as well, and as curiously, as most Surveyors: Yea, some of them will do it better than some Surveyors, especially those Workmen who understand the Theorick part of Building, as well as the Practick.[34]

While Richard Neve in his *The City and Countrey Purchaser, and Builder's Dictionary* of 1703, wrote as his definition of 'the architect':

> A Master-Workman in a Building; 'tis also sometimes taken for the Surveyor of a Building, viz. He that designs the Model, or draws the Plot, or Draught of the whole Fabrick; whose business it is to consider the whole Manner and Method of Building, and also the Charge and Expence.[35]

By the time Campbell was writing his *London Tradesman* in 1747 he takes it for granted that all the masters of the major building trades will be able to read English, draw and design their own work and be acquainted with the architectural trends of the time.

Architectural and building publications can give us much valuable information. But it is information which must be treated with circumspection as it must always to some extent represent the ideal rather than the actual. If we wanted to investigate building or design practice today we would be very foolish to take the perfect procedures laid out in the manuals as evidence of actual office or on-site practice. Neither can the contemporary literature tell the whole story. On most of the matters with which this book is concerned they are frustratingly silent. Booksellers and publishers were working in a largely untried market. Some types of publications, such as architectural treatises and measuring and surveying books, were obviously the result of changing conditions in the style and construction of buildings. These books were responding to a recognizable demand. But others such as *Mechanick Exercises* were more experimental and it is impossible to know how far they were a result of a need or desire for such publications, or how far they were trying to create new areas of publishing interest.

However, despite the problems of the contemporary literature as a source for information on building knowledge and practice, there are certain conclusions that can be drawn from it. Firstly, the information contained in the practical works assumes the reader is a novice in the matter. Secondly, it does not give any indication as to what the style or the formal characteristics of the building should be. All the works, apart from the books of designs and books on the orders, contain very few illustrations, and few of these show elevations or contain details conveying stylistic information. Moxon does include a diagram for a timber house, which is an elevation, and one for a brick house[36] (see figures 18 and 19), but the poor graphic quality and vagueness of delineation in the engraving make this no more than a generalized guide as to form. It would seem that there was no direct relationship between a particular kind of publication and a certain style and method of design, as there was for the eighteenth-century speculative house. Some books, particularly measuring and surveying books, provided technical and practical information which did have a direct input into the building process. Books of designs and books on the orders were being produced in increasing numbers in English. But their influence on the speculative house, which was only semi-classical, was slight. None of them contain designs for the kind of wood-panelled rooms or plain brick facades which were actually built. On the other hand there is evidence that some craftsmen owned books and were probably acquainted with the more theoretical works. This knowledge formed more a general design background to their work on middle-level houses than a direct source of patterns and ideas. Yet because the literature does not contain a form type similar to that which was built in vast numbers, this does not mean that there was no preconception or presumption as to what that form should be, nor that there was not a wider understanding or agreement about what sort of shape and detailing was appropriate for it.

How else then might design have been formulated and conceived? It is to studies on the Italian Renaissance that we must turn to see by what methods non-paper-based design might have proceeded. These show that some early Renaissance classical buildings were designed without the systematic use of drawings, or pattern books, or treatises. A new style was developed but it was realized initially by using existing methods for designing and constructing buildings. This has been shown most clearly in relation to Brunelleschi, who both in his own lifetime and subsequently has been regarded as having restored the 'manner of building called alla Romana or all antica', as his biographer Manetti recorded.[37] He was also one of the pioneers of one-point perspective which he applied to his buildings with dramatic results. Yet as one who had been trained first as a goldsmith and then as a sculptor he continued to think and design in a three-dimensional and materially orientated way. We know from Manetti and Vasari that models and written instructions were as important as drawings for Brunelleschi's design method.[38] When he won the commission for the design of the dome of Florence cathedral he achieved this through a written and spoken account: 'Filippo's programme and specification given in writing and in many words uttered frankly remained the basis [of the work].'[39] It was for this reason that when Brunelleschi feigned illness in order to receive due credit for the design, that Ghiberti was unable to continue the operation because there were not sufficiently detailed drawings or models to guide him. What this example demonstrates is that a new approach to architecture was achieved using traditional (i.e. primarily non-drawn) design methods. The change in thinking about architecture was not matched by an immediate change in the methods for executing that architecture.

The situation was comparable in late seventeenth-century England. The limited use of drawings at St Paul's Cathedral has already been described. Kerry Downes suggests that it was models and moulds which acted as the principal method of resolving and refining the design as the building went up.[40]

> At St Paul's, however, the part played by final drawings on the scaffold is in itself doubtful: a typical joiner's payment in the accounts is for 'makeing Models & Molds, Templetts &c'. (*Wren Soc.* XIII, p.124) Numerous models were also made for parts of the building by the masons; thus while there was no complete model its function as a source of solid information was diffused into many particular and occasional part models.[41]

Comprehension of design came through the physical object and the written or spoken word as it had for hundreds of years previously. Nicholas Stone described a plot he had been involved in building at Covent Garden as, 'being in proportion like a carpenter's square'.[42] In other words he described the plot not as being L-shaped, which is an abstract concept, but in physical terms in relation to an existing tangible object.

One way of designing was by precedent or through comparison with a built example. This is the essence of vernacular or traditional design methods and there is plenty of evidence for this approach being used for urban housing. For example, a building agreement at Exeter House stated that William Edge, bricklayer, who had contracted to build two houses shall, 'pave the front with black and white paving like the paving in Crane Court, Fleet Street'.[43] However, more often it seems existing buildings were held up as examples to ensure that the multiple units which made up a development carried out by different builders coalesced into a uniform whole. When James Burkin was building in Mincing Lane in the City, where Barbon had already done some work, he told his workmen that they should make the exterior of the house, 'agreeable to the outward ornaments of the houses of the said Nicholas Barbon new built within his yard on the east side of Mincing Lane'.[44] To be agreeable in contemporary eyes the houses had to be uniform and conform with one another. Precedent-based design was therefore the perfect solution. This is made clear in a building agreement for Red Lion Fields which states that, 'the houses so agreed to be built as aforesaid, for materials, strength, scantlings and uniformity of buildings, shall be equally good or better than the houses built on the west side of a street called Brook Street lately erected and built in the garden called Brook Garden in the said county of Middlesex'.[45]

Uniformity of appearance was largely achieved, as the quotation given above indicates, through a harmonization of material and structural components. Standardization was the final method by which the form of the house was determined, through the use of off-the-shelf components such as doors, windows and balusters. Builders also used the provisions of the 1667 Rebuilding Act as a guide for their own developments, which provided a framework, literally, within which to work. Neve, quoting Leybourn, seems to suggest that cornices were produced off-site and sold by the foot:

Some Cornices (says Mr. Leybourn) are valued by the piece, dearer, or cheaper, according to their Largeness, goodness of the stuff, and curiosity of workmanship: others are measur'd and rated by the Foot Running measure, i.e. by the number of Feet in length only. Experienced carpenters tell me, that for making of plain Cornices (without any carving) under the eves of a house, they commonly have 1s per foot, Running measure. Mr. Wing tells us, that cornices are valu'd according to their Nature, and bigness; a modilion-cornice (of free-stone) of 18, or 20 inches thick, is worth (says he) 5 or 6s per foot, running measure. He also tells us (in Joyners Work) that a modilion-cornice, with its carved work, is worth 7s per foot. And a plain modilion-cornice of 12, or 14 inches (says he) will be worth 3s 6d or 4s per yard running measure. A brick-cornice (as some workmen tell me) 2s 6d per foot.[46]

It seems that these rates refer to finished cornices, rather than being rates of pay for carrying out the work. This would seem to suggest that cornices were pre-produced off-site, in which case the design would firmly rest with the joiners' or bricklayers' team.

Who determined the form of the standardized elements is much harder to ascertain. The published works on building practice give very little information on this. As standard patterns became common so must have the cutting plates and tracings used to make them. Moxon's definition of 'molding' in 'An Explanation of Terms Used in Carpentry' suggests a process highly amenable to large-scale production: 'Moldings are stuck upon the edges of stuff to ornament it: As on Chimney-pieces, the inner edges of Window-frames, shelves etc.' [47] Equally when he is writing about window frames, he notes that the frame is often bevelled where it meets the glass: 'And upon that Bevel is commonly stuck a molding (for ornament sake) according to the fancy of the Workman, but more generally according to the various Mode of the Times.' [48]

The genesis of the word 'moulding' provides a useful insight into the subtle variations and gradual shift in meaning of such terms and the related, although often not simultaneous, shifts in design practice. Chambers described a mould as follows:

> Mould, in the Mechanick Arts etc, a Cavity artfully cut, with design to give its form, or Impression to some softer Matter applied therein. Mould, among Masons, a Piece of Hard Wood or Iron, hollowed within side, answerable to the Contours of the Mouldings or Cornishes, etc. to be form'd. [49]

The word 'mould', which is usually related to an older type of architectural design, is therefore the source for the term 'mouldings' which is generally associated with the classical style. Mouldings could be either cast in a mould or template or carved:

> Moulding, anything cast in a Mould, or that seems to have been so; tho' in reality it were cut with the Chissel, or the Ax. [50]

If the original meanings of these terms are resurrected we uncover a vocabulary in which the design process is presented as a far more physically orientated and well-established procedure than the subsequent evolution of these words might suggest.

Moxon described how to make moulds for brick cornices and fascias and he mentioned using moulding for wooden ornamentation as well. [51] His information is aimed at tradesmen, and it seems that the person who determined the form of the mould would be the same person who went on to make it by the complex process that Moxon describes. However, we can not be sure about this and in large workshops this is not so likely to have been the case.

Ultimately therefore we have too little evidence to answer the question as to who was responsible for the design of mass-produced components. Sometimes it might have been the brickmaker or joiner making that feature, sometimes it might have been their master. Occasionally it is possible that someone from outside the craft team may have suggested or initiated a design. This could be so in the case of Barbon, for example. Often probably it was a combination of some or all of these. Design even for mass production was still a collaborative activity.

Although a new style was being used, traditional methods of creating, resolving and communicating form continued to be employed. Joseph Rykwert has stressed the importance of verbal ways of transmitting ideas through example, training and debate.[52] Verbal communication through discussion, instruction and description was far more effective in the early modern period in which communities were so much smaller. It is possible, particularly from building specifications, to find evidence of some of that language and thus gain a greater insight into the comprehension and meaning of form and style at the time. The terms used to describe buildings or their features can be broken down into various types. These are descriptions by age, material, size, position, quality and appearance. Many of these categories may seem too commonplace to be worthy of investigation. But by doing so the wide range of formal characteristics that can be indicated through spoken language becomes clearer.

The first type of categorization by age is one of the most common ways of describing buildings throughout the cases, so descriptions of 'new' houses abound. Very often this term is combined with another categorization, by material. This resulted in the term 'new brick messuages' which can be found being mentioned in many building leases and agreements.[53] The two terms went together and when the word 'new' is used on its own in relation to houses, in the London context at this time, this automatically means a brick house. The size of the house or group of houses is also often mentioned; the words used here are usually 'large' or 'small', 'great' or 'little', and 'substantial'. These words obviously relate to the amount of space, as in an inventory for a music house in Lamb's Conduit Fields which lists both the 'great dining room' and the 'little dining room',[54] but they also convey more than that. The words 'great' and substantial', in particular, signified levels of social prestige and importance as well. Size could also be described in words, without necessarily using numbers. The width of a stone, for example, could be determined in relation to another object: 'a hollow stone to go over the door ... two posts in breadth'.[55] Or at Essex House a passage is planned, 'from the Strand as wide as Little Essex Street and open to the sky'.[56] In other words it was not just other buildings which were used as a physical reference source but any object or space which provided a useful comparison.

The next category of differentiation was through positioning. Again these are not socially neutral terms relating solely to physical location, but also convey the building's place within the spatial hierarchy. Inside the house there is the 'back' and 'fore' garret, and the 'back' and 'fore' chamber,[57] with the principal rooms usually being to the fore. A distinction was also made between 'back' buildings set back from the road and 'front' buildings which meant houses built on the street line.[58] However, 'back' houses were not always subordinate to 'front' houses, as is discussed in Chapter 8 in relation to dwellings in the City.

Moving on to written descriptions of buildings themselves, two distinctions can be made. Firstly, properties were defined by the quality of finish or workmanship. It was common to agree to carry out a job 'in a workmanlike manner'.[59] At the Middle Temple Barbon agreed to build, 'in an artificial and workmanlike manner'.[60] Yet at Mincing Lane the houses he built were described as, 'incomplete, imperfect, unfinished, and such works as were done were so ill and artificially done'.[61] Secondly, buildings are described through adjectives relating to their form or appearance. These are extremely limited in number and by twentieth-century terms in scope also. The most common terms are: 'good', 'fair', and 'substantial' again. So we find for example: 'a good deal door',[62] 'very fair tenements',[63] 'two or more sufficient and substantial houses of brick' etc.[64] Sometimes terms are used which relate to the notion of propriety, for example 'ornaments proper and fair',[65] or the 'large and substantial music house' which had, 'all conveniences meet and proper for an entertaining house'.[66] The word 'commodious' also appears as a term of approval.[67] The only other term to appear with any regularity is the word 'uniform'. We hear of 'uniformity of buildings'[68] and 'uniform well-built houses'.[69] It was also used in an attempt to describe a terrace, a term which was clearly not current at the time. The houses, 'shall take up as a continuous building the whole front of the said ground' and 'the front to range in a straight line and uniform with the houses to be there built'.[70] A terrace at the time meant either an outdoor bank of earth, or a balcony, open gallery or flat roof in a building.[71]

Here we see both the strength and weaknesses of contemporary vocabulary in relation to design. On the one hand the language does not yet seem to have incorporated words like 'terrace' which provided a terminology for new forms. What is remarkable about the language usage is how general the terms are. Adjectives like 'good' and 'fair' and 'great' were obviously not specific to buildings or houses, or attempts to convey particularities of form and style. Design vocabulary was imprecise, but this does not mean that there was any confusion as to meaning. It is quite clear that it was well known what was meant by a 'new brick house' or by 'fair ornaments'. There was a consensus among the people arguing these cases about what form was and what it should be. We can no longer reconstruct their meaning because we see form, design and style in a way quite alien to their thinking. At this date a notion of style or form separate from the object, that is a paper conception, only existed among the architectural and intellectual elite. For most people an understanding of form was a physical and tangible experience. The lack of a specific design terminology is evidence that form and making were inextricably linked in this period. And yet this extraordinarily imprecise vocabulary does seem strange given that this restricts yet another possible channel of communication. This throws us on to the making process and the use of built examples as the main methods for transmitting new forms and ideas. In other words there was a built vocabulary which was accepted and understood as a means of expression, albeit that it was evolving. There was not yet a parallel written or spoken vocabulary to articulate it in language.

Notes

1 Eileen Harris, *British Architectural Books and Writers, 1556-1785*, Cambridge, Cambridge University Press, 1990, p. 25.

2 See: John Summerson, *Georgian London*, 1945, Harmondsworth, Penguin, 1987 edn, pp. 72-5; Dan Cruickshank and Peter Wyld, *London: The Art of Georgian Building*, London, Architectural Press, 1975, pp. 3-17; Rudolf Wittkower, 'English Literature on Architecture', in his *Palladio and English Palladianism*, London, Thames & Hudson, 1974, pp. 95-112; Harris, *British Architectural Books*, pp. 23-37 and individual entries for authors.

3 Cruickshank and Wyld, *The Art of Georgian Building*, gives examples, see for instance: pp. 90-5, 110-23, 154-9.

4 Harris, *British Architectural Books*, pp. 513-16.

5 Wittkower, 'English Literature on Architecture', pp. 99-102.

6 Joseph Moxon, *Mechanick Exercises, Or, the Doctrine of Handy-Work*, London, 1683, p. 163.

7 Moxon, *Mechanick Exercises*, p. 163.

8 Joseph Moxon, *Vignola or The Compleat Architect*, London, 1695.

9 Harris, *British Architectural Books*, pp. 35-6.

10 Harris, *British Architectural Books*, pp. 36, 379-80.

11 Harris, *British Architectural Books*, p. 379.

12 Pierre Le Muet, *The Art of Fair Building*, English edn by Robert Pricke, London 1670, Frontispiece.

13 Information on Emmett from: *Wren Society*, Vol. XX, 1943, p. 65; and Royal

Academy of Arts, *Sir Christopher Wren and the Making of St Paul's*, London, Royal Academy of Arts, 1991, p. 50, which relates how he produced a 'bootleg' set of engravings of St Paul's in *c.* 1702-03 working from inside information and imaginative calculation. Another member of the family, Stephen, can be found working as a bricklayer in the building of Smith Square, Westminster (PRO C6/351/22).

14 Lorna Weatherill, *Consumer Behaviour and Material Culture, 1660-1760*, London and New York, Routledge, 1988, p. 8; p. 88, Table 4.4; p. 185, Table 8.2.

15 See among others: L. Febvre and H.-J. Martin, *The Coming of the Book*, London, Verso, 1976; E. L. Eisenstein, *The Printing Press as an Agent of Change*, 2 Vols, Cambridge, Cambridge University Press, 1979.

16 J. M. McKean, 'Sebastiano Serlio', in *Architectural Association Quarterly*, Vol. 2, No. 4, 1979, pp. 4–13.

17 Harris, *British Architectural Books*, p. 11.

18 Harris, *British Architectural Books*, p. 41.

19 See Harris, *British Architectural Books*, pp. 55-60, on the publishing industry.

20 William Leybourn, *The Compleat Surveyor*, London, 1653, frontispiece.

21 William Leybourn, *Pleasure with Profit*, London, 1694, p. 1.

22 Leybourn, *Pleasure with Profit*, p. 1. Also see, C. E. Kenny, 'William Leybourn 1626–1716', *The Library*, Series 5, V, No. 3, 1950, pp. 159-71.

23 Harris, *British Architectural Books*, p. 292.

24 William Leybourn, *Architectonice, or A Compendium of the Art of Building*, in V. Scamozzi, *The Mirror of Architecture*, London, 1700.

25 William Leybourn, *The Art of Measuring: Or the Carpenters New Rule Described and Explained*, London, 1669.

26 William Leybourn, *A Platform, Guide, Mate, for Purchasers, Builders, Measurers*, London, 1668, frontispiece.

27 Stephen Primatt, *The City and Country Purchaser and Builder*, 1667, 'To the Reader'.

28 William Leybourn, *Panarithmologia: An Appendix containing Heads of Daily Use to All Traders*, London, 1693.

29 For the definitive biography on Moxon see, Herbert Davies and Harry Carter, eds, *Mechanick Exercises on the Whole Art of Printing 1683-84 by Joseph Moxon*, London, Oxford University Press, 1962 (2nd edn), Introduction. Davies and Carter state that Moxon appears to have given up printing in 1650-55 and turned to globe- and map-making and hydrography. Moxon's trade card, undated but catalogued as 1650, survives in the British Museum (Crace XXXVIII, 22). This describes his services and expertise in: 'Astronomy, Geography, Celestial and Terrestial Globes, Sun Dyalls, Nautical matters and Triangulation.' The origin of the date of 1650 is unclear, but it is certainly pre-Fire, as a view of London, which includes old St Paul's, runs along the bottom.

30 Moxon, *Mechanick Exercises*, Preface.

31 Benno M. Forman, Introduction, in Joseph Moxon, *Mechanick Exercises*, ed. Charles F. Montgomery, New York, Washington and London, Praeger Publishers, 1970.

32 Harris, *British Architectural Books*, pp. 55-7.

33 Harris, *British Architectural Books*, p. 38.

34 Moxon, *Mechanick Exercises*, p. 252.

35 Richard Neve, *The City and Countrey Purchaser, and Builder's Dictionary: Or, The Compleat Builders Guide*, London, 1703, p. 12.

36 Moxon, *Mechanick Exercises*, 1683 edn, p. 147; 1703 edn, p. 266.

37   A. Manetti, *The Life of Brunelleschi*, ed. H. Saalman, Pennsylvania and London, Pennsylvania University Press, 1970, p. 34.

38   Giorgio Vasari, *The Lives of the Artists*, trans. George Bull, Harmondsworth, Penguin, 1965, pp. 133-73. Also see Henry A. Millon, 'Models in Renaissance Architecture', in Henry A. Millon, ed., *The Renaissance from Brunelleschi to Michaelangelo: The Representation of Architecture*, London, Thames & Hudson, 1994, pp. 19-75.

39   Manetti, *Brunelleschi*, p. 80.

40   The Royal Academy of Arts 1991 exhibition, *Sir Christopher Wren and the Making of St Paul's*, included three of these models.

41   Kerry Downes, *Sir Christopher Wren: The Design of St Paul's Cathedral*, London, Trefoil in association with the Guildhall Library, 1988, pp. 27-9.

42   PRO C8/84/53.

43   PRO C8/263/91.

44   PRO C10/181/4.

45   PRO C9/294/7.

46   Neve, *The City and Countrey Purchaser*, p. 119.

47   Moxon, *Mechanick Exercises*, pp. 169-70.

48   Moxon, *Mechanick Exercises*, p. 149.

49   Ephraim Chambers, *Cyclopaedia: Or An Universal Dictionary of Arts and Science*, 2 Vols, London, 1728.

50   Chambers, *Cyclopaedia*.

51   Moxon, *Mechanick Exercises*, p. 268.

52   Joseph Rykwert, 'On Oral Transmission of Architectural Theory', *AA Files*, No. 6, May 1984, pp. 14-26.

53   For example see, PRO C7/152/40.

54   PRO C5/187/61.

55   PRO C10/422/30.

56   PRO C8/269/79.

57   PRO C7/120/1.

58   PRO C7/120/1.

59   For example, PRO C5/314/25, C5/113/35.

60   PRO C8/230/72.

61   PRO C7/543/52.

62   PRO C7/210/27.

63   PRO C8/230/72.

64   PRO C8/263/91.

65   PRO C7/543/52.

66   PRO C5/178/4.

67   PRO C8/404/37.

68   PRO C9/294/7.

69   PRO C9/74/112.

70   PRO C8/263/91.

71   Sources: *OED*; Samuel Johnson, *A Dictionary of the English Language*, London, 1755; Chambers, *Cyclopaedia*.

8 Housing the city: tradition and innovation in the urban terrace

> It is true that before the Fire of London, the streets were narrow ... and
> the houses all built of timber, lath and plaster, or, as they were very
> properly called paper work. But the manner of building in those days,
> one storey projecting out beyond another, was such, that in some nar-
> row streets, the houses almost touched one another at the top, and it
> has been known, that men, in case of fire, have escaped on the tops of
> the houses, by leaping from one side of a street to another ... How this
> has been regulated, how it was before, and how much better it is now,
> I leave to be judged, by comparing the old unburnt part of the city with
> the new.
>
> (Daniel Defoe, *A Tour through the Whole Island of Great Britain*,
> 1724-26, pp. 296-70)

The late seventeenth century saw the beginnings of a revolution
in housing in Britain. Within the space of twenty or so years, from
the late 1660s to the 1680s, the housing stock of the capital city was
transformed. In the process a new prototype for urban housing was
established which became adopted all over the country and has
remained the model for domestic housing to the present day. Yet
this revolution, which saw the birth of the modern house, for all
its magnitude and long-term significance has been given very little
attention in architectural histories of the period and the late seven-
teenth- and early eighteenth-century London house remains little
known or recognized. This is partly because of the difficulty of
fitting late seventeenth-century architecture into canonical histories of stylistic development in Britain, as discussed in the
Introduction, and also because of its position as a housing type
between vernacular and polite buildings. This chapter will seek to
identify the characteristics of the house, to assess how novel it was,
and to place it within the existing context of housing in the capital.

In order to do this we must go back to the situation before 1660.
Until the Great Fire London was a city of timber-framed buildings
interspersed with a few stone monuments, largely ecclesiastical,
which towered above the densely packed streets below (see figure
1).[1] However, in the 1630s a new style of brick terraced house began
to be introduced. This was essentially of two types. The first was a
form of Serlian-influenced mannerism, which offered a natural

progression from the equally eclectic native Jacobean approach. As
Timothy Mowl and Brian Earnshaw correctly stress in their book
on the period, *Architecture Without Kings: The Rise of Puritan Classicism under Cromwell*, it was Serlio not Palladio who was the
dominant influence for seventeenth-century English architecture.[2]
Developments in the West End such as those at Henrietta Street
(1630-33) and King Street (1631-37) exemplified the style with their
busy facades of elaborate cut and moulded brickwork and multiple
projections and additions to the wall-plane in the form of gables,
balconies and pilasters. None of these terraces survive today but
good individual examples of the type can be seen further out at
The Presbytery, Crooms Hill, Greenwich, *c.* 1635 and at Cromwell
House, Highgate, 1637-38 (figure 14).

The second style of house drew more directly from the classical
repertoire and took the pedimented front with giant pilasters as its
principal organizing device. Inigo Jones's scheme for Covent Garden had pioneered the use of the temple facade for urban housing.
It had also been employed at William Newton's developments of
Great Queen Street and Lincoln's Inn Fields of the 1630s to 1650s.
Jones's original plans for the Bedford development eschewed the
giant order and instead adopted an astylar approach, which Mowl
and Earnshaw have labelled 'Puritan minimalism'. This was
dropped after the intervention of Charles I who persuaded the Earl
to adopt a more grandiose scheme for the new piazza. However, it
was this minimalist aesthetic that was to dominate after the Restoration and to become the predominant building style for an
entire city. The brick terrace was not therefore a result of the 1666
Fire, but as with so many aspects of London's growth in this period
was already evident in the period prior to 1660. This provided a

14] Cromwell House,
Highgate Hill, N6, 1637–3

blueprint after the Restoration for the new urban house once the rate of development accelerated.

The movement towards a new housing type was consolidated by the disastrous Great Fire of 1666 and the Act for the Rebuilding of the City of London of 1667 which followed it.[3] This specified that all new buildings were to be of brick or stone and established four classes of houses. The first were those fronting 'by-streets and lanes' which were to be two storeys high. The second fronting 'streets and lanes of note and the Thames' were to be three storeys high, while the third 'fronting high and principal streets' were allowed four storeys. The fourth sort were mansion houses for people of quality which could not be greater than four storeys.[4] In each case the wall thicknesses and room heights were specified apart from for the fourth sort, where they were left to the builder's discretion. The external decoration of the house was not specified but generally conformed very broadly to a certain type. As Mowl and Earnshaw comment: 'The 1667 Act for the Rebuilding of the City of London was no daring post-fire innovation, it simply formalised Puritan Minimalism with a few additional fire-precautions and a crude class structure.'[5] Its prohibitive restrictiveness, as with the Crown's control over the granting of licences for new developments, undermines the myth that London was developed purely by private interests with virtually no state intervention.

In fact what it did was to provide a template for the new house which established its frame, dimensions and general typology. Although it was seemingly stylistically neutral, in effect it dictated the new urban vocabulary of uniformity, regularity and minimalism. The provisions of the 1667 Act only applied within the City of London, but the standards for construction that it provided were used elsewhere in both London and the provinces.

15] 'A house of the type built by Nicholas Barbon between 1670 and 1700', from John Summerson, *Georgian London*, 1945.

Figure 15 shows a generalized exterior of a plain brick elevation with a tiled roof. This is very much a notional representation which will be discussed more critically in due course. But it will serve for the present to give an indication of the basic construction and form of the new house. The main characteristics of the house were its brick, symmetrical frontage and double-depth plan. The house displays a radical reduction of decorative elements down to a few key essentials. The wooden ornament consisted of a simple dentil cornice under the eaves and a panelled door with surround. Besides this there were brick or stone string courses and segmental brickwork above the windows with stone keystones. Not shown in this drawing are the balconies and roof terraces which were popular at the time and which can be seen in figures 6 and 56. Cornelius Batty who had a house built for him in Essex Garden specified that his house should have a stable, racks and a manger, plus two vaults, a 'belcony' and a platform or open area on top of the building.[6] It was common for building agreements also to mention coach houses and ancillary outbuildings.

A wonderful description of the essential requirements for the house, particularly as regards servicing, is given in a report of the building agreement for a house in Great Russell Street.[7] In the kitchen there were to be three stoves, a broiling place, a boiler, an oven, a dresser beside the window and one in the middle of the room also. The work to be done included: painting the doors and 'lattees' (slats) in the kitchen all the same colour; plastering the wash house and the closet; setting up shelves in the closet; and providing a broad dresser to iron upon. In the wash house there was to be a chimney and a copper, as there was likewise for brewing in the servants' hall. Very good brass locks were to be fitted for the three middle storeys with master-keys. A door was to be made in the middle of the two rooms on the second floor and a partition for a closet to be made by the chimney in one of the garrets; a hanging shelf or shelves to be put in the storeroom; and window shutters to be made for the two back rooms on the second floor and closets.

Of those who have discussed the type outlined above, the best-known published accounts today are John Summerson's in *Architecture in Britain, 1530-1830*, where he has two pages on the late seventeenth century at the beginning of a chapter called 'The House and the Street in the Eighteenth Century,'[8] and his treatment of the subject in *Georgian London*, including the schematic elevation shown in figure 15.[9] For Summerson, this style of house represented the beginnings of the modern London house and the forerunner of the Georgian buildings with which he was principally concerned. The kind of structure that Summerson delineated demonstrates a recognizable and significant shift away from the timber-framed medieval house which preceded it. However, although new it is questionable if it can be labelled Renaissance, although it is obviously post-medieval. Summerson certainly did question their provenance and consequently found them wanting, for they were not classical in the way in which he understood the term, which was primarily a Palladian interpretation.

Summerson's preference for Palladianism is made clear in *Georgian London* in which it forms one of the two themes around which the book is structured: providing the 'taste' which formed the city along with the 'wealth' in Summerson's analysis. The earlier Jonesian-style developments come in the critical chapter 2 'Foundation Stones: Taste', while the Georgian house is placed in chapter 5 'The London House and its Builders'. Sandwiched in between in the chapters on 'Wealth' and 'The Mercantile Stronghold', the late seventeenth-century house is to be found, an aberration in Summerson's eyes. As he wrote in his conclusion to the chapter on 'Taste', 'Palladian taste represents a norm to which classical architecture in this country returned over and over again'.[10]

Summerson's approach typifies the problems of accommodating the late seventeenth century within a traditional architectural chronology. It is an irritant because it disrupts the smooth flow of the Palladian stream, from Inigo Jones through Webb to Lord Burlington and the neo-Palladians. It took only a notion of regularity and some, but by no means all, of its detailing from the classical vocabulary. It used neither the applied orders to express the classical system, as earlier houses at Great Queen Street and Lincoln's Inn Fields had done, nor did it relate to the Palladian approach, which although astylar, adopted a rational organizing principle through its use of strict proportioning and hierarchy of levels with an emphasis on the *piano nobile*. (See figure 35 which shows a comparison between an early eighteenth-century and a Georgian terrace at Queen Anne's Gate.) At the same time because it has been written about from within the Palladian classical tradition, a somewhat misleading and over-simplistic interpretation of the late seventeenth- and early eighteenth-century house prevails, which is necessary if these objects are to be incorporated within the essentially linear construction of British classicism which has predominated to date. This is most evident in Summerson's elevation in *Georgian London* which for thousands of people represents the true picture of the 'new' town house (see figure 15).[11] It gives an over-regularized view of the house using almost eighteenth-century proportions and including a basement which was not always standard at the time (although an innovation that Barbon incorporated in his developments), so that the house truly looks like a less sophisticated version of the Georgian house.

To what extent did the new urban house follow Summerson's model? First of all the switch to brick was not as absolute as the exterior alone might suggest. An examination of the structure of the house reveals that behind the brick facade wood continued to play a critical role, for the entire interior of the house was of timber construction.[12] R. Campbell in *The London Tradesman*, 1747 commented on the immense reliance on timber technology that the supposedly new brick town house employed: 'a City-House, where the Carpenter by the strength of Wood, contributes more to the standing of the House than all the Bricklayer's Labour'.[13] The outer brickwork was very much a shell without interior masonry walls. The internal timber wall and flooring system, which was built into the brickwork, gave it structural stability.[14] The carpenter was also responsible for the wooden roof structure, increasingly a trussed

one from the late seventeenth century onwards,[15] and especially
on soft ground for strengthening the foundations by driving
timber piles into the ground. The walls were timber partitions
covered over with lath and plaster.

With its internal wooden structure and roof it could be argued
that the 'new house' was still partly conceived in traditional technological terms, that is as a timber- framed building but with a
brick skin. Such a view is particularly supported by the use of a
double brick skin. The outer layer was purely for show while the
inner skin in conjunction with the timber frame took all the structural load. The narrow brick piers between the windows and the
use of bonding timbers within the brick walls, wherever an extra
load such as a girder was to be placed, all suggest a framing rather
than a walling conception of structure. The house at this time was
to some extent an experimental model, initially taking different
forms and not having yet evolved into the standard type that it
became in the eighteenth century. The evidence suggests that the
late seventeenth-century house was the product of a transitional
technological stage between a timber framing and a masonry walling system of construction. This is true to a lesser extent of the

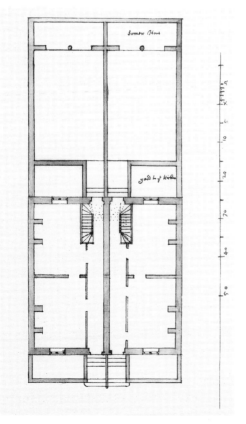
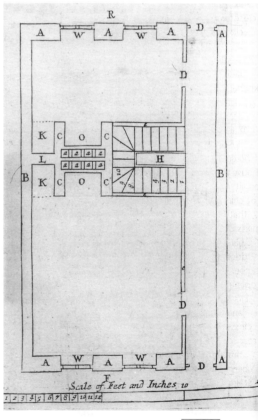

Georgian house as well, where as Dan Cruickshank writes, 'what is certain is that timber was regarded as an essential addition to a brick structure'.[16] Technologically there was no major adjustment to be made in the production of this building type. Brick was not completely new for small town houses. The major change here was the quantities of the material required rather than a change in technology.

Turning now to the footprint of the house, Summerson showed a plan of what later became the accepted London layout very similar to that in figure 16, with the chimney stacks firmly anchored to one wall and the staircase on the opposite side adjacent to the rear room. This produces a plan in which the front room is usually larger than the back, with a closet wing sometimes being attached to the rear of the building. However, as Frank Kelsall has shown in his article 'The London House Plan in the Later 17th Century', in fact this arrangement took some time to evolve. He argues that the plan form for London houses in the period 1660-80 was by no means settled and was a mixture of old and new types.[17] His article shows that the smaller London house (up to 25 ft frontage) retained elements from vernacular architecture, primarily the central staircase, until c. 1680. Kelsall argues that a preoccupation with seeing these houses as precursors of the Georgian house, has blinded us to the elements that they retained and subsequently adapted from existing urban vernacular architecture. The house plan in this period was both experimental and transitional.

Joseph Moxon in *Mechanick Exercises* discussed the problems of incorporating the traditional central position of the staircase within the essentially linear plan of the urban terrace house, which deprived it of light, and offered top-lighting as a solution.

> Stairs are either made about a *Solid Newel*, or an *Open Newel*, and sometimes mixt, viz. with a Solide Newel for some few Steps; then a sraight or Foreright Ascent, with *Flyers* upon the side of the square Open Newel, and afterwards as Solid Newel again. Then reiterate &c.
>   The last, *viz.* the *Mixt-Newel'd Stairs*, are commonly made in our *Party-walled Houses* in *London*, where no Light can be placed in the Stair-Case, because of the Party-walls; so that there is a necessity to let in a *Sky-light* through the Hollow Newel: But this sort of Stair-Cafes take up more room than those with a single solid Newel; because the Stairs of a solid Newel spread only about one small Newel, as the several Foulds of the Fans Women use spread about their Centre: But these, because they sometimes wind, and sometimes fly off from that winding take therefore the more room up in the Stair-Case.[18]

Moxon illustrated such a plan in the 1703 edition of his book and William Leybourn in his guide to building of 1668 shows a similar arrangement in his illustration for floor framing.[19] Moxon's plan

16 *facing, left*] Design for a pair of houses in what became the standard London plan: two rooms deep, an entrance passage and stair to the rear, with the stacks on the opposite wall, 43 × 43 ft. Although absent from this plan there was often an extending closet wing to the rear as well. The yards to front and back indicate a basement, the latter is labelled 'yard to ye kitchen'. At the rear of the garden is a 'Somer Hous'.

17 *facing, right*] Joseph Moxon, *Plan of A Brick House*, 1703. Plan of the house in figure 18 showing an alternative arrangement of chimneys and staircase to that in figure 16. Key: 'A. piers of brick B. flank walls C. jambs of chimneys D. doorcase of timber E. timber partitions F. front H. open nuel to give light to stairs K. clossets L. a brick and a half between clossets. O. chimneys R. rear front W. windows of timber a. funnels of chimney 1,2,3,4 steps of stairs called fliers 8.9.10 steps of stairs called winders.'

shows a chimney stack supporting a stairwell to one side (figures 17 and 18). He says of this 'draught of a ground plat': 'You may imagine this design to be the ground floor, having no cellar beneath it ... and because we do suppose this building to have Houses adjoining it on each side, therefore we have drawn the stair-case with an open nuel to give light to the Stairs; but if the House had stood by itself, without other houses adjoyning, then we might have had light to the Stairs from the Flank wall.'[20]

The problem with this plan, besides the lack of light, was that it was very wasteful of brick in a terrace and also of floorspace. It was in order to economize on land and money that the optimum solution of a chimney stack set against the party wall with a separate rear staircase evolved. The positioning of the staircase against the back wall reduced the amount of space previously taken up by the stairwell to light and support the stair. Instead the stair could be lit by windows at half-levels in the rear elevation, and attached to the back wall for structural support. This plan, shown in figure 16, was described by Roger North in c. 1695-96 as, 'The manner ... that is used in the citty, and is the common forme of all late built houses ... where divers houses stand contiguously in a range.'[21]

18] Joseph Moxon, *Elevation of A Brick House*, 1703. Key: 'A. water table B. first fascia C. second fascia D. 3 chimnies G. gable end H. streight arches W. shas frame S. shas lights K. door-case L. window-lighte over door.'

19] Joseph Moxon, *Elevation of A Timber House*, 1683, 1703. The house is designed as a shop with O being the shop windows. Regarding the plan Moxon wrote that there could not be a standard division between front and back since 'nor all Shop-keepers Houses alike, for some Trades require a deeper, others may dispense with a shallower Shop'.

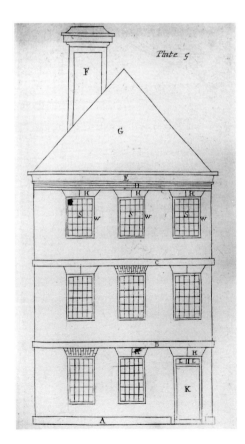

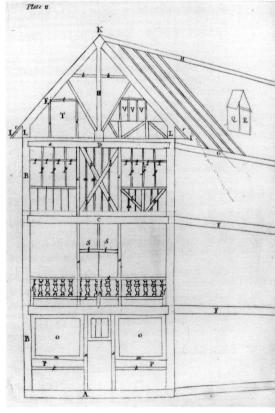

Turning to the elevation of the house, Moxon again provides us with a very different representation from that of Summerson. Significantly his illustration for the brick house was not included in the first edition of the work in 1683, which gave instead a diagram and instructions for the building of a timber-framed house (figure 19). The second edition of 1703 included the brick elevation but significantly also retained the timber one as well (see figure 18). Instead of Summerson's modulated and well-proportioned facade, we find a far more pragmatic design in which there is no obvious proportioning system in use. Above all, the house maintains the gabled roof shape, and the roof and chimney, far from trying to conceal themselves behind a uniform parapet, are major features in the design. Detailed contemporary illustrations of the average London house at this time are extremely rare, so it is perhaps telling that one of the few elevations, besides Moxon, which is known shows a similar style of house.

The second drawing comes from a collection largely of ground plans in the Bodleian Library. They are mainly of ordinary houses, of a variety of types. Alison Maguire, who has studied the drawings, suggests that they were made in the years 1685-90.[22] The plans shown in figures 16, 21 and 22 are also from this collection. Among these plans is one elevation which shows a pair of houses of a type similar to Moxon's (figure 20). These houses are two bays wide instead of three and appear to contain shops probably with cellar storage below, as is indicated by the small windows at street level. They have the same pitched roof form, this time with a dormer window and a heavy cornice beneath. The windows are casements rather than sashes. (Figure 23 shows a surviving casement window.) Most houses of this type have not survived. They have either been demolished or had their gables incorporated into raised storeys or rebuilt parapet roof lines. The plan for the design is arranged to provide a large room at the front for the shop (see figure 21). There is therefore no hall passage and a central staircase is used to divide the open room at the front from either private rooms or storerooms to the rear. This centrally divided plan was the standard one for commercial properties and can also be seen in figure 12 for shops along the Broadway in Westminster. It survived in use for businesses, long after it was abandoned for residential houses, as can be seen in the many similar plans for premises in the City throughout the eighteenth century in the Crace Collection.[23]

Topographical views of the time show similar hybrid houses as having been built in both the City and the West End on a large scale (see figures 6 and 55). The fact that Moxon included a house very similar to this as his prototypical example, in a book as late as 1703, points I would suggest to a far more widespread use of this type in the late seventeenth- and early eighteenth-century town than has been imagined previously.

There is some surviving built evidence of these transitional houses. Most notably the brick terrace of houses at Nos 52-55 Newington Green, which date from 1658 according to the exterior panel (figures 24-26). Although built on the outskirts of town these houses follow the West End fashion of Great Queen Street and Lincoln's Inn Fields in the use of giant pilasters.[24] However, instead of the straight roof line of a classical house, the roof has been built in the familiar gabled shape of a timber-framed building, although converted into the new building material, brick. The Newington Green houses have always been seen as an idiosyncratic aberration. But although they date from the Commonwealth period there is a similarity between them and Joseph Moxon's elevation for a brick house published in 1703. This is particularly so in the notional gable ends and the prominent chimneys, now much less visible at Newington Green than they would have been originally. The plan is essentially the same as Moxon's with the rooms entered by a passage running down one side of the house, and a centrally placed stack and staircase, although at Newington Green the stack is split supporting the staircase in the middle rather than to one side as in Moxon's plan. The staircases were lit by an internal

20] A drawing of an elevation of a house of the late seventeenth century, possibly in the City. The ground-floor shutters, which opened outwards (shown by blank squares), indicate a shop or other commercial premises requiring display space.

21] Ground plan of figure 20, 34 × 32 ft, showing the large shop area to the front with increased windows and no hall passage to maximize space, and two positions for a centralized staircase either attached to the side wall or within an enclosed central support system. This centrally divided plan seems to have been maintained for commercial premises as the best arrangement long after it had been abandoned for residential houses. Many similar examples can be found throughout the eighteen century, in Crace Vol. IX, a portfolio of plans of property in the City.

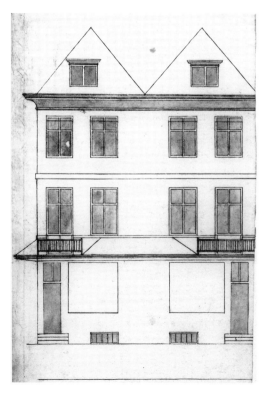

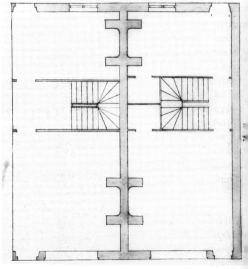

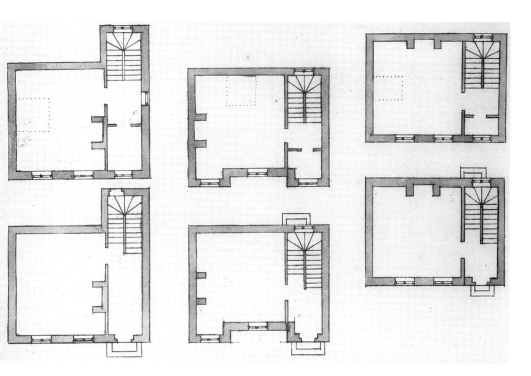

22] Three designs for what are presumably town houses of 32 × 34 ft with varying chimney stack, entrance hall and staircase arrangements at the ground and first-floor levels. The steps up to the houses at the front and the steps to the rear at ground level, where no door is shown, would suggest a basement storey below. The single-depth plan three bays wide is here combined with the town house arrangement of hall passage and rear staircase. No. 237 Hoxton Street has a similar plan but with the entrance and staircase placed centrally giving one room with a fireplace on either side.

23] Englefield House, 23 Highgate High Street, N6, 710, with double casement window in basement.

24] Nos 52–55
Newington Green, N1, 1658

25] Nos 52–53
Newington Green, N1, 1658

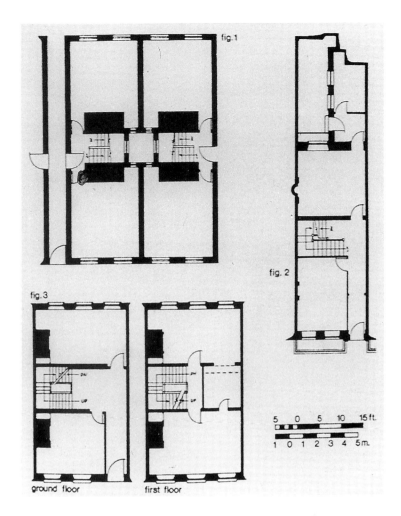

fig.1

fig. 2

fig.3

5 0 5 10 15 ft.

1 0 1 2 3 4 5 m.

ground floor   first floor

26] Nos 52–55 Newington Green, plan from Frank Kelsall. Since this plan was drawn up Kelsall thinks that all four houses had entrances from the front as well as from the side or in the case of the middle two houses via the passage. There is no doubt that the entrances from the passage were original, however he does not think these were the sole or principal access points. Kelsall provides examples of other centrally placed staircases at Nos 10 and 20 Buckingham Street, 13 and 14 Essex Street, 107 Great Russell Street and 12 Bloomsbury Square. Of these only the Newington Green houses had a centrally placed chimney stack as well.

lightwell between the two houses, as Moxon had described, and such lightwells were common features, particularly in City houses, with their cramped linear plots.[25]

In the newly developing areas of what became known as the West End, we find a second type of house conforming much more closely to Summerson's prototype. Odd houses survive from some of Barbon's developments at Essex Street and Bedford Row (figure 27). All of these are notable for their extreme plainness, with decoration kept to an easily repeatable pattern and only a slight variation in height between the different storeys. This model can be seen used at other developments in an even more reduced form as in the Great Ormond Street area and in one surviving example in Gray's Inn Road (figures 28 & 29). The minimalist approach was enthusiastically embraced by the building industry in the late seventeenth century as the optimum solution for a complex product which needed to be manufactured on a large scale within a

27] No. 33 Bedford Row, WC1, c. 1693, refronted early–mid-eighteenth century, hence the windows being set back rather than flush with the brickwork. This is remarkably close to Summerson's elevation (figure 15), for which it may have served as the model, with the exception of the change in the windows from sashes to casements and the replacement of the original wooden dentil cornice.

short time period in a highly competitive market. The regularity and formulaic nature of classicism made it perfectly suited to the consumer and industrial requirements of the period. Its essentially geometric forms could be used for both short- and long-run production with variations of detail and scale being possible within the overall frame. From the aristocratic enclave of St James's Square, to the smallest first-rate house in a back alley of the City, to a grand mansion on the outskirts of the town the same basic features were adopted. The flexibility and adaptability of the rectangular shell with applied ornamentation allowed it to be adopted in varying formats by different social groups. This was true not just for this kind of housing but for other types of institutions and forms of accommodation as well. This can be seen at a number of surviving hospitals, such as Chelsea (1682-91), or almshouses such as the Geffrye ones in Shoreditch (1712-16) or Trinity Almshouses, Mile End (1695) (see figure 52).

The possibility for modification allowed for variations and individual choice within the house as well as between houses. A number of houses survive in Denmark Street, including some, such as Nos 6 and 7, which maintain a great deal of their interiors intact (figure 30).[26] Nos 5-10 Denmark Street were built *c.* 1687, in plan they are two rooms deep with a rear staircase.[27] The terrace demonstrates the new kind of house with a narrow frontage, some proportioning in the facade (the first-floor windows are larger than

those above) and a simplification of detail to key motifs. Decoration on the facade is limited to the brick and stone string courses between storeys and the prominent keystones over the windows. A specification for six other houses in Denmark Street stated that the houses were to be the same height as those already built, 'with the like free stone tables on the front of such houses so agreed to be built as were in most of the said houses already built in Denmark Street'.[28] Raised or sunk panels of this type between windows were a common feature on the exterior.

The interiors of Nos 6 and 7 Denmark Street raise interesting questions in relation to Summerson's comments in *Georgian London* on Barbon's interiors. Summerson had the advantage in 1945 of being able to examine some of Barbon's output, most of which today has been either demolished or irrevocably altered. This was his verdict on what he saw:

> The houses he built were all very much alike, economically planned to the point of meanness, with coarse ornaments which repeated

30] Nos 5–7 Denmark Street, WC2, c. 1687. The first-floor windows of Nos 6 and 7 have been dropped in varying length but those of No. 5 to the left retain their original height. The parapets, above which there are dormers, were added late The eaves line would originally have been marked by a wooden cornice.

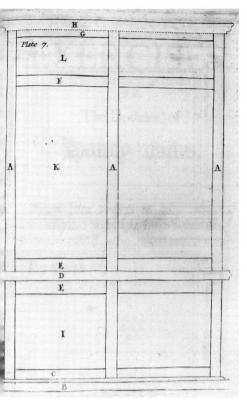

themselves over and over again. The design of the panelling and staircases of his houses never varies, and his carpenters must have turned out thousands upon thousands of the twisted balusters whose slick modernity was calculated to engage the eye of the bumpkin in search of his first town house.[29]

If there was a remarkable consistency of form to be found in Barbon interiors this was not the case everywhere. Nos 6 and 7 Denmark Street were built together, yet there are significant variations between the panelling in each house. In both houses the surviving panelling dates from the 1690s, but it is remarkably different in detailing and quality. This can be explained by the fact that panelling was specified by the tenant and not the builder. This might also occur with staircases.[30] At No. 6 Denmark Street the panelling is extremely plain and simple and laid as flat strips along the wall in a similar fashion to the diagram for wainscotting in Moxon (figure 31). At No. 7 the panelling is much grander with raised mouldings stuck on to the plain panelling below, creating bolection moulding. Edward Hatton in his glossary of artistic terms defined this as follows: '*Bolection* (by some called Polection-work) is the Moulding of Frames wherein the Pannels of Wainscot are set, the Work is either Bolection laid in, or Bolection swelling, and each of these with, and without *raised* Pannels.' For an example see figure 40.

In 1668 William Landen who had rented a house in the newly built Southampton Street in Bloomsbury wanted to move out and asked his landlord Thomas Cox, a doctor, for a credit of £80 for the money 'he had spent on wainscot and other charges, since the house was new and with bare walls when he had moved in'.[31] In another property owned by Cox, this time in Bloomsbury Square, he threatened to remove wainscot and pictures belonging to the tenant to satisfy a debt he claimed was owing to him.[32] Panelling then was personable, movable property provided by the lessee and not part of the infrastructure of the house. It was, in other words, the contemporary equivalent of wallpaper.

There are examples at 75 Hampstead High Street and 55 Newington Green of painted panels surviving on plaster. It is thought that these were mock-ups to show clients what potential panelling might look like. In the case of Newington Green it has been suggested that this was an adaptation of an early seventeenth-century technique of wall decoration to a newer style of panelling.[33] These examples show that even within speculative developments consumers had some choice and control over the interior fitting-out

33] No. 15 Queen Anne' Gate, SW1, *c.* 1704. The wooden cornice, dorme attic storey and grotesqu carved keystones are a visible.

34] No. 17 Queen Anne' Gate, SW1, *c.* 1704. Carv wooden canopy.

of the building. This raises the interesting question as to why this choice was not available in Barbon's buildings. Were they aimed at a different sector of the market? Or if his competitors were offering their customers a choice, was his appeal based on the price reduction that standardization might bring?

It is important to realize that even within the West End there was a variation in how the standard model might be interpreted. Not all developments were as streamlined as Barbon's. Perhaps the best-known examples of a more highly ornamented and crafted approach are the early eighteenth-century houses in Queen Anne's Gate. Other examples survive further out at Albury Street, Deptford (*c.* 1709) where the mariners' houses have doorhood brackets hand-carved to individual designs and at Kensington Square of 1685 onwards (figure 32).

The oldest surviving houses in Queen Anne's Gate were built in 1704 and known as Queen Square.[34] They were built on land belonging to Christ's Hospital and there were originally two streets, Park Street to the east and Queen Square to the west. Park Street was developed first, around 1686, as we know from the date of two building leases which survive.[35] The 1704 houses were originally of three storeys with attics and basements, elaborately carved doors and grotesque carved keystones (figures 33–35). It is possible that they, too, represent a type which was once more prevalent than the surviving evidence suggests. They rely for their effect on

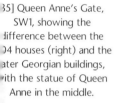

[35] Queen Anne's Gate, SW1, showing the difference between the [17]04 houses (right) and the [l]ater Georgian buildings, [w]ith the statue of Queen Anne in the middle.

detailing, texture and elaborate ornamentation, unlike Georgian houses in which compositional proportion is paramount.

In the City where new houses were rebuilt on existing plots, either by their owners or as small speculative developments of usually a few houses, the different development pattern and social composition of the area resulted in a more elaborately decorated version of the new style with a modified layout. The courtyard and alley had been the dominant pattern of the pre-Fire City and much of the area was rebuilt according to its existing street plan. Figure 36 shows the common arrangement of a continuous street frontage of houses with an arch giving access to an alley behind, off which there are further alleys and plots. Whereas the shops along Fetter Lane are uniform, the variety of the houses behind is striking. Most of them are accessed through gateways off Nevills Alley and are placed to the rear of their sites. The frequent use of the terms 'front houses' and 'back houses', suggests that such arrangements were common. Roger North produced a 'Model of a city house lying backwards', which showed a large house reached down an alley and set behind the 'houses fronting ye street'.[36] Front and back houses are also mentioned outside the City at

36] 'A Plott of the Buildir upon the Ground of Sr Nicholas Bacon Kt of the Bath in Fetter Lane in the Parish of St Dunstan in th West London together with the names of thos Persons to whome the same ware First Grantec by John Gostyng, 1670. A copy of the original plan The similarity of the elevations of the house along Fetter Lane to that shown in figure 20 is striking. Notice the contrast between these and the larger mansion houses set to the rear o their plots off Nevills Alle A plan for a garden desi is shown in the middle c the drawing.

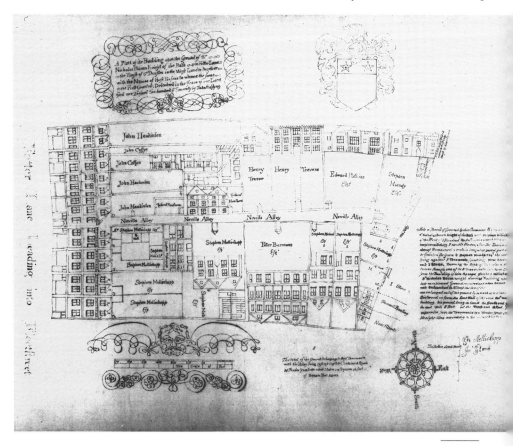

174

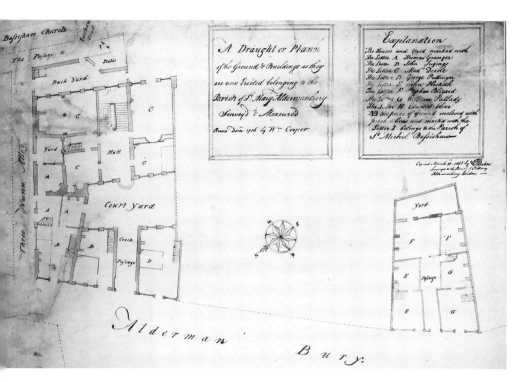

A Draught or Plann
of the Ground & Buildings as they
are now Erected belonging to the
Parish of S. Mary Aldermanbury
Survey'd & Measured

Anno Dom 1726 by W.m Cooper

Explanation
The House and Yard marked with
the Letter A Thomas Granger
the Letter B John Ingine
the Letter C Mad Doxile
the Letter D George Pottinger
the Letter E John Hoskick
the Letter F John Olizard
the Letter G William Pollexfen
the Letter H Edward Olive
NB the piece of Ground inclosed with
prick'd lines and marked with the
Letter I belongs to the Parish of
S. Michel Bassishaw

7] 'A Draughtt or Plann of he Ground & Buildings as they are now Erected belonging to the Parish of St Mary Aldermanbury, urvey'd & Measured Anno om 1726 by Wm Cooper', copy of 1815. The letters on the plan relate to the st of occupiers and show large and small houses grouped around a system f internal courtyards and alleys.

developments in St Martin's Lane and Red Lion Fields.[37] While details of the estate of Joseph Collins, the builder and developer of St Martin's Lane, mentions his 'dwelling house and two front houses belonging to it.' (see p. 99 above).[38] Layout plans then were by no means immediately universalized into the modern street pattern, and in smaller developments or those on the fringes of the City this was even more true.

The grouping of houses around a courtyard was another medieval arrangement which survived the Fire. Large mansions could occupy the entire space around the courtyard.[39] Such grand houses were both private homes and business complexes, as was the case with the house of Peter Parraviceene, merchant, in Mincing Lane, whose property consisted of a 'great house', stable, coach-house, counting-house and garden.[40] The print of Sir Robert Viner's residence shows how inadequate the term 'house' is for these places which functioned as both centres of commerce and palaces of pleasure and lavish entertaining (figure 38). A plan of the site of the house shows the entrance passageway off Lombard Street opening out into the central courtyard with a further passageway leading out to link into an alleyway to the rear.[41] A plan of Sir John Houblon's property, another City magnate and Lord Mayor, shows a mansion house 80 ft wide, with a counting-house to one side, a stable and other buildings on the other, and a large garden to the rear.[42] Roger North's City house plan places the

garden before the house and the kitchen and stable courtyard to the rear. Edward Hatton in his *New View of London* in 1708 described both the situation and sumptuousness of these magnates' City mansions:

> Those especially about half a mile in compass round the Royal Exchange, particularly eastward therefrom, are so numerous and magnificent with courts, offices and all other necessary apartments enclosed to themselves, and noble gates and frontispieces of some towards the street, but chiefly so ornamental, commodious and richly furnished within, that it would require too much room to give the names and situations, much less can their descriptions, as magnitude, beauty and usefulness be expected particularly to be accounted for in this book. They are for conveniences aforesaid, and because of the great quantity of ground they are built on, generally situate backward, and by that means the City appears not to strangers who walk the street near so stately and beautiful as it really is and would show itself were these ornaments exposed to public view.[43]

The nature of the sites available for redevelopment also led to an increase in density, as Defoe realized, despite the seemingly greater spaciousness of the rebuilt areas:

> But though by the new buildings after the fire, much ground was given

38 *facing*] Sutton Nicholls, *View of the Old General Post Office in Lombard Street, formerly Sir Robert Viner's house*, 1710. This shows the central courtyard at the heart of the City mansion of a wealthy banker. Viner was at one time Lord Mayor and this view belongs in a tradition of representing the Lord Mayor's mansion, which later became known as '*The* Mansion House'. The quality of the detailing is evident in the fenestration patterns of the gables, the brick arches above the windows and the elaborate cornice. It is interesting to note that the upper storey with sashes and the lower with casement windows do not match up. The apparent difference in levels between the two sides of the courtyard can be explained by the fact that Viner enlarged his site after the Fire by incorporating the neighbouring tavern. Two employees can be seen sitting at the far end at counting tables on which they have small square packages, while two similar structures can be seen unoccupied on the left.

up, and left unbuilt, to enlarge the streets, yet 'tis to be observed, that the old houses stood severally upon more ground, were much larger upon the flat, and in many places, gardens and large yards about them, all which, in the new buildings, are, at least, contracted, and the ground generally built up into other houses, so that nothwithstanding all the ground given up for beautifying the streets, yet there are many more houses built than stood before upon the same ground; so that taking the whole city together, there are more inhabitants in the same compass, than there was before. So many great houses were converted into streets and courts, alleys and building, that there are, by estimation, almost 4000 houses now standing on the ground which the Fire left desolate, more than stood on the same ground before.[44]

Barbon's own town residence was in the City at Crane Court, off Fleet Street which he built in 1670.[45] He dwelt in 'the capital messuage' at the north end of the court, which was destroyed by fire in 1877. No. 5 and its neighbour No. 6 are the only two survivors from this date (figures 39 and 40). No. 6 was probably first occupied by Samuel Vincent, Barbon's partner in the fire insurance and other schemes.[46] These houses, which were rather brutally restored in 1971, are larger and more individualistic than those that Barbon built elsewhere. The level of ornamentation and decoration in particular stands out as being different in character from his West End houses. Both houses have spectacular first-floor rooms with magnificent plaster ceilings and fine bolection panelling. Barbon's own house had a similar ceiling, and English Heritage suggests that this rich plasterwork was probably added after building to meet the requirements of the first tenant.[47]

We have a vivid picture from evidence given in two Chancery cases of what the entrance way to the courtyard once looked like.[48] Barbon and the other people living or owning property in the court – William Morgan, John DeChaire gent, Humphrey Dove gent, Mary Green widow, and Charles Titford gent – decided that 'for the ornament thereof', the court should 'be paved with black marble and white purbeck stone, well rubbed, and of such a square and dimension as might be most durable as well as ornamental for the design proposed'.[49] Besides this they arranged with Richard Hutchinson the mason carrying out the work, 'that he should make for each house in the said court several circular curled steps of Portland stone, with a ball and fillet round the edge thereof, well rubbed'.[50] Strype's eye was caught by these features and he wrote of No. 2 Crane Court as 'a very handsome open Place with a Free-stone pavement, and graced with good Buildings, well inhabited by Persons of Repute; the front House being larger than the rest, and ascended up by large Stone Steps'.[51] The original residents did not stop there but also wanted to 'adorn the entrance into the said court with necks and balls of stone and other advantages that the place might require'.[52] These advantages consisted of 'one white marble stone with golden letters placed over the gate of the entrance into the said Crane Court, and ... two pissing places placed within the said court at the entrance therinto out of Fleet Street'.[53]

Further evidence of buyers 'customizing' a house prior to moving in can be found at a small development in Mincing Lane. Two of the people buying (not leasing) houses from Barbon wanted to have 'additional ornaments' inside: 'They being desirous for their own convenience and pleasure and for the greater beauty of the said house to have several alterations and amendments made therein other than were designed at the time of the making of the aforesaid articles.'[54] The 'ornaments of beauty and pleasure' they wanted included: 'in four of the rooms of the said house, where designed, four marble chimney pieces or mantle pieces with foot places also of marble, each of them of one entire piece with the ornaments proper and fair'.[55]

Barbon's involvement at Crane Court does not necessarily make these typical City houses. However, they follow the City trend in being more richly ornamented than their plainer West End neighbours. Summerson characterized City houses built after the Fire as being, 'rarely of a kind to satisfy educated taste'.[56] He cited the

39] No. 18 Red Lion Court, EC4, c. 1670. This is the rear elevation and courtyard of Nos 5–6 Crane Court. The size and layout of the rear wing suggest a commercial usage. Notice the brick dentil cornice and pediment just visible to the right. The arch over the gateway has a similar feature.

40] No. 5 Crane Court, EC4, first-floor front room. Showing bolection panelling and fine plasterwork ceiling, probably installed by the first tenant.

houses on Laurence Pountney Hill as an example of this, 'vigorous but impolite' he called them (figure 41).[57] However, one can only be impolite if one intends to be polite and there is no evidence at this date that a single dominant notion of politeness had been accepted. As Peter Earle has shown, the economic boom of the late seventeenth century fostered a strong and separate cultural identity among Londoners of the middling sort, of which their elaborate and costly City dwellings were but one manifestation.[58] Their differences from West End fashions should not be understood in terms of decline or degeneration from a universally accepted standard but rather as a deliberate means of differentiation and distancing from their gentry neighbours.

The Laurence Pountney houses are illustrative of these more individually ornamented City houses which are distinguished by their richly carved wooden detailing.[59] The entrances to both Sir Robert Viner's and Sir Robert Clayton's houses were also through similarly flamboyant concave shell hoods.[60] Exuberant decorative carving was not confined to the City, however, as the example of Queen Anne's Gate demonstrates. On the exterior of the house the carver might work on the doorcase, consoles and brackets, and the carved cornice.[61] Nos 33-35 Mark Lane (now demolished) was a very elaborate City house of the early eighteenth century with rich exterior and interior ornamentation, principally carving (figure 42).[62] The mansion was entered via a huge carved archway, which can now be seen in the shop at the Victoria and Albert Museum; the visitor then proceeded through the courtyard to enter the house through a door surmounted by a Baroque-inspired segmental curved pediment encasing putti, scrolls and twirling ornament within an ogee frame. The rest of Mark Lane lived up to the fanfare made at its entrance with pilasters and overmantels carved with naturalistic foliage in Grinling Gibbons style and ornamented plaster ceilings in the principal rooms. The staircase provided a procession of individually carved balusters all varying in shape and design with marquetry panels set along the wall. However, not all mansion houses sustained the Baroque approach that their street presence proclaimed. Sir Robert Clayton's house was large but plain and astylar behind its enormous shell entrance way.[63] Sir John Houblon's house was similar in character with a pitched roof with dormers, both being in style like giant versions of the new minimalist town house.[64] A similar surviving house may be seen in figure 43.

A fourth form of house can be identified around the fringes of the urban core.[65] Hoxton, on the northern edge of the City, provides some interesting examples of this type. Its proximity to the centre led to the development in the 1680s of two squares on the West End model, Hoxton Square in 1683 and Charles Square in 1685. The houses in these two developments followed the new style (see figures 43 and 44). Despite its location near to the commercial heartland Hoxton failed to develop as a fashionable residential

43] No. 16 Charles Square, N1, early eighteenth century. A large mansion house just outside the City

44] No. 32 Hoxton Square, N1, 1680s/90s. The facade has been restored in the manner of a house of the 1720s, but its height and overall proportioning spring from its earlier antecedents.

5] No. 237 Hoxton Street,
N1, 1700–30.

area and attempts to establish a market quickly foundered. Instead it acquired a rather different identity which to some extent traded on its semi-rural location. This was sustained largely by its long-established function as a feeding ground for the city through its nurseries and market gardens and enhanced by a new role as a centre for Nonconformism, schools and hospitals. Hoxton was an area whose strengths lay in being a backwater, but a relatively genteel one, in which problematic activities such as housing the sick and insane could be accommodated without disturbing a large resident population. It may have been that this both contributed to and supported the maintenance of an alternative building tradition even on the very edge of the commercial centre itself and ensured the continued survival of these buildings unmodernized throughout the eighteenth century.

Along its main artery, Hoxton Street, a mixture of dwellings developed embracing both standard second- and third-rate houses and hybrid vernacular/polite houses. No. 237 Hoxton Street (1700-30) is a rare survivor of a housing type which may once have been common in the area (figure 45). The house as we see it today is a late seventeenth-century building which was remodelled in the early eighteenth century. The surviving structure retains traces of the earlier building which was itself built on an existing site. It is a single-pile house, five bays wide. The proportions are lower and broader than those traditionally associated with urban houses of the period. It originally had five windows at first-floor level which were altered to three in the early eighteenth century. The plan consisted of two rooms set either side of a central staircase, with chimney stacks against the side walls. The archaeological evidence suggests that the dormers are in their original position set within the pantile roof. The dormers have been restored as have the Kentish mud stock bricks of the elevations.[66]

The *Survey of London* and photographic evidence of demolished buildings in the area suggest that there were other similar buildings in the neighbourhood. The *Survey* details houses such as Nos 46-48 Hoxton Street which is of the same type and period as No. 237, although L-shaped in plan.[67] No. 47 Charles Square is an early to mid-eighteenth-century survivor of a vernacular-type house with low proportions and floor heights (figure 46). The wider plot front-ages and hence lower building line of these Hoxton houses are typical of development outside the fashionable core. In these areas land prices were lower and plots were often developed individually or in small groups.[68] This was not estate development and a piece-meal system of building was one factor in maintaining a more generous layout and variety of plan.

Other examples of similar houses may be found in other parts of London. Some houses such as 30 Romford Road, Stratford or 24 Hampstead High Street, both of the early eighteenth century, had a complete timber frame internal structure. No. 30 Romford Road (*c.* 1700) is a weatherboarded building yet proportioned and de-tailed in accordance with the new classical systems (figure 47). Romford Road at this date was an arterial road on the outskirts of London and instances of such fully weatherboarded houses in the centre were probably rare. However, there is plenty of evidence of partial weatherboarding particularly to the side and rear of build-ings. This may still be seen, for example, in Spitalfields at Nos 5-7 and 30 Elder Street, 1722-25, and in Hampstead at 24 Hampstead High Street and 112-14 Heath Street, both early eighteenth century. Photographic evidence shows that some of the late seventeenth-

46] No. 47 Charles Square, N1, early–mid-eighteenth century. It is interesting to compare this house which is in fact located on the backside of the square facing Pitfield Street, with the more visible house fronting the square shown in figure

47] No. 30 Romford Road, E15, c. 1700.

48] Nos 58–60 Highgate High Street, N6, late seventeenth–early eighteenth century.

century houses in Wellclose Square were weatherboarded over at a subsequent date,[69] and it was probably a common technique for making repairs and extensions to brick buildings throughout the eighteenth century. It was also used for commercial buildings, and a corn merchant's premises at 58-60 Highgate High Street survives in the same weatherboarded state in which it was originally built in the late seventeenth or early eighteenth century (figure 48). On the outskirts of the town a semi-rural idiom and culture predominated and an alternative building tradition which mixed old and new prevailed.

Despite the survival of vernacular features on the periphery, in the centre one of the remarkable features of the post-Restoration London developments and rebuilding was the speed and comprehensiveness with which a totally new form of architecture was embraced on a wide scale. There is no doubt that there was a broad consensus as to the form and style that the house should take. In Moxon, for example, it is clear in his illustration of the brick house that he sees a certain set of decorative features and elements as being appropriate to it, and not appropriate to the wooden framed house and vice versa. The elevation for the brick house includes a cornice, brick string courses and sash frames with brick arches above. In the text he describes how to make brick fascias and cornices for use with the new house.[70] In the 'Art of Joynery', when he describes how to wainscot a room, he presents the information as if this is the only acceptable way of decorating certain kinds of rooms, rather than just one of a variety of designs or options available.[71] While the precise form of the house was by no means fixed at this stage there was a prevailing notion, judging from surviving examples and the written evidence, as to the general form and style that it should take.

We should also consider the late seventeenth- and early eighteenth-century house as a product for a newly emerging consumer society. It consisted essentially of a brick and wood shell that was decorated with applied ornamental features which were cheap and easy to produce, thus allowing for changes in fashion and style to be accommodated while the basic structure remained unchanged. This ability to change and up-grade the structure plus the high level of maintenance which the new house required, particularly in the painting of woodwork, made it perfectly suited to a consumer economy geared towards the continual renewal and replacement of products.

In summary, there were four distinct types of ordinary London houses at this time, all of which maintained some connections with previous housing types and structures. Firstly, evolutionary brick houses which incorporated elements from previous housing forms and combined them within the new constraints of the terrace. Secondly, the new West End Barbon-style house which was revolutionary in its use of consistent, standardized parts, and in its regularity and hence repeatability of form and detailing. Thirdly, there were City houses in which a delight in a display of individualistic carving is evident and which in typology might be more varied. Fourthly, a hybrid house existed on the fringes of the town. All four were distinctive from the eighteenth-century Georgian town house.

It is essential that we begin to see these houses in their own terms and not just through a Palladian prism. They are not products of a misinterpreted or undigested classicism for that was not their aim. The late seventeenth- and early eighteenth-century house was a transitional building which combined traditional elements with new classical features. This was also the approach adopted for the majority of architecture of the time, particularly in the Pratt-inspired country house, which mixed a regular double-pile plan with hipped roofs and dormers. There was no conception that the two must be separated nor that some form of design blueprint existed which invalidated such an approach. Instead it was seen as but one alternative from among the new styles currently available and unlike the expensive full-blown stone-built Baroque that most suited for the production of mass urban housing.

Notes

1 For houses before *c.*1660 see, John Schofield, *Medieval London Houses*, New Haven and London, Yale University Press, 1994.

2 Timothy Mowl and Brian Earnshaw, *Architecture Without Kings: The Rise of Puritan Classicism under Cromwell*, Manchester, Manchester University Press, 1995, p.128.

3 19 Charles II.

4 For more information see: T. F. Reddaway, *The Rebuilding of London after the Great Fire*, London, Jonathan Cape, 1940; Stephen Porter, *The Great Fire of London*, Stroud, Sutton, 1996.

5 Mowl and Earnshaw, *Puritan Classicism*, p.5.

6 PRO C8/306/118.

7 PRO C10/422/30.

8 John Summerson, *Architecture in Britain, 1530-1830*, Harmondsworth, Penguin, 1983, pp.383-84 and see pp.209-10.

9 John Summerson, *Georgian London*, 1945, Harmondsworth, Penguin, 1978 edn, pp.47-51. For other accounts of the London house of the period see: Nathaniel Lloyd, *A History of the English House*, London, Architectural Press, 1931; Edmund Gray, *The British House: A Concise Architectural History*, London, Barrie & Jenkins, 1994; Dan Cruickshank and Peter Wyld, *London: The Art of Georgian Building*, London, Architectural Press, 1975, pp.40-53.

10 Summerson, *Georgian London*, p.36.

11 Summerson, *Georgian London*, p.47.

12 See Peter Wyld's excellent axonometric survey in Cruickshank and Wyld, *The Art of Georgian Building*, pp.222-3.

13 R. Campbell, *The London Tradesman*, London, 1747, p.159.

14 For more on this see, David Yeomans, 'Structural Carpentry in London Building', in Hermione Hobhouse and Ann Saunders, eds, *Good and Proper Materials: The Fabric of London since the Great Fire*, London, London Topographical Society, 1989, pp.38-47. Also see a series of articles in the *Architects' Journal* called '18thC Timber Construction': 10 July 1991, 17 July 1991, 24 and 31 July 1991, 7 August 1991, 14 August 1991; especially: David Yeomans, 'Floor Structures', 17 July 1991, pp.46-51; David Yeomans and Anthony Cleminson, 'Walls and Partitions', 7 August 1991, pp.43-6.

15 David Yeomans, 'Roof Structures', *Architects' Journal*, 24 and 31 July 1991, pp.45-50.

16 Dan Cruickshank and Neil Burton, *Life in the Georgian City*, London, Viking, 1990, p.108. However, he then goes on to argue that the bonding timbers had little actual effect in holding the building together structurally.

17 Frank Kelsall, 'The London House Plan in the Later 17th Century', *Post-Medieval Archaeology*, Vol. 8, 1974, pp.80-91.

18 Joseph Moxon, *Mechanick Exercises, Or, the Doctrine of Handy-Works*, London, 1683, p.151.

19 William Leybourn, *A Platform, Guide, Mate, for Purchasers, Builders, Measurers*, London, 1668.

20 Moxon, *Mechanick Exercises*, p.265.

21 Howard Colvin and John Newman, eds, *Of Building: Roger North's Writings on Architecture*, Oxford, Clarendon Press, 1981, pp.69-70.

22 Alison Maguire, ed., with contributions by Howard Colvin, 'A Collection of

Seventeenth-Century Architectural Plans', *Architectural History*, Vol. 35, 1992, pp. 140-82.

23 See especially, Crace, IX, 'Plans of Property in the City'.

24 Information on Nos 52-55 Newington Green from: EH Files, ISL 40; RCHM, *London: West*, Vol. II, London, HMSO, 1925, pp. 92-3; VCH, *The County of Middlesex*, Vol. VIII, Institute of Historical Research, London, Oxford University Press, 1985, pp. 41-2.

25 See, for example, Crace VIII, 48; IX, 120; IX, 128.

26 I am grateful to Zöe Croad of English Heritage and Bill Newman of Newman Associates for arranging access to Nos 7 and 27 Denmark Street.

27 The developers were Samuel Fortrey and Jacques Wiseman, neither of them building craftsman, according to EH Files, CAM 87. Also see, *Survey of London, St Giles-in-the-Fields*, Pt II, Vol. V, London, Athlone Press, 1914, pp. 142-3.

28 PRO C8/375/48.

29 Summerson, *Georgian London*, p. 45.

30 I am very grateful to Ivan Hall for corroboration of this information and a detailed discussion of Nos 6 and 7 Denmark Street.

31 PRO C8/163/54.

32 PRO C6/239/53.

33 EH Files, ISL 40.

34 RCHM, *London: West*, Vol. II, 1925, pp. 138-41; *Survey of London, St Margaret Westminster*, Pt I, Vol. 10, London, Athlone Press, 1926, pp. 78-141.

35 Guildhall Library, Christ's Hospital Records, MS. 13,064, 13,065. There is also a plan of the area in 1697 with Park Street clearly marked, Guildhall Library, Christ's Hospital Records, MS. 22635/8.

36 Colvin and Newman *Of Building*, Pl. 11.

37 PRO C7/120/1, C9/461/173.

38 PRO C7/120/1.

39 For an example of a courtyard house built after the Fire see, Bridget Cherry, 'John Pollexfen's House in Walbrook', in J. Bold and E. Chaney, eds, *English Architecture Public and Private*, London, Hambledon Press, 1993, pp. 89-105.

40 PRO C8/306/118.

41 Crace, IX, 106. The plan is consistent with the arrangement shown in Sutton Nicholls' illustration.

42 Crace, VIII, 72.

43 Edward Hatton, *A New View of London*, London, 1708, as quoted in A. Saint and G. Darley, *The Chronicles of London*, London, Weidenfeld & Nicholson, 1994, p. 127.

44 Daniel Defoe, *A Tour through the Whole Island of Great Britain*, 1724-26, ed. Pat Rogers, Harmondsworth, Penguin, 1971, p. 297.

45 PRO C7/225/4.

46 EH Files, CITY 30. Also see, RCHM, *London: The City*, Vol. IV, London, HMSO, 1929, pp. 163-4.

47 EH Files, CITY 30.

48 PRO C8/219/41, C8/219/42.

49 PRO C8/219/41.

50 PRO C8/219/41.

51 J. Strype, *The Survey of London*, London, 1720, Vol. I, Bk III, Ch. XII, p. 277.

52 PRO C8/219/42.

53 PRO C8/219/41.

54 PRO C7/543/52.

55 PRO C7/543/52.

56 Summerson, *Georgian London*, p. 59.

57 Summerson, *Georgian London*, p. 59.

58 See: Peter Earle, *The Making of the English Middle Class: Business, Society and Family Life in London, 1660-1730*, London, Methuen, 1989 and *A City Full of People: Men and Women of London, 1650-1750*, London, Methuen, 1994.

59 RCHM, *London: The City*, pp. 103-4.

60 Crace XXIII, 19; XXI, 52-3.

61 Cruickshank and Wyld, *Georgian Building*, pp. 202-6.

62 See: RCHM, *London: The City*, p. 186; and for a visual record the London Metropolitan Archives 69.0 MAR and Crace XXIII, 43, 68.

63 Crace XII, 49-53.

64 Crace XXII, 4.

65 See, Elizabeth McKellar, 'The City and the Country: The Urban Vernacular in Late Seventeenth and Early Eighteenth-Century London', in Neil Burton, ed., *Georgian Vernacular: Papers Given at the 1995 Georgian Group Symposium*, London, Georgian Group, 1996, pp. 10-18.

66 I am grateful to Julian Harrap Architects for information on No. 237 Hoxton Street.

67 *Survey of London, St Leonard, Shoreditch*, Vol. VIII, 1922, pp. 134-5, Pls 59-64.

68 See for example, M. J. Power, 'East London Housing in the Seventeenth Century', in Peter Clark and Paul Slack, eds, *Crisis and Order in English Towns, 1500-1700*, London, Routledge & Kegan Paul, 1972, pp. 237-62.

69 London Metropolitan Archives, Photograph Library, Wellclose Square Nos 74/13959, F1657, 75/13136.

70 Moxon, *Mechanick Exercises*, p. 268.

71 Moxon, *Mechanick Exercises*, pp. 105-6.

Open spaces in the city: from fields to squares and gardens

9

> Our real social experience is not only of the country and the city, in their most singular forms, but of many kinds of intermediate and new kinds of social and physical organisation.
> (Raymond Williams, *The Country and the City*, 1973, p. 289)

Raymond Williams' emphasis on intermediacy and indeterminacy are particularly apt in relation to late seventeenth- and early eighteenth-century London. The process of urban growth generated a series of changes whereby old spaces became transformed into new ones, open land and countryside were swallowed up by bricks and mortar, and outlying villages and farms were transmuted into first suburban and then in time inner-city areas. Foremost among the new forms of spatial organization were the square and the small inner-city garden. Yet these were also to some extent intermediate spaces. Gardens of varying types had a long pedigree in the city, and the square itself was a development out of other older and existing urban patterns. These small spaces sat like a series of Chinese boxes within the larger network of streets, alleys, walls and gateways which formed the built core and this in turn was situated within the wider context of the surrounding hills, fields, watercourses and villages.

London was a river city set within a rich agricultural region, the economic importance of which was fundamental in a still predominantly rural society. Defoe placed London within a rich luxuriant landscape which both contributed towards and enhanced the city's growing reputation as a new world centre.

> It is not easy to describe the beauty with which the banks of the Thames shine on either side of the river ... the river sides are full of villages, and those villages so full of beautiful buildings, charming gardens, and rich habitations of gentlemen of quality, that nothing in the world can imitate it ... The banks of the Sein are not thus adorned from Paris to Roan, or from Paris to the Loign above the city; the Danube can show nothing like it above and below Vienna, or the Po above and below Turin ... here is a plain and pleasant country, a rich fertile soil, cultivated and enclosed to the utmost perfection of husbandry, then bespangled with villages; those villages filled with these houses, and the houses

surrounded with gardens, walks, vistas, avenues, representing all the
beauties of building, and all the pleasures of planting.[1]

The interconnected nature of this network of roads, vistas and
villages is evident in contemporary topographical views of London
which often included the countryside within the view (see figures
1 and 53). Maps such as Strype's show that outside the central core
of the City, the West End and Southwark there existed a fringe area
in which town and country intermixed (see figure 4). This semi-
rural zone played an important role in contemporary life but its
existence and significance has largely been ignored by architectural
historians who have generally accepted Raymond Williams' division of city and country as two discrete and fundamentally
contrasting environments. Williams' pioneering and massively influential book laid out much of the terrain over which historians
of both pastoral and metropolitan ideas have been tramping ever
since, reinvigorated by post-modern theory which has presented
country and city as mutually defining and reinforcing binary
oppositions.[2]

The intermediate zone around the capital was often mentioned
in accounts of metropolitan life, such as Pepys' diaries, and written
about by contemporary commentators including Fiennes and De
Sassure. Daniel Defoe in his *Tour* included a line of measurement
which defined London, giving a total of 36 miles, 2 furlongs and
39 rods. He also devoted a section to the villages surrounding London which showed that, besides their primary agricultural
function, they were heavily used as playgrounds and dormitories
by the London population. It was also evident that many settlements were becoming absorbed into the city itself. As he wrote of
Chelsea, '[it] seems to promise itself to be made one time or other
a part of London, I mean London in its new extended capacity,
which if it should once happen, what a monster must London be,
extending from the farther end of Chelsea west, to Deptford-Bridge
east, which I venture to say, is at least eleven miles'.[3]

All contemporary writings on London presented these outlying
areas as forming part of the experience of the city. F. Colsoni in his
guide to London of 1693 written for German and French visitors
outlined some of the varying attractions and features of the different areas.[4] Greenwich should be visited by boat for its wonderful
set-piece architecture, Chelsea for its hospital, Kensington and
Hampton Court for the royal palaces. A tourist itinerary not very
different from that of today. He also wrote that Chatham should
be seen for the great warships, Hackney for its schools and Stepney
for its churches, which were packed with people from all over the
capital attending the parish church of St Dunstan and the Non-

49 *facing*] T. Bowles, *A New and Exact Prospect of the North Side of the City of London, taken from the upper Pond near Islington*, 1730. Islington's proximity to the City and the course of the New River through its fields made it a popular place for taking the air and walking. The New River Head with its pumping house and attendant buildings dominate, while to the left of the picture are grouped the various spas and the Sir Hugh Myddleton Inn. It is noticeable that despite the relatively crowded nature of the area and the fashionableness of the visitors' dress a similar architectural transformation has not been effected and the entertainments remain housed in adapted vernacular buildings.

conformist chapel, where Matthew Mead attracted the largest congregations in London.[5]

Spas were one of the most popular entertainments and when it came to taking the waters Londoners were spoilt for choice. Defoe wrote: 'the nobility and gentry go to Tunbridge, the merchants and rich citizens to Epsome; so the common people go chiefly to Dullwich and Stretham; and the rather also, because it lies so near London that they can walk to it in the morning and return at night'.[6] By the time Defoe was writing in the 1720s the most fashionable spas were at Tunbridge Wells, Epsom, Hampstead and Islington. Colsoni outlined Islington's various rival establishments of which Sadlers Wells and the New Tunbridge Wells or Islington Spa were the best known (figure 49). In these places, according to Colsoni, besides sampling the waters one could take coffee, gamble, play various games and listen to concerts. It is also clear from Colsoni's guide that perhaps the greatest attraction was the moral and physical corruption to be encountered there and he made a point of highlighting this as a feature, while at the same time naturally warning of its dangers. Defoe wrote of the popularity of commuting to Epsom, reinforcing his characterization of London as a centre intimately connected to a satellite constellation of villages: 'The greatest part of the men … may be supposed to be men of business, who are at London upon business all the day, and thronging to their lodgings at night … for 'tis very frequent for the trading part of the company to place their families here, and take their horses every morning to London, to the Exchange, to the Alley, or to the warehouse, and be at Epsome again at night.'[7]

The cities of London and Westminster existed within a larger geographical and regional nexus. Although the nature of the surrounding environment might appear stable it was being affected by the dynamic centre in its midst. Many of the areas closest to London, as with Hoxton, were developing new identities, besides their traditional agricultural functions, as dormitory villages, pleasure resorts or as centres for other commercial enterprises. Conflicts arose when these open areas became engulfed by new buildings and it was in the process of this interchange between urban and rural, built and unbuilt that both new and intermediate types of spaces evolved.

The square

Rasmussen, as part of his rehabilitation of Georgian architecture in the 1930s, identified the square as one of its defining elements. He wrote of, 'the London square with its character of unity

surrounded as it is by dignified houses, all alike'.[8] He contrasted it
with European squares of a similar date.

> The architecture of the Baroque square is generally united into a grand
> crescendo. It leads the vision of the spectator from one place to the
> other, the whole lay-out has a distinct tendency and an architectural
> climax, a monument or a monumental building. Each square is a sub-
> ordinate element in a great composition. The English square or crescent,
> on the contrary, is a restricted whole as complete as the courtyard of a
> convent.[9]

Rasmussen characterized the square as a modernizing form of urban organization and this interpretation has been strengthened by the recent historiography on the late seventeenth- and eighteenth-century town. Both Peter Borsay and Mark Girouard have presented the square as one of a number of innovative forms of public space which allowed for new forms of social interaction and were central in helping to both define and shape polite society.[10]

In John Summerson's blueprint for development in this period the square also played a crucial role. It formed two of his three principles of development: firstly, he claimed that the leading role of aristocrats in the development process was reinforced through their presence in the squares they built by maintaining their own houses there. Secondly, the square formed the centrepiece of the new urban landscape which also included a market, secondary streets and perhaps a church. These principles had been established, Summerson asserted, in the two first post-1660 developments, Bloomsbury Square and St James's Square.[11]

However, as with the house there are differences between the squares of the late seventeenth and early eighteenth century and what became the accepted model in the Georgian period. Squares were not considered indispensable in urban planning at this time and many successful developments took place without including one; such as those along the Thames which replaced the great aristocratic mansions of the Strand, and the area around Piccadilly developed from the 1680s onwards. Another significant development, Seven Dials of 1693, with its wheel of seven spokes radiating from a central axis, also rejected the square to advance a more radical alternative to set-piece planning. (All of these can be seen in figure 50.) An ambiguity as to the square's status and character in this period arose from several things: its heterogeneous architectural sources; a confusion as to its purpose and function; and its place within the debate over the growth of the city at this time.

The first two squares in London, Covent Garden of 1631 and Lincoln's Inn Fields of c. 1640, demonstrate both the creative architectural mix which formed the English square and the competing demands made on these new urban spaces. Covent Garden, designed by the great Inigo Jones and called a 'piazza', was the epitome of imported European classicism.[12] The design of the scheme combined elements from the piazza at Livorno and the Place des Vosges in Paris of 1605. Its Italianate style (rather than French or Dutch influenced), its arcades and the monumental palazzo scale distinguished it from subsequent developments. It was particularly notably at the time for its uniformity in style and conception. In its original form, however, terraces were built on

50 *facing*] Robert Morden and Philip Lea, *London, Westminster and Southwark*, 1690. This section of the map shows various stages in the development of the square: the early schemes of Covent Garden and Lincoln's Inn fields; the irregular space of Leicester Fields with its prominent pathways; Red Lion Square and the similarly radiating Seven Dials; and the more conventional arrangements such as Soho and St James's Squares. The map also shows the great majority of buildings, for example along the Strand, Drury Lane, St Martin's Lane and Haymarket, which were developed without the use of a square as a centrepiece.

———

two sides of the central area only, the third being formed by the church and the fourth by the Earl of Bedford's garden (see figure 50). This lack of absolute geometry and enclosure was not, however, seen as a disadvantage by contemporaries. Strype in his comments on Covent Garden related how the ground was an oblong rather than a square and praised, 'its open and large Piazza or Garden, so delightful to walk in'.[13] He stressed its open character and the benefits of the Bedford garden, 'The South Side lieth open to Bedford Garden where there is a finall Grotto of Trees, most pleasant in the Summer Season; and in this Side there is kept a Market for Fruits, Herbs, Roots and Flowers every Tuesday, Thursday and Saturday; which is grown to considerable account, and well served with choice goods, which makes it much resorted unto.'[14] Nor did its layout lead to a general association between the word 'piazza' and an open regular space. In 1708 Edward Hatton defined the term as follows: 'Piazza, a lower or Ground-walk covered over but open at one side; the same as Cloister (as commonly understood)'.[15] Although the houses on the piazza had originally been intended for gentlemen, from the first the population of the area was very mixed and the commercial function came to dominate over the residential one. The expansion of the market in 1670 and the removal of the Russells as residents from the area in 1700 contributed towards its long-term transformation into a Bohemian neighbourhood. If the area was an experiment in creating a new kind of socially exclusive environment then it most

51] John Kip, *The Prospect of Lincoln's Inn*, from Strype's edition of Stow's *Survey*, 1720. Lincoln's Inn Field is on the left with the walkways across it dominating the 'square'. The 'New Square' of Lincoln's Inn of *c*. 1685–97 is shown with the gardens beyond laid out in the 1660s, after the fashion of 'the Walks' established at the neighbouring Gray's Inn in *c*. 1600 by Sir Francis Bacon.

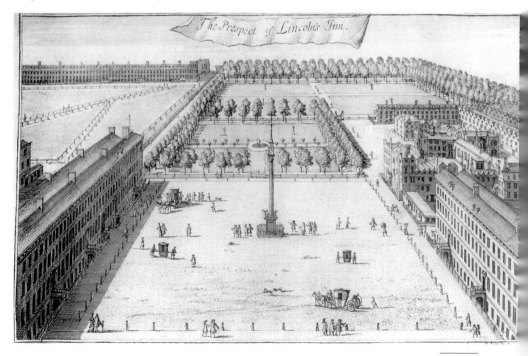

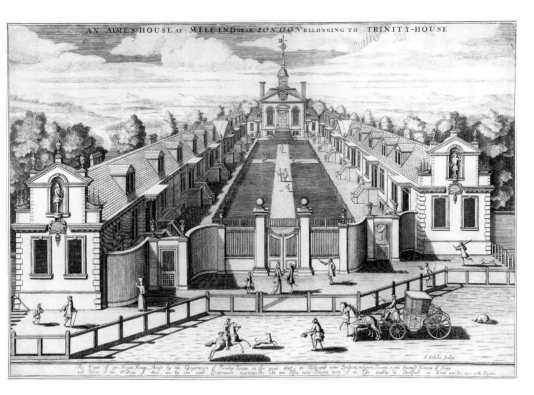

52] S. Gribelin, *An Almes House at Mile End, near London, belonging to Trinity House, built by the Corporation, 1696, for Decayed Masters of Ships and Pylots*, n.d. This view shows both the importance of spaces like the almshouse quadrangle as precedents for the London square, and the adaptability and flexibility of the new form of architecture at a range of scales and for a variety of building types.

certainly failed. Instead the development's main impact was in shifting the retail axis of the metropolis westwards away from the City.

Lincoln's Inn Fields represents a different strand in the creation of this quintessential London space. Although often discussed as a square,[16] an examination of both its formation and its layout make such a view problematic. At Lincoln's Inn Fields the maintenance of a large open area at the centre of the new terraces is directly attributable, not to any classicizing aesthetic, but to a prolonged and successful campaign stretching back to 1613 by the Society of Lincoln's Inn to protect the open character of their neighbourhood.[17] In 1617 a petition was presented to the Crown suggesting that the Fields be converted into walks in a similar manner to those at Moorfields. Indeed Jules Lubbock goes so far as to argue that it was the latter which should be regarded as the first London square.[18] The fact that the houses there were not built around the fields in direct relation to the space does I think put Moorfields in a different category. The Lincoln's Inn petition was approved by the Privy Council who sent a letter on 4 May 1617 to the relevant parties commending the project, which they said:

> wilbe a meanes to frustrate the covetous and greedy endeavors of such persons as daylie seeke to fill upp that small remaynder of Ayre in those partes with unnecessary and unproffittable Buildinges, which have been

SOUTHAMPTON OR BLOOMSBURY SQUARE

found the greates meanes of breedinge and harbouring Scarcity and Infection, to the general inconvenience of the whole Kingdome.[19]

In 1638 this policy was overturned when William Newton was granted a licence to build on the Fields. However, he was forced to agree to keep the central area free of buildings and open for walking and other recreational purposes, as were later builders who completed the surrounding terraces by 1659.

The large expanse of ground left unbuilt created an extremely open feel different from the enclosed squares of subsequent periods (see figure 50). The site was and remained 'fields' with walks across it, bounded by houses on its perimeter. The terraces in this instance could be said not to have created a new space but instead to have given emphasis and greater definition to an existing entity, Upper Lincoln's Inn Field. Strype wrote of the Fields: 'The East side lieth open to Lincolns Inn Garden, which gives a delightful prospect to the inhabitants: It is a great thoroughfare both for Horse and foot.'[20] The accompanying illustration to his text shows how this type of planning, consisting of ranges of buildings situated around open rectangular spaces, was nothing new in this part of London (figure 51). The Inns of Court, along with their architectural cousins the Oxbridge colleges, with their spacious gardens surrounded by blocks of chambers arranged around quadrangles provided another precedent for the London square. Lincoln's Inn Fields in Strype's view looks like nothing more than an extension of the landscape of the adjacent Lincoln's Inn and Gray's Inn. This continuity of tradition is reflected in the terminology used for the new spaces of the city. Bedford Row next to Gray's Inn Walks was originally known as Bedford Walks and the nearby Red Lion Square was sometimes referred to as Fishers Walks, after the Fisher family who had previously owned the land. Rasmussen's characterization therefore of the London square as being 'like the courtyard of a convent' comes from its roots in an existing planning tradition – essentially for contemplative purposes – leading back from the inns of court to the quadrangle and the cloister, and also incorporating spaces such as the almshouse and the convent (figure 52).

Two traditions created the London square. On the one hand it came out of a long history of open land in towns and formed part of a struggle to maintain common land against private interests. This is the tradition that Jules Lubbock has highlighted in his account of the formation of the London square. He cites Moorfields as the paradigm and criticizes Summerson's attribution of Covent Garden as the first square as that of a modernist: 'It is a very neat story which published as it was by a powerful advocate of town planning at the very time that the 1947 Town and Country Plan-

53 facing] Sutton Nicholls, *Southampton or Bloomsbury Square*, 1746. The plainness and openness of the space is typical of the early squares. The houses fronting the square are narrower and less prestigious than those on Great Russell Street which have large rear gardens and a prospect of the northern heights of Hampstead, Highgate and Islington. It is significant that this urban view incorporates the countryside beyond the city indicating the important umbilical link between the two.

ning Act began its journey to the statute book, divides the credit between the state and a great architect-planner.'[21] It is equally unsurprising that Lubbock as someone who has been closely associated, at least at times, with the Prince of Wales's campaign to champion community-based and socially responsive architecture is keen to promote an alternative communitarian history. In fact both elements – the communitarian (the Lincoln's Inn Fields tradition as I prefer to call it) and the authoritarian (the Covent Garden exemplar) – combined, initially uneasily, in the making of the late seventeenth-century square.

The squares developed after the Restoration drew on both these legacies. On the one hand there was a move towards creating the kind of unified urban set-piece that Covent Garden provided, and on the other the spatial ambiguity evident at Lincoln's Inn Fields remained. At Red Lion Fields in the mid-1680s Barbon originally intended to build over the whole area. It was only after his clash with the Society of Gray's Inn that he conceded leaving an open square in the middle of the development. Barbon said that as a result of the opposition that he had encountered he, 'did at last with great pains and charges overcome the difficulties ... although he was by the said troubles forced to break his design and model'.[22] In 1684 he reported that the development would consist of, 'fair large houses for persons of estate and value, before which this defendent intends to leave a very large square unbuilt with pleasant walks therein in which the gentlemen of the said Society or any the persons of quality that visit them may walk and take the air if they please'.[23] This may help explain the unusual star-fish arrangement of the space, Fishers Walks, begun in 1685, which seems designed to facilitate numerous entry points and diagonal access across the square in a similar fashion to the access which the turnstiles allowed on to Lincoln's Inn Fields (see figure 50).

The first of Summerson's two pioneering post-Restoration developments was Bloomsbury Square of 1661, where the dominant aristocratic presence was inescapable. It was originally called Southampton Square, after its creator the Earl of Southampton, and consisted of nothing more than two parallel terraces, Allington Row and Seymour Row, which flanked Bedford House at their northern end. The fourth side consisted of a road called Vernon Street. Figure 53 shows a representation of the square by Sutton Nicholls in which the view is from on high and from the square to the house. The square created a pleasant prospect for the Earl and it could be argued that this, in fact, was the dominant viewpoint, looking from house to the square rather than vice versa. Although topographical views depict it the other way round this arises from the artist's wish to focus on the family's house; a con-

54 *facing*] Plan of the Old Parish of St Martin's, *c.* 1690. This portion of the map shows St James's Park at the bottom of the map with its canal and avenues of trees, and Buckingham House on the left. The new area around St James's Square can be seen, along with completed and proposed developments in the Soho area to the north. Some of the great mansions along Piccadilly, such as Berkeley House and Burlington House, survive with their gardens, while in between, the new streets, which Evelyn deplored, are beginning to take over.

vention which was paralleled in depictions of country seats, such as those of Knyff and Kip, which also used the bird's-eye viewpoint to incorporate the surrounding landscape of the estate.[24]

Southampton Square therefore could be seen as doing little more than creating a courtyard fronting Southampton House which helped maintain a prospect and open aspect to the fore of the property as well as the rear. This raises questions as to how far Borsay's characterization of such places as forging grounds for a new kind of society was inherent in their original conception. The square has been presented for the eighteenth century as a new kind of modern, public space. But Bloomsbury or rather Southampton

A. Panton Street.

B. Green Street.

Leicester Square.

55 facing] J. Overton del.,
J. Bowles pub., View of
eicester Square, towards the
North, 1727. The houses
ere are of the second sort
and according to the 1670
building agreement were
ntended to have balconies;
nly two houses are shown
vith them, the first at the
bottom left and one
half-way along on the left.
Although shops were
originally forbidden this
was relaxed in the 1690s
nd some stalls can be seen
n front of Leicester House
as well as at either end of
ie left-hand terrace. Some
of the houses have had
their original roofs
eplaced by a fourth storey
with a parapet. It is also
noticeable how many of
ie new houses behind the
square have the dormer
gables of earlier building
ypes. All the houses have
railings in front of them,
besides those around the
quare which was enclosed
in the 1720s. The formal
planting of the square is
typical of this date. The
large gardens which
originally existed to the
ear are also visible. Sutton
Nicholls' earlier view of
1721 (also published by
Bowles) shows these as
having been infilled with
smaller houses, except
directly behind Leicester
House itself. This view of
1727 therefore, although
ater, must represent the
earlier state of the area.

_____

Square can be read as also arising from the traditional great house courtyard layout reworked within the context of an expanding, commercialized city. Covent Garden piazza and Leicester Square were also created in front of existing aristocratic palaces. At Soho Square a brand new mansion, Monmouth House, was manufactured on one side of the square for the Duke of Monmouth, illegitimate son of Charles II. The connection with Monmouth was not however of benefit to the scheme after his abortive rebellion and subsequent execution in 1685.[25] Colsoni in his guide of 1693 still called the area 'Monmouth Square' reinforcing the notion of these spaces, as at least initially, deriving some of their value from traditional hierarchical associations.[26]

St James's Square, by contrast, did not include a grand house as part of its scheme, although the whole development only existed in relation to and dependent upon the most important mansion of all, the palace of St James's (figure 54 and see figure 50) It was conceived and built as a square in which the house of the Earl of St Albans was indistinguishable from those of his neighbours. Strype summarized its salient characteristics admirably, 'a large handsome Place, encompassed with Rails, and graced on all Sides with large Buildings. Inhabited chiefly by the Nobility, except on the South, which is the Back Part of the North Row of Buildings in the Pail Mail.'[27] St James's followed the lead established at Covent Garden of creating a coherent and unified architectural composition and this is particularly noteworthy given that this was the one scheme where plots were sold off freehold rather than leasehold. There is evidence that the Crown did exert control over the design of the houses[28] and that it approved a plan drawn up in 1665 for the layout of the new development.[29] However, unlike the Earl of Bedford in the 1630s St Albans was also successful in his aim of attracting and retaining residents of quality.

An impression of these developments as unified in composition has subsequently arisen partly from topographical depictions which for the sake of clarity often have a tendency to simplify and homogenize. The visual record, however, can be misleading and even in the premier squares of St James's and Bloomsbury absolute conformity along the terraces was not achieved. It is worth remembering that many of the most famous views, such as those by Sutton Nicholls, were not produced when the squares were first built but in the early to mid-eighteenth century, by which time both the squares themselves and architectural tastes had changed. Bowles' view of Leicester Square of 1727 provides an example of the distortions that can arise in such representations (figure 55). If one compares this view with maps such as Morden and Lea's (see figure 50) it is clear that Bowles, or rather his draughtsman Overton, has portrayed what we can see from the map to be an irregular layout as a regularized square thus disguising its true shape. The irregular space arose from existing plots which pinched the square in towards the south. It had previously formed part of the the common field of St Martin's where parishioners had rights of way and other common rights. In the licence to build these were not mentioned but strict limits were given for the ranges of building. The space was originally open and accessible to all. Both here and at St James's Square a few trees left over from hedgerows in the fields continued to grow.[30] The railings and fences shown in Overton's view were not erected until the 1720s.[31] The walkways across the fields feature prominently in maps of the period and it continued to be called Leicester Fields as late as Rocque's map of 1746. Like Lincoln's Inn Fields, Leicester Fields was an existing and known landscape which only evolved into a new entity, Leicester Square, gradually.

Not all West End squares included aristocratic mansions; there were none at Golden Square, Red Lion Square or Queen Square for instance. It does seem that a shift took place throughout the period with a square becoming a more common feature as time went on. In the 1660s and 1670s squares tended to be used in the most exclusive developments while other schemes dispensed with them

56] Sutton Nicholls, *Devonshire Square*, 1714. Unlike its West End counterparts this square i shown as being uniform. The houses are of four bays although the door an window details do vary, some of the latter are sashes and some casements. The raised viewing points which wer a feature at the time car be seen in the rooftop balcony of the middle house (centre picture) an in the flat roof terrace o the block behind. The railings in front of the basement appear to be wood cut to look like iror The square is cobbled an in an unusual arrangemer is left open but fringed with trees.

DEVONSHIRE SQUARE

altogether. From the 1680s onwards it becomes more common to find squares used in all types of large-scale development ranging from the grandest to the most modest. This occurred not only in the West End but also in the City and the suburbs. In the City, Heydon Square was built around 1682 and Devonshire Square (c. 1680) was one of two squares to be found off Bishopsgate, the other being Crosby Square (c. 1671). Bridgewater Square, on the site of Bridgewater House, was developed from 1688. These squares tended to be smaller in scale and their houses naturally followed City rather than West End patterns of planning and detailing (figure 56). Many squares were built in the suburbs. Wellclose Square, off Ratcliffe Highway, was a brave attempt to introduce fashionable architecture to the East End with limited success. As Defoe commented in his *Tour*, it was 'so remote from houses, that it used to be a very dangerous place to go over after it was dark, and many people have been robbed and abused in passing it'.[32] On the other side of town Kensington Square was built way out in the fields in 1685 by Thomas Young, a London woodcarver, a brave decision as William and Mary did not purchase what became known as Kensington Palace until 1689. (See figure 32 which shows one of the surviving houses in the square.)

A cluster of squares was built to the north of the City around Shoreditch consisting of: Hoxton Square 1683; Webb's Square, Shoreditch, 1684; Charles Square, Hoxton 1685; St Bartholomew's Square, Old Street c. 1700-08. The surviving evidence in Hoxton shows that there was an attempt to differentiate these buildings from the more vernacular style of houses in Hoxton Street outlined in Chapter 8. No. 32 Hoxton Square conforms much more closely to the West End type although it is smaller than its inner-city counterparts. No. 16 Charles Square is really a City mansion placed just outside the square mile but interestingly built as part of a square rather than as a freestanding house (see figures 43 and 44). Following the Southampton/St James's model a licence was obtained for a market to be situated between the two squares in 1687/88, but it was never successful, perhaps because of the superabundance of market gardens nearby which made such a retail outlet unnecessary in an outer-city location.

Squares therefore were not solely a West End phenomenon. Besides being applied to these new types of spaces in all parts of town the word 'square' was used as an interchangeable term with those of 'court' and 'yard' for small open spaces. The maps of the period reveal places being called squares which are really just glorified courtyards, or sometimes not even those. An example of the latter is Queens Square, Westminster, in reality a street (later Queen Anne's Gate), or Jeffrey's Square off Lime Street which is a courtyard. In figure 6 of the Monument the three-sided rectangular space behind the column was called Fish Street Square. Strype wrote of Bear Garden Square, Thames Street, Southwark as, 'a new built Court well inhabited ... so called as built in the Place where the Bear Garden formerly stood until removed to the other side of the Water: which is more convenient for the Butchers and such like, who are taken with such rustic sports as the baiting of Bears and Bulls'.[33] The use of 'square' in a general sense to describe an open space was common usage; Edward Hatton, for example, described Billingsgate as, 'a kind of Square, which is a commodious Place for Hoys &c. to lie, and take in and unlade Goods'.[34]

The squares of London in the period 1660–1720, like its houses, were a mixture of existing and new ways of organizing space. The new integrated planning was important but most developments maintained the imprint of earlier landscape formations, buildings and patterns of usage. The evolutionary nature of the square in this period is evident in the lack of consensus about the layout that the square should adopt. The arrangement of streets leading off the square was not standardized. They were sometimes placed in the sides of the square as at St James's, sometimes in the corners as at Golden Square or in the starfish arrangement of Red Lion Square (see figure 50), while the pragmatic aspect in the making of squares can be seen in figure 5 where Wells Close is caught as an irregular arrangement of buildings and space in the process of transition from an open field, as it is shown in William Morgan's map of 1682, to its eventual designation as Well Close Square in John Rocque's map of 1747. In this intermediate period its character is definitely more that of medieval close than prototypical urban piazza.

This lack of clarity about the form, if not the shape, of the square was paralleled by an uncertainty as to what and for whom the square was intended. The accessibility and permeability of the early squares allowed for multiple but often conflicting uses. At Lincoln's Inn Fields the Act of 1735, which allowed for regulation of the Fields, outlined the problems that this had created:[35]

the great Square, now called Lincoln's Inn Fields ... hath for some Years past lain waste and in great Disorder, whereby the same has become a Receptacle for Rubbish, Dirt and Nastiness of all Sorts ... but also for Want of proper Fences to enclose the same great Mischiefs have happened to many of His Majesty's Subjects going about their lawful Occasions, several of whom have been killed, and other maimed and hurt, by Horses which have been from Time to Time aired and rode in the said Fields; and by reason of the said Fields being kept open many wicked and disorderly Persons have frequented and met together therein, using unlawful Sports and Games, and drawing in and enticing

young Persons into Gaming, Idleness and other vicious Courses; and
Vagabonds, common Beggars, and other disorderly Persons resort
therein, where many Robberies, Assaults, Outrages and Enormities have
been and continually are committed.[36]

Open access proved incompatible with the type of environment
that the inhabitants of such places increasingly came to desire as
new definitions of gentility and acceptable behaviour evolved.
The lack of enclosure of the early squares, both physically and
socially, began to change in the early eighteenth century as the
capital expanded and became more regularized and privatized. It
was this trend which led towards the enclosing and railing in of
squares resulting in the more contained and socially segregated
spaces of the 1720s onwards. At St James's the central area was
originally open and unadorned, as can be seen in Kip's view of 1710
(see figure 2). In due course this became cluttered up with booths
and rubbish leading in 1726 to the residents successfully petition-
ing Parliament for an Act to improve the square.[37] This provided
the powers to enclose, maintain and police the square. In the
period 1720-25 the building of Hanover Square (1717-19), Cavendish
Square (*c.* 1720), Grosvenor Square (1725 onwards) and Smith Square
(1726) initiated a new phase in which the square became more
central to the development scheme and more integrated within
the overall plan. The increasing ornamentation and design of the
square was partly the outcome of the beginnings of the idea of the
square as a garden but also a practical, physical means of effecting
social exclusion and control.

In the early developments the centre of the square was generally
gravelled or cobbled and left open reflecting its multi-functional
use. Low posts were sometimes used to keep carriages and riders
out of the central area as at St James's and Bloomsbury Squares
(see figure 53). With the shift towards greater enclosure increased
emphasis was given to the central area. The Swiss-French visitor
De Saussure in 1725 wrote of the: 'fine open spaces called squares,
because they are of that shape. The centres of these squares are
shut in by railings of painted wood, and contain gardens with
flowers, trees and paths. Those of Soho, Leicester Fields, of the Red
Lion, and the Golden Square are in this style.'[38] Bowles' view of
Leicester Square shows the increased centrality and the square-
within-a-square effect that this produced (see figure 55). A
building specification of 1687 for what was later to become Smith
Square in Westminster prescribed a similar layout.[39] What was
described as 'the court' before the houses was to be 180 ft one way
and 120 ft the other with 'the square' in the middle being 60 ft
by 100 ft. The square was to have 'gravel walks, grass platts and
lime trees'. It was to have a summer house in the middle with

palisado pales of wood four inches high 'resembling those of iron at the Countess of Devon's house in Gerrard Street'. Although the new-style squares incorporated some natural planting, this was kept to a minimum. Thomas Fairchild in his *The City Gardener* of 1722 commented unfavourably on: 'The plain way of laying out Squares in Grass Platts and Gravel Walks' and instead wanted to see them designed more 'in a Country manner'.[40]

The importance of prospect was evident in the careful siting of ornamental features and objects within the square which were placed to create views and axial vistas. These were partly for decoration but features such as summer houses or seats also provided places for contemplation and repose, which was held to be one of the purposes of a garden. Water elements were considered desirable particularly fountains, the water being conveyed by wooden or lead pipes from cisterns (figure 57). At St James's Square by 1728 an octagonal railed area had been created with a basin of water with a fountain at its centre. Obelisks, statues and sundials were other popular garden features. Strype described Soho Square as, 'a very large and open Place, enclosed with a high Pallisado Pale, the square being neatly kept, with Walks and Grass-Plots, and in the midst is the Effigies of King Charles the Second, neatly cut in Stone, to the

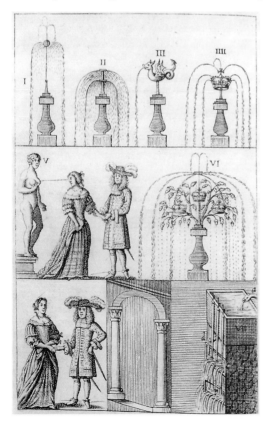

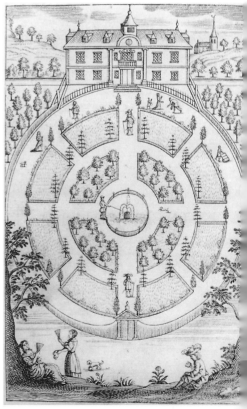

57 facing, left] John Worlidge's, *The Art of Gardening*, 1688 edn, designs for fountains. Key: '*I* The Ball raised by a Spout of Water. *II* The Water representing a double Glass, the one over the other. *III* A Dragon or such like, casting Water out of its Mouth, as it runs round on the Spindle. *IIII* A Crown casting Water out of several Pipes as it runs round. *V* A Statue of a Woman, that at the turning of a private Cock, shall cast Water out of her Nipples into the Spectators Faces. *VI* the royal Oak with Leaves Accorns, and Crowns dropping and several small Spouts round the top. *VII* The Cistern into which the Water flows by the Pipe *a*. the Air issueth out at the Pipes *bbb*. the ends whereof make the Musical sounds in the Trough of Water at *c*. which is supplied with Water, by the Pipe *d* which in time dreins the Cistern, which wast Water precipitates into *e* and from *e* into the common Drein.'

58 facing, right] John Worlidge, *The Art of Gardening*, 1688 edn, a formal country garden, of which he wrote: 'A draught of the square Garden I have given you, which may be varied as every Designer pleaseth; each principal Walk is bordered with Flowers; each principal Corner with Flower-pots, and the middle of the greater Squares with Statues' (p. 17). It was this style of garden, he said, which was popular in the town.

Life, standing on a Pedestal'.[41] The square was in fact becoming seen as a garden.

The garden

The interest in gardening was a relatively recent phenomenon, as Defoe wrote:

> the strange passion, for fine gardens, which has so commendably possessed the English gentlemen of late years, for 'tis evident it is but of late years ... the king began with the gardens at Hampton-Court and Kensington, and the gentlemen followed everywhere, with such a gust that the alteration is indeed wonderful throughout the whole kingdom.[42]

The style of gardening adopted in late seventeenth-century England was drawn from Renaissance traditions and contemporary French and Dutch designs.[43] As with the square, fashionable gardens of the period were notable for their formality, minimal natural features, geometrical patterns and regular layout. The formal garden was developed for aristocratic, rural seats but its emphasis on hard surfaces, geometricity and ordered visual effects made it a perfect model for the urban environment. It could be adopted at all scales, from the large expanses of the newly formed St James's Park, to the square and the grandee's town garden, through the small inner-city plot, down to a symmetrical arrangement of rectangular planters around a doorway.

John Worlidge described and illustrated such a garden in his book *Systema Horticultura: or, the Art of Gardening* of 1683.

> The Square is the most perfect and pleasant form that you can lay your Garden into, where your ground will afford it, every Walk that is in it being streight, and every Plant and Tree standing in a direct line ... You may divide your Square into three parts by Pallisades, the long way beginning at your House, the middle third part containing a large Gravel walk, adorned of each side with a border of your most Select Plants, Shrubs, and Flowers, between those borders and the Pallisades, green walks with Borders next the Pallisades, on which you may plant Perennial Greens, and your more ordinary Plants and Flowers.[44]

It would seem that this style of garden with its gravel walks, borders, surrounding walls and internal divisions was transferred directly from the country to the town (figure 58). However, Worlidge makes an interesting observation suggesting a reverse influence: 'The new mode of Gravel Walks and Grass-plots, is fit only for such Houses or Palaces, that are scituated in Cities and great Towns, although they are now become presidents for many stately Country Residencies.'[45] The division of the garden into small rectangles suited the shape of regular urban plots. The lack

of flowers was a huge advantage in the city where gardeners waged
a constant battle against the effects of pollution, and as Thomas
Fairchild in his *The City Gardener* of 1722 said: 'I find that every
thing will not prosper in London ... because of the Sea-Coal does
hurt to some plants.'[46]

Although the popularity of gardening in the late seventeenth
century was inspired by the Court it is unclear how far the new
style of urban garden was limited to the wealthy alone in London.
The large aristocratic mansions maintained their grand formal
gardens, some of which can be seen in figure 54. Gardens had long
existed in the City, the Livery Company's gardens being particularly well-known examples.[47] The grandest houses in the City
continued to allow space for gardens where possible. A building
agreement for a mansion house in Mincing Lane specified that
about 30 ft was to be left for a garden.[48] The situation in the new
areas of town is unclear. Some developments dispensed with
gardens altogether, others provided small backyards, while some
included a fairly generous allowance of open space to the rear
(which would not necessarily be used as a garden). Little attention
has been given to town gardens in this period and a lack of visual
and documentary evidence means that our knowledge of them is
fragmentary and impressionistic. Contemporary newspapers and
printed sources would suggest an interest in gardens given the
frequency with which they are mentioned. Advertisements for
houses, for example, mention gardens attached to properties suggesting that they were desirable features. The Friday 24 May
edition of *A Collection For Improvement of Husbandry and Trade* of
1695 carried advertisements for a house in Highgate 'with a large
Garden and Orchard' and one in Westminster near the Abbey likewise 'with a garden'. The paper also carried advertisements for
suppliers and sales of plants and trees.[49] Neil Burton writes that,
'the ordinary town house garden is a product of the eighteenth
century'.[50] He suggests that town gardens first came into common
use around 1720 with the upper classes in locations such as the
Grosvenor Estate in London and in Bath. Todd Longstaffe-Gowan
has demonstrated how in the eighteenth century gardening became a major leisure pursuit and arena for consumption for the
urban middle classes.[51]

Some maps and views from the earlier period do provide
evidence of gardens within the central area, although how widespread these were and the precise nature of their design are
impossible to gauge from these sources alone. In Morgan's survey
of 1682 and Strype's of 1720 many of the new streets are depicted
with their individual plots clearly shown albeit in outline only,
while Morden and Lea's map, based on Morgan's, shows a plethora

of gardens throughout the town (see figures 5 and 50) There had long been a tradition of gardening on the fringes of the city where Strype wrote of 'the Gardens Planted Every where without the Houses of the Suburbs the Citizens have Gardens and Orchards planted with Trees, large, beautiful, and one joying to another'.[52] These can be seen in figure 5 which shows gardens throughout the eastern fringe of the town and on the Southwark side of the river too. Interestingly these occur not just in the old villages and river settlements but also in the new developments in Spitalfields and Whitechapel, particularly around Goodmans Fields. The map suggests that these gardens were allocated as an integral part of the new housing here. Many of these gardens disappeared under the impact of subsequent infilling and rebuilding at a higher density from the 1720/30s onwards. Figure 50, showing the western part of the map, also details gardens across the city. Most significantly the new buildings in Soho, Piccadilly and the Haymarket are for the most part clearly shown with gardens. The planting layouts indicated often seem to be larger than would be possible for the plot of an individual house and Bowles' engraving of Leicester Square of 1727 gives us an indication of what such grounds may have looked like (see figure 55). Large gardens are clearly visible to the rear of the houses, particularly those to the north and west. For the most part these are not divided up into individual plots but seem to form communal rear gardens as a supplement to the open space of the square at the front. Like those in Spitalfields these too became subject to later infilling. It may have been that the urban areas built at this time were more spacious in layout with a greater number of gardens than has been realized, as the original settlement pattern was almost immediately annihilated by subsequent accretions. As the centre of London moved inexorably westwards from the 1720s onwards and architectural fashions began to change, the areas built in the preceding era were vulnerable to rapid redevelopment at higher densities as a result of which any gardens that had once existed were rapidly obliterated.

We know more about the situation at Bloomsbury Square where the yards behind Allington and Seymour Rows were small and cramped but the gardens behind Great Russell Street were highly esteemed as much for their views as for their generous size (see figure 53). Strype praised it as: 'a very handsome large and well built Street, graced with the best Buildings in all Bloomsbury, and the best inhabited by the Nobility and Gentry, especially the North Side, as having Gardens behind the Houses: and the Prospect of the pleasant Fields up to Hamsted and Highgate. Insomuch that this Place by Physicians is esteemed the most healthful of any in London.'[53] Sutton Nicholls' view of 1746 shows a variety of garden layouts dominated by the clipped topiary which Switzer was deploring as early as 1712: 'Our British Gardeners ... instead of humouring Nature, love to deviate from it as much as possible. Our Trees rise in Cones, Globes and Pyramids. We see the marks of the Scissors upon every Plant and Bush.'[54]

Sir Henry Johnson moved into a house in Great Russell Street in 1708. He ordered that the garden was to be planted with evergreens and fruit trees. The garden was to be designed, 'as Mr Ettricks, except the greens'.[55] A rolling stone was to be provided with an iron handle to roll the gravel, which was the usual material for making walks within a garden. Worlidge in the *Art of Gardening* suggested an undercourse of bricks below and at the sides of the gravel to prevent weeds growing. A layer of unscreened gravel would be set down first followed by a top layer of red fine gravel. John Rea, another popularizing writer on gardens, in his *Flora* of 1665, recommended 'cat-brained binding gravel' as being the best.[56] Palisades were to be made at the lower end of Sir Henry's garden, the rest of which appears to have been walled. Brick and stone were considered the best walling materials but increasingly cheaper alternatives were being utilized, particularly wood, just as they were in the construction of houses. For the fencing within the garden Rea commented, 'you must make use of some under-standing Joyner to work them; first he must be made acquainted with the Draught'.[57]

Worlidge gave full details for the design and construction of fences:

> These open fences are made of Board of about three or four inches broad, and three or four foot long, either nailed to, or let throw two Rails, with heads cut either round or like a Lance, and painted white with Linseed Oyle, and white head, two or three times over, to make them endure the Weather.
> But the best material to make these Pallisades withal is Iron, so framed as are the Iron Balconies in London, save only that these appear above the Rails with square painted Heads ... This fence is also permanent and needs no repair.
> In imitation whereof, there is newly made in some few Gardens a Pallisade of Boards ... being cut with square pyramidical points, do very much resemble those made of Iron. As you stand against them they appear open, and every thing very conspicuous through them like the Iron ... These Pallisades although they require somewhat more timber and workmanship than the ordinary foil, yet are by far the more com-pleat and beautiful, every motion of your Body from its place, begetting a variety in the object.[58]

Sir Henry also ordered that the two brick houses at the end of the garden should be removed and rebuilt on a grander scale. They were to have sash-windows installed on two sides giving views both to the field and towards the house. They were to be wainscotted and floored with deals and the roofs and ceilings were to be painted. A garden pavilion is visible in one of the Great Russell Street gardens in figures 53. For Worlidge it was the banqueting house, above all, that could combine the two essential elements of the garden: ornament and retreat. A banqueting house at this date was not intended for full-scale banquets but meant a small summerhouse or pavilion where desserts and confectionery could be consumed and other recreations could take place.

> Arbours, Benches and Seats are very necessary, being present expedients for them that are weary; but that which crowns the pleasures of a Garden is a place of repose, where neither Wind, Rain, Heat nor Cold can annoy you.
>
> This small Edifice usually term'd a Pleasure-house or Banquetting-house, may be made at some remote Angle of your Garden: For the more remote it is from your House, the more private will you be from the frequent disturbances of your Family or Acquaintance, and being made at an Angle, part within your Garden and part without, you will have the priviledges and advantages of Air and View, which otherwise you will want and which render it much more pleasant than to be without them.
>
> The Windows and Doors, the one or other respecting every Coast, may be glazed with the best and most transparent Glass, to represent every Object through it the more splendid, with Skreens of printed and painted sarcenet to prevent in the day, and flutters of thin Wainscot, in the night, others from disturbing your solitary repose …
>
> In the other corner of your Garden, or some opposite place to such Pleasure-houses, may you erect another of the same Form to answer it as to your view, which may serve as a place to preserve your tender Plants in, during the extremity of the Winter, and it is usually term'd a Greenhouse, because several Winter Greens are therein preserved, that will not endure the severity of that season; in it also may you dispose on shelves your dry Roots of Flowers and Seeds, until the time of the Year mind you of interring them.
>
> On these small Edifices may you bestow what cost you can afford, and make them (as they deserve to be) the principal Ornaments of your Ville.[59]

Rea recommended an octagonal summerhouse, 'finely painted with Landskips and other conceits, furnished with Seats about, and a Table in the middle'.[60] This he suggested would be useful for putting boxes on and sitting at to write out plant labels and other things. The desire for a place of escape might be felt even more keenly in the urban context; to judge by Worlidge's remarks, banqueting houses in larger town houses were a grander forerunner of the male preserve of the garden shed. The matching building in the city garden often contained the house of office or privy. Symmetry of prospect was thus maintained while the restrictions of space determined a more directly functional use. There is a tradition too of the privy as a place of escape and thought, but the smells were probably too overpowering.[61] Figure 12 shows a plan of new houses in Westminster with some gardens with privies on one side and sheds with corner chimneys on the other, while figure 16 (showing the typical new house layout) includes a 'Somer Hous' at the far end of the garden and a 'yard to ye kitchen' adjacent to the rear of the house.

The proliferation of books on gardening for both professionals and amateurs in the period testifies to its growing importance and popularity (figure 59). John Worlidge wrote in the Preface to his *Art of Gardening*, 'this Art which is of late years much improved in every part ... And as this Art hath with its Subjects encreased of late years to have the Instructions or Treatises written to that effect been multiplied: The affections of our Countrymen so naturally tending that way, have given great encouragement to such Publications.'[62] Worlidge wrote that his intention was that the style of his book should be plain and 'suited to the vulgar'.[63] However, the delights of the garden were not limited to those living in the country:

Neither is there a Noble or pleasant Seat in England but hath its Gardens

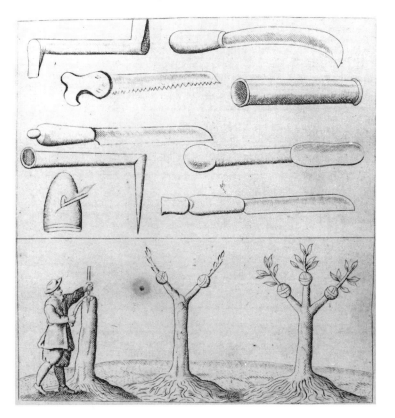

59] Leonard Meager, *Th[e] Compleat English Gardene[r]* 1710, showing tools and demonstration of grafting, evidence of th[e] new interest in gardenin[g] and the market for explanatory books on th[e] subject.

for pleasure and delight; scarce an Ingenious Citizen that by his confine-
ment to a Shop, being denied the priviledge of having a real garden, but
hath his boxes, posts, or other receptacles for Flowers, Plants etc. In
imitation of it, what curious Representations of Banquets of Fruits,
Flower-pots, Gardens and such like, are painted to the life, to please the
Eyes, and satisfie the fancy of such that either cannot obtain the Felicity
of enjoying them in reality, or to supply the defect the Winter annually
brings.[64]

Both Thomas Fairchild, whose *The City Gardener* of 1722 is
testament to the increase in urban horticulture, and Leonard
Meager commented on the growing popularity of container
gardening. This took place both in the garden, and outside and
inside the house. Fairchild included a chapter on 'Ornaments and
Decorations for Balconies, and the Outside of Windows in Large
Streets'. He wrote, 'if we have convenience of a Place to set Pots
abroad, or without Doors, we may have most of the Annual
Flowers to interchange from Time to Time, as it may be judg'd
proper'.[65] Meager wrote of the way the garden was coming into
the house, 'many are very much taken and affected with furnishing of their Flower-pots for the Adorning of some Rooms in their
Houses etc'.[66]

John Rea in his *Flora* of 1665 makes it clear that he is writing for
an inexperienced garden owner but one who cannot afford a full-
time gardener: 'I shall now proceed to inform all such as desire to
be florist, how they may do as I have done, make their own Gardens themselves, assisted onley by ordinary Labourers … and in so
plain and easie a method, that every person of any capacity may
be enabled thereby to be his own Gardener.'[67] Another solution
was to employ a part-time gardener or one who might combine
this with other duties. An advertisement in 1695 stated, 'I want a
sober, quiet Coachman of middle Age, that understands something
of Gardening to serve a Gentleman.'[68] George London and Henry
Wise, the royal gardeners, in their 'Advertisement' at the front of
their edition of Jean de la Quintinie of 1699 criticized these un-
skilled gardeners:

There is also a sort of Men who call themselves Gard'ners, and of them
not a few, who having wrought at labouring work at the new making
of some Ground, or in a Garden, where a great many Hands are employed; and after the young beginner hath exercised the Spade and the
Barrow for twelve Months or thereabouts, he then puts on an Apron,
sets up for a professed Gard'ner, and a place he must have; he hears some
honest Country Gentleman is in London, and want a Gard'ner; he goes
to him, and tells him his story of what great matters he is capable of,
and that he hath been at new making of such a Ground, may be he gets
a favourable Letter, or at least some recommendation from some of
those sellers of Trees before mention'd; for then he is hired.[69]

London was the undisputed horticultural centre of seventeenth-century England.[70] The gardening elite consisted of a close circle of professional gardeners and nurserymen and their patrons. The increased activity in gardening led to the growth of the trade as a demand for a commercial supply of seeds and plants developed. London and Wise distinguished between three sorts of dealers in plants and seeds.[71] Firstly, there were seedsmen operating via shops and catalogues; secondly, those that traded from the Exchange and Westminster Hall; and thirdly, nursery men. Being nurserymen themselves, naturally they recommended the latter, and Fairchild also counselled against buying from fruiterers in markets, where he had, 'seen Plants that were … as uncertain of Growth as a Piece of Noah's Ark'.[72]

Among the range of open spaces available in London in this period the individual private garden was the most uncommon and least available to the majority of the population. Small individual gardens existed in all parts of the town but how widespread they were or whether courtyards and paved areas predominated is impossible to tell from the evidence assembled here. If there was a lack of demand for gardens for the middling ranks this could be explained partly by the newness of gardening as a leisure pursuit, also by the evolutionary nature of the new developments themselves and by the tradition of accessibility to open spaces in the city. Londoners of all classes still considered open space in and around the city, including squares, to be theirs to use and enjoy. The countryside was near enough to visit easily and some people who lived in the centre kept a plot or garden on the outskirts. Above all at this date the city was not viewed as a series of compartmentalized boxes in which the 'ownership' of open space could only be made through the purchase of a private garden. Under the impact of the new notion of politeness that concept of spatiality began to change around 1720, as squares became private rather than public arenas and the introduction of small town gardens began. The city began to be shaped as a series of bounded spaces, both physically and socially, where enclosure ensured exclusion and exclusion ensured exclusivity.

Notes

1 Daniel Defoe, *A Tour through the Whole Island of Great Britain*, 1724-26, ed. Pat Rogers, Harmondsworth, Penguin, 1971, pp. 174-7.

2 For a fuller version of this argument see, Elizabeth McKellar, 'The City and the Country: The Urban Vernacular in Late Seventeenth and Early Eighteenth Century London', in Neil Burton, ed., *Georgian Vernacular: Papers Given at the 1995 Georgian Group Symposium*, London, Georgian Group, 1996, pp. 10-18. The literature for the town has already been detailed. Some of the most significant

works on the country include: Mark Girouard, *Life in the English Country House: A Social and Architectural History*, New Haven and London, Yale University Press, 1978; James Ackerman, *The Villa: Form and Ideology of Country Houses*, London, Thames & Hudson, 1990; Tom Williamson, *Polite Landscapes: Gardens and Society in Eighteenth-Century England*, Stroud, Sutton, 1995; Nigel Everitt, *The Tory View of Landscape*, New Haven and London, Yale University Press, 1994.

3 Defoe, *Tour*, pp. 345-6.

4 F. Colsoni, *Le Guide de Londres*, London, 1693.

5 The banning of Nonconformists from preaching within five miles of London in 1665 lead to the migration of many dissenting communities to the outlying areas.

6 Defoe, *Tour*, p. 66.

7 Defoe, *Tour*, pp. 170-1.

8 Steen Eiler Rasmussen, *London: The Unique City*, 1934, Cambridge, Mass: and London, MIT Press, 1982, p. 166.

9 Rasmussen, *London*, pp. 198-9.

10 Peter Borsay, *The English Urban Renaissance: Culture and Society in the Provincial Town, 1660-1770*, Oxford, Clarendon Press, 1989; Mark Girouard, *The English Town*, New Haven and London, Yale University Press, 1990.

11 John Summerson, *Georgian London*, 1945, Harmondsworth, Penguin, 1978 edn, p. 42.

12 *Survey of London, St Paul's, Covent Garden*, Vol. XXXVI, London, Athlone Press, 1970; John Summerson, *Inigo Jones*, Harmondsworth, Penguin, 1966.

13 J. Strype, *The Survey of London*, London, 1720, Vol. II, Bk VI, Ch. VI, p. 87.

14 Strype, *Survey*, Vol. I, Bk VI, Ch. VI, p. 89.

15 Edward Hatton, *A New View of London*, London, 1708, p. 811.

16 See for example, Timothy Mowl and Brian Earnshaw, *Architecture Without Kings: The Rise of Puritan Classicism under Cromwell*, Manchester, Manchester University Press, p. 136.

17 *Survey of London, St Giles-in-the-Fields*, Vol. III, Pt 1, 1912, pp. 7-13.

18 Jules Lubbock, *The Tyranny of Taste: The Politics of Architecture and Design in Britain, 1550-1960*, New Haven and London, Yale University Press, 1995, p. 30.

19 PRO PC3/fos 315-16.

20 Strype, *Survey*, Vol. II, Bk IV, Ch. IV, p. 75.

21 Lubbock, *Taste*, p. 30.

22 PRO C9/457/109.

23 PRO C9/92/3.

24 Leonard Knyff and John Kip, *Britannia Illustrata*, London, 1707.

25 The house remained largely empty until 1713 and unfinished until 1719. See, *Survey of London, St Anne, Soho*, Vol. XXXIII, 1966, pp. 107-9.

26 Colsoni, *Le Guide de Londres*, p. 17.

27 Strype, *Survey*, Vol. II, Bk VI, Ch. VI, p. 81.

28 See *Survey of London, St James, Westminster*, Vol. XXIX, 1960, pp. 56, 61, 63.

29 PRO MPE/556. This does not survive and its authorship is therefore ambiguous, although an eighteenth-century copy does exist in the PRO. The square as delineated on the map and as actually built are slightly different. For more on this see, *Survey of London, St James, Westminster*, p. 60.

30 Norman Brett-James, *The Growth of Stuart London*, London, London and Middlesex Archaeological Society with George Allen & Unwin, 1935, p. 375.

31 *Survey of London, St Anne, Soho,* Vol. XXXIV, 1966, p. 433.

32 Defoe, *Tour,* pp. 298-9.

33 Strype, *Survey,* Vol. II, Bk IV, Ch. I, p. 28.

34 Hatton, *London,* p. 7.

35 *Survey of London, St Giles-in-the-Fields,* Vol. III, Pt I, 1912, pp. 19-20.

36 Act 8 Geo. II cap. XXVI.

37 *Survey of London, St James, Westminster,* Vol. XXIX, 1960, pp. 66-67.

38 C. de Saussure, *A Foreign View of England in 1725-29,* trans. Madame Van Muyden, London, Caliban Books, 1995, p. 44.

39 PRO C7/210/27.

40 Thomas Fairchild, *The City Gardener,* London, 1722, p. 12.

41 Strype, *Survey,* Vol. II, Bk VI, Ch. VI, p. 87.

42 Defoe, *Tour,* pp. 174-6.

43 The best introductions are: Reginald Blomfield, *The Formal Garden in England,* 1892, reprinted London, Waterstone & Co., 1985; Roy Strong, *The Renaissance Garden in England,* London, Thames & Hudson, 1979; John Anthony, *The Renaissance Garden in Britain,* Princes Risborough, Shire, 1991.

44 John Worlidge, *Systema Horticultura: Or, the Art of Gardening,* n.p. [London?], 1683, p. 17.

45 Worlidge, *Art of Gardening,* p. 18.

46 Fairchild, *The City Gardener,* p. 5.

47 See, Mireille Galinou, ed., *London's Pride: The Glorious History of the Capital's Gardens,* London, Anaya, 1990, particularly the essays by Peter Stott on medieval gardens and Vanessa Harding on the Tudor and early Stuart period.

48 PRO C5/144/1.

49 *A Collection For Improvement of Husbandry and Trade,* Vol. 7, No. 147, 2 and 24 May 1695. I am grateful to Michael Harris for this information.

50 Dan Cruickshank and Neil Burton, *Life in the Georgian City,* London, Viking, 1990, p. 190.

51 Todd Longstaffe-Gowan, 'Gardening and the Middle Classes, 1700-1830', in Galinou, *London's Pride,* pp. 122-33.

52 Strype, *Survey,* Vol. II, Appendix, p. 12.

53 Strype, *Survey,* Vol. II, Bk IV, Ch. IV, p. 85.

54 As quoted in Laurence Fleming and Alan Gore, *The English Gardener,* London, Michael Joseph, 1979, p. 79.

55 PRO C10/422/30.

56 John Rea, *Flora: Sen, De Florum Cultura. Or, a Complete Florilege,* London, 1665, p. 3.

57 Rea, *Flora,* p. 6.

58 Worlidge, *Art of Gardening,* pp. 26-8.

59 Worlidge, *Art of Gardening,* pp. 39-41.

60 Rea, *Flora,* p. 9.

61 Isaac Ware commented on the problems of siting benches near privies. See, Cruickshank and Burton, *Georgian City,* pp. 193-4.

62 Worlidge, *Art of Gardening,* Preface.

63 Worlidge, *Art of Gardening,* Preface.

64 Worlidge, *Art of Gardening,* p. 3.

65 Fairchild, *The City Gardener,* p. 66.

66 Leonard Meager, *The English Gardener: Or, a Sure Guide to Young Planters and Gardeners*, 1670.

67 Rea, *Flora*, p. 2.

68 *A Collection For Improvement of Husbandry and Trade*, Vol. 7, No. 147, 2 May 1695.

69 George London and Henry Wise, 'An Advertisement to the Nobility and Gentry', in Jean de la Quintinie, *The Compleat Gard'ner*, London, 1699.

70 See: George Plumptre, *The Garden Makers*, Pavilion, London, 1993; Galinou, *London's Pride*, particularly the essays by Rosemary Weinstein and Todd Longstaffe-Gowan.

71 London and Wise, 'Advertisement', in de la Quintinie, *Compleat Gard'ner*.

72 Fairchild, *The City Gardener*, p. 68.

Conclusion

The image of late seventeenth-century London as a phoenix rising reinvigorated from the ashes of the Great Fire has been a powerful and persuasive one. The understandable emphasis placed on rebirth by contemporaries, as exemplified by the Monument (see figure 6), has been echoed by historians. The ritual cleansing of the medieval city has provided a convenient symbol for the birth of a new era in the history of the capital. Yet this emphasis on modernity has obscured the underlying continuities between the pre- and post-Restoration metropolis, whose expansion westwards was already well under way prior to the Fire. Summerson, as a modernist living in a war-ravaged city, subscribed to theories of historical fracture, wholesale physical change and above all a notion of 'the urban'. But as we have seen, the 'modern city', although undeniably radically different and new, developed out of existing housing types and traditional layouts and maintained links with the countryside and older patterns and associations of land usage. The creation of modern London was an evolutionary not a revolutionary process.

As far as architectural and building practice is concerned this book has argued that many features which were thought to have occurred in the eighteenth or nineteenth centuries actually originated much earlier. This was part of a wider transformation taking place in all the trades, as a result of which independent small-scale capitalists became the dominant producers for the expanding consumer markets. If we place the shifts in building within this wider context, we may perhaps avoid some of the confusions which an isolationist approach to architectural history has perpetuated. A new type of building practice was established in the late seventeenth century which set the pattern for the construction industry well into the nineteenth century. In the later period the scale of operation expanded and the increasing involvement of the state and big corporations as clients resulted in new kinds of contracting and building organization. However, most smaller scale works, particularly housing, continued to be put up by small entrepreneurs operating through sub-contracting and the building lease system. A nineteenth-century speculative housing development would have been carried out in a fashion essentially the same as that of its late seventeenth-century precursors. The situation changed in the twentieth century with a governmental role in the provision of housing and the rise of large specialist speculative house builders such as Barratt and Wimpey. However, many small building firms and individual tradespeople still operate today in a similar way to an early modern tradesman. The major difference being the replacement of the measure and value system by fixed contracts. What this book has shown is that if we are looking to explain changes in the building industry and architecture over the past three hundred years, we should not seek to do so on the basis of the pre- and post-capitalist assumptions on which so much of the literature rests.

This period saw the beginnings of a new understanding of built form and a transitional stage in the transmission and articulation of that form in design procedures. It has been demonstrated that the introduction of classicism did not immediately result in the use of the techniques usually associated with its design and production. The language of building was in the process of evolving and being adapted to varying circumstances. However, this experimentation operated inside strictly defined limits, and within these we find a remarkable consensus about what the form of the house should be. It is important to raise the question of what this new vocabulary represented and, most particularly, the extent to which we may consider these houses as classical. When Sir John Summerson looked at these houses he found them wanting as they did not accord with the notion of classicism he had so lucidly outlined in *The Classical Language of Architecture*.[1] His book allowed for a variety of approaches to the antique in different periods but it dealt only with the polite language of classical architecture and not with the vernacular. The classical language of architecture has other dialects, accents and levels than the ones which Summerson detailed. Even the notion of 'the' classical language is now being questioned, most notably in John Onians' book *Bearers of Meaning*,[2] which shows the multiplicity of ways in which it has been understood and the different meanings attached to it in different periods. Like any language, classicism was always evolving and changing its meanings and usages. There was no one form of classical architecture in Britain but a complicated mosaic of varying interpretations at different places at different times with different purposes. The particular confusion in seventeenth-century England arises because classicism was being adopted at two levels simultaneously, but that does not mean it was being done in the same way or for the same reasons. The late seventeenth- and early eighteenth-century London house is then a regional dialect or a vernacular variant of the classical language. In our own post-modern age we should have no problem in understanding a culture which did not privilege one form over another but instead preferred to operate on the basis of stylistic diversity and eclectic plurality.

The London house was a new kind of object. It was perfectly suited in both structure and form to fulfil the demands of an increasingly commercialized, mass-consumption housing market arranged around the continual renewal and replacement of products. However, the house would only have been successful if it had met the social and cultural needs of the time, as well as being economically viable. The transmission of the ideas underlying the new house could only take place within a climate of cultural consensus. This was a consensus not just between producers but between producers and consumers as well. They, of course, were often the same people and the social acceptability and cultural authority that the new style rapidly established must ultimately have been dependent on this fact. Exactly who those consumers were is still not clear. We do not know the extent to which such houses were occupied solely by the gentry, or by the gentry and middle-class groups. It seems in London that from the very first both types of people occupied the new housing and that it cannot therefore be defined in terms of a distinct social group or culture. Peter Borsay's model of the new urban housing as a product of social emulation cannot therefore be sustained in the context of late seventeenth- and early eighteenth-century London.[3] Borsay is right to stress the adoption of urban classicism by both the gentry and middle classes as a means of cultural differentiation from the rest of society. But the precise use and meaning of that architecture for those two groups, and the way it moved between one and the other, has yet to be explained and explored. Until we know more about the people who bought and lived in these houses the picture will remain incomplete. There was, however, a spatial realignment along social lines in this period, with the withdrawal of the gentry and pseudo-gentry from the City to the West End. Social segregation occurred but articulated more through location than through style.

This book was written partly as a response to the eastward expansion of London in the 1980s. The poverty of much of the Docklands design then threw up pressing questions about the interaction between architecture and the economic system that produces it, and the planning procedures which control it. The relationship between architecture, society and the market is a complex and changing one. It is important to examine how these factors played out in the past, to investigate how our cities developed and the forces to which they were subject. The existing literature has too frequently failed to portray the social and economic reality within which the eighteenth-century city existed. Instead by concentrating on the physical landscape that was left behind, it has offered a false paradigm to those who seek an escape from what they perceive to be the current urban malaise. Compared to the chaos and incoherence of current development, the physical cohesion and order of the Georgian city is understandably seductive. What must be remembered is that in each era buildings were put up under an essentially identical economic system, as speculative developments within a free-market economy. It may be that the history of the twentieth century has contributed to a false notion of how architecture and building operated in the past. The massive state building programme which resulted in the employment of large numbers of architects in the public sector, plus professionalization, led to the isolation of architects from the market economy until relatively recently. Whereas in fact for most of the early modern and modern period, in the seventeenth, eighteenth and nineteenth centuries, this is the arena in which architects and craftsmen worked. Today with the virtual elimination of the public sector, the decline in professional status for architects and possible deregulation, and the legislation permitting design and build - as a result of which the design and construction functions are no longer legally separated - we may be coming full circle once more.

We must be under no illusions that the late seventeenth- and eighteenth-century city was not produced by a system other than one as competitive and market-orientated as our own. There is, however, one difference in that architecture was able to function more easily within the market, because of a much greater degree of social consensus about cultural identities and a shared value system between the producers and consumers of these buildings. It was this, not a difference in the economic conditions or a labour force more interested in notions of skill than profit, that created a successful urban environment. In the post-industrial, pluralist society in which we live such a consensus would be an impossibility and those who propound solely formalist solutions to the problems of the modern city would do well to take account of this. Until those architects and architectural historians who look to the past for urban solutions to today's problems, acknowledge the reality of what that past was - a past every bit as competitive, capitalist and commercialized as our own - we will continue to take illusory comfort from a past that never was, establishing false traditions which do little to help us to face up to the challenges of the future.

Notes

1 John Summerson, *The Classical Language of Architecture*, 1963, London, Thames & Hudson, 1980.

2 John Onians, *Bearers of Meaning: The Classical Orders in Antiquity, the Middle Ages and the Renaissance*, Princeton and New Jersey, Princeton University Press, 1988.

3 Peter Borsay, *The English Urban Renaissance: Culture and Society in the Provincial Town, 1660-1770*, Oxford, Clarendon Press, 1989.

Appendix

Schedule of leases attached to a plan of the Ormond Street area, BL Crace XV, 27

This is a transcription of the schedules of leases attached to figure 10. The schedules cover the period 1702-20 and appear to be originals, unlike the plan of 1752, and are in two different hands. The schedules are evidence of the wide range of people taking building leases, including the builders Ragdall, Hawkins and Betts, gentry such as Sir John Smith and Thomas Wentworth Esq. and one woman, Elizabeth London. There is also a division between those such as London who inhabited the houses they financed and those instances where the property has been let to tenants. The right-hand schedule also shows the considerable time taken to build this development, which was still underway at the time the schedule was drawn up as the later peppercorn rents indicate.

NB Spellings and layout given as in the original, although 's' has been substituted for 'long s'.

—— = illegible word

do = ditto

Mid = Midsummer

Mich = Michaelmas

Cartouche inscription

At Xmas 1686. A Lease of the Under Menshon[d] Ground was granted to D[r] Nich[s] Barbon, by the ffeofees of Rugby School for 50 Yrs at 50£ ann. and sometime after the D[r] assignes y.[e] same to S[r] W[m] Milman K[t] and in 1702 by a decree in Chancery y[e] s[d] ffeofees did Grant to S[r] W[m] A farther term of 43 Y[rs] from the Expira[n] of y[e] beforemenshon[d] lease at 60£ ann whic S.[d] lease will expire at Xmass 1779.

Left-hand schedule

An Inventory or Schedule of all the Building Leases Given by S[r] W[m] Milman Kt dece[d]. of the several houses in and Ab[t] Great Ormond Street, Including y[e] West side of the Lower End of Red Lyon Street & Conduit Street wth the Dates of the Leases, to whome Given, Time of Commencem[t]. Dates of Leases & Tenants in possesion. Anna[l]. Rents.

Dates of Leases	To Whom Given and time of Commencmt and term	Tenants in possession	Annual rents			Time of Expiration
			£	s	d	
1702 Feb 18	Lease to Jos Walker for 61 years from Ladyday 1703	Walker	4	0	0	Ladyday 1764
do	To Sim^n Betts for 61 years from Ladyday 1703	Degley	4	0	0	do
do	To W Ragdall Lamp Office for 61 yrs from Ladyday 1703	Johnson	3	0	0	do
do	do	Major Aldee	4	8	0	do
do	To John Ragdall 61 years from Ladyday 1703	Ragdall	3	10	0	do
26	To Wm Hawkins for 61 yrs from Xmas before	do	5	0	0	Xmas 1763
do	do	Palmer	6	0	0	do
do	To David Fifield for 60 yrs from Ladyday 1703	Harcourt	8	0	0	Ladyday 1763
Mar 5	To J—— Bedford for 60 yrs from Ladyday 1703	Child	6	0	0	do
do	To Paul Gainsford for 60 yrs from Ladyday 1703	Crew	6	0	0	do
do	To —— Sparks for 60 yrs from Ladyday 1703	Fifield	6	0	0	do
1703 Ap 6	To Edwd Buckingham for 61 yrs from Mids 1704	Holl	8	0	0	Mid 1765
Sep 25	To Jo^n Kent for 61 yrs from Ladyday 1704	Bush	8	0	0	Mid 1765
26	To —— Sparks for 61 yrs from Ladyday 1704	——	8	0	0	do
do	To Wm Hawkins for 61 yrs from Xmas before [sic]	Dennis jn	4	0	0	Xmas 1763
do	To W Ragdall for 61 yrs from Ladyday 1704	Dickenson	4	12	0	Ladyday 1765
do	To —— for 61 yrs from Xmas ——	Latham	4	0	0	Xmas 1764
1705 Ap 3	To David Fifield for 58 yrs from Ladyday 1705	Fifield	6	0	0	Ladyday 1763
do	To James Paget for 58 yrs from Ladyday 1705	Pagett	6	0	0	do
July 2	To Wm Dagell [Dagett?] for 50 yrs from Midd 1705	Millington	8	0	0	Xmas 1764
Nov 5	To R^d Stokes for 61 yrs from Xmas 1705	Lucas	4	0	0	Xmas 1766
do	To do for 60 yrs	do	4	0	0	Mich ms 1765
do	To —— Sparks for 61 yrs from Michs before	Stevens	4	0	0	Mich 1766
Feb 20	To Sim^n Betts for 61 yrs from Xmas 1705	Ingram	4	0	0	Xmas 1766
26	To Matt Allam for 61 yrs from Ladyday 1706	Bedford	4	0	0	Ladyday 1766
do	To do from do for do	do	4	0	0	do
1706 Ap 20	To Thos Wentworth Esqr for 58 yrs from Ladyday 1706	Wentworth	8	0	0	Ladyday 1764

Dates of Leases		To Whom Given and time of Commencmt and term	Tenants in possession	Annual rents			Time of Expiration
				£	s	d	
May 8		To do for stables for do	do	2	0	0	Ladyday 1764
	5	To Joⁿ Kent for 61 yrs from Midd 1706	Md^m Finch	7	17	6	Mid 1767
	do	To Joⁿ Ragdall for 61 yrs from Midd 1706	Dagley	7	17	6	do
	do	To Simⁿ Betts for 61 yrs from Midd 1706	Md^m Pearse	7	14	0	Mid 1767
	2	To Jos Walker for 61 yrs from Midd 1706	Chisledon	7	9	6	do
1710	Mar 12	To Mr Barlow for 61 yrs from Ladyday before	Barlow	5	0	0	Ladyday 1770
	do	To do for do from do	Yate	4	0	0	do
	do	To do for do from do	Yate	1	—	6	do
1710	May 29	To Edwd Chapman for 61 yrs from Ladyday before	Eales	14	0	0	Ladyday 1771
1711	May 1	Mr Brownjohn for 61 yrs from Mid 1711	Brownjohn	10	0	0	Mid 1772
1710	July 20	to Edw Chapman for 50 yrs from Mid 1716	Eales	12	10	0	Mid 1775
1717	Apr 10	to Dennis Sen for 54 yrs from Ladyday before	Dennis	3	0	0	Ladyday 1771
			Total	228: 14 00			

Right-hand schedule

An Inventory or Schedule of all the Building leases which Wee the Heirs of the late Sr Wm Milman K^t dec^d. according to his articles wth Joⁿ Richbell Joⁿ Ragdall & Edwd Chapman builders of a piece of ground part of Lambs Conduit Fields, lying on the East side of Red Lyon & Conduit Street, for 61 yrs from Ladyday 1717 at 180£ p.ann: subj^t to Taxes

Dates of Leases		To Whom Given and time of Commencmt and term	Tenants in possession	Annual rents			Time of Expiration
				£	s	d	
1719	May 16	To Thos Mead for 61 days from Ladyday 1717	Mead	7	0	0	Ladyday 1778
	do	To Edwd Symson do do	Sympson	7	7	0	do
	do	To Eliz^b London do do	London	6	0	0	do
	May 29	To Willm Pain do do	Pain	5	0	0	do
	do	To do	do	5	0	0	do
	Aug 5	To —— Nurse do	Nurse	6	0	0	do
	Sep 22	To Joⁿ Ragdall do	Martin	6	0	0	do
	do	do	do	6	0	0	do
	do	do	Mills	5	0	0	do
	do	To Joⁿ Richball do	Reevs	6	0	0	do
	do	do	Frower	7	0	0	do
	do	do	Dry	7	0	0	do
	Jan 14	To Brown & Grey do	Mr Smith	7	7	0	do
1720	Sep 27	To Sr John Smith do	S^r Joⁿ Smith	7	0	0	do
	Oct 21	To Joⁿ Ragdall do	Ragdall	5	0	0	do

Dates of Leases	To Whom Given and time of Commencmt and term	Tenants in possession	Annual rents			Time of Expiration
			£	s	d	
do	do	do	5	0	4	do
do	To Walker & Hiron do	Walker & Hiron	5	18	0	do
do	To Math Allum do	Allam	5	0	0	do
do	To Jon Gifford do	Gifford	5	0	0	do
do	To Edwd Symson do	Symson	5	0	0	do
do	To Jon Cooper	Cooper	8	8	0	do
1720 Oct 21	To Edwd Chapman do	Chapman	7	7	0	do
do	do	do	7	14	0	do
do	do	do	6	0	0	do
do	do	do	5	0	0	do
do	do	do	5	0	0	do
do	do	do	8	8	0	do
do	do	do	5	16	8	do
	To Jon Ragdall	Pepper Corn				do
	do					do
	do					do
	do					do
	do					do
	do					do
	do					do
	do					do
	To Jon Richbell	Pepper Corn				do
	do					do
	do					do
	do					do
	do					do
	do					do
	To Edwd Chapman	Pepper Corn				do
	do					do
	do					do
	do					do
	do					do
			£ 180: 00: 00			
	Brought Over		228: 14: 00			
	Total Ground Rents		408: 14: 00			

Select bibliography

Contemporary secondary sources and treatises

Alberti, Leon Battista, *The Ten Books of Architecture*, ed. J. Leoni (1755), New York, Dover Publications, 1986

Aubrey, John, *Brief Lives*, 2 Vols, ed. A. Clark, Oxford, Clarendon Press, 1898

Barbon, Nicholas, *An Apology for the Builder Or A Discourse Shewing the Cause and Effects of the Increase of Building*, London, 1685

Barbon, Nicholas, *A Discourse of Trade*, London, 1690

Campbell, R., *The London Tradesman*, London, 1747

Chambers, Ephraim, *Cyclopaedia: Or An Universal Dictionary of Arts and Sciences*, 2 Vols, London, 1728

Colsoni, F., *Le Guide de Londres*, London, 1693

Defoe, Daniel, *A Tour through the Whole Island of Great Britain*, 1724-26, ed. Pat Rogers, Harmondsworth, Penguin, 1971

De la Quintinie, Jean, *The Compleat Gard'ner*, London, 1699

Evelyn, John, *Diary*, ed. E. S. de Beer, Oxford, Clarendon Press, 1955

Evelyn, John, *Fumifugium: Or the Inconveniencie of the Aer and Smoak of London Dissipated. Together with some Remedies humbly proposed*, London, 1661

Evelyn, John, *Sylva, Terra and Pomona*, London, 1679

Evelyn, John, 'An Account of Architects and Architecture', Preface to Roland Fréart, *A Parallel of the Antient Architecture with the Modern*, 1664, English trans. by John Evelyn, London, 1707

Fairchild, Thomas, *The City Gardener*, London, 1722

Fiennes, Celia, *Journeys*, ed. Christopher Morris as, *The Illustrated Journeys of Celia Fiennes 1685-c. 1712*, Stroud, Sutton, 1995

Francine, Alexandre, *A New Book of Architecture*, London, Robert Pricke, 1669

Hatton, Edward, *A New View of London*, London, 1708

James, John, *The Theory and Practice of Gardening*, trans. of A. J. D'Argenville Dezallier (1709), London, 1712

Johnson, Samuel, *A Dictionary of the English Language*, London, 1755

Lawson, William, *A New Orchard and Garden*, London, 1618

Lawson, William, *The Countrie Housewife's Garden*, London, 1618

Le Muet, Pierre, *The Art of Fair Building*, English edn by Robert Pricke, London, 1670

Leybourn, William, *The Compleat Surveyor*, London, 1653, 1674

Leybourn, William, *A Platform, Guide, Mate, for Purchasers, Builders, Measurers*, London, 1668

Leybourn, William, *The Art of Measuring: Or the Carpenters New Rule Described and Explained*, London, 1669

Leybourn, William, *Architectonice or A Compendium of the Art of Building*, in V. Scamozzi, *The Mirror of Architecture*, London, 1700

Mandeville, Bernard, *The Fable of the Bees*, ed. Philip Harth, Harmondsworth, Penguin, 1989

Manetti, A., *The Life of Brunelleschi*, ed. H. Saalman, Pennsylvania and London, Pennsylvania University Press, 1970

Meager, Leonard, *The English Gardener: Or, A Sure Guide to Young Planters and Gardeners*, 1670

Moxon, Joseph, *Mechanick Exercises, Or, the Doctrine of Handy-Works*, London, 1683, 1703

Neve, Richard, *The City and Countrey Purchaser, and Builder's Dictionary: Or, The Compleat Builders Guide*, London, 1703

North, Roger, *Of Building: Roger North's Writings on Architecture*, ed. Howard Colvin and J. Newman, Oxford, Oxford University Press, 1981

North, Roger, *The Autobiography of the Hon. Roger North*, ed. Augustus Jessopp, London, D. Nutt, 1887

Palladio, Andrea, *The Four Books of Architecture*, ed. Isaac Ware (1738), New York, Dover Publications, 1965

Pepys, Samuel, *Diary*, ed. Robert Latham and William Matthews, London, Bell & Hyman, 1970-83

Pratt, Roger, 'Notebooks', ed. R. T. Gunther, *The Architecture of Sir Roger Pratt*, Oxford, printed for the author at the University Press, 1928

Rea, John, *Flora: Sen, De Florum Cultura. Or, A Complete Florilege*, London, 1665

Saussure C. de, *A Foreign View of England in 1725-29*, trans. Madame Van Muyden, London, Caliban Books, 1995

Serlio, Sebastiano, *The Five Books of Architecture*, English edn (1611), New York, Dover Publications, 1982

Strype, J., *The Survey of London*, enlarged edn of John Stow, London, 1720

Vitruvius, *The Ten Books on Architecture*, trans. Morris Hicky Morgan, New York, Dover Publications, 1960

Worlidge, John, *Systema Horticultura: Or, the Art of Gardening*, n.p. [London?], 1683

Wotton, Henry, *The Elements of Architecture*, London, 1624

Secondary sources

Ackerman, James S., 'Architectural Practice in the Italian Renaissance', *Journal of the Society of Architectural Historians*, Vol. 13, 1954, pp. 3-11

Airs, Malcolm, *The Making of the English Country House, 1500-1640*, London, Architectural Press, 1975

Alford, B. W. E. Barker, T. C., *A History of the Carpenters Company*, London, Allen and Unwin, 1968

Anthony, John, *The Renaissance Garden in Britain*, Princes Risborough, Shire, 1991

Barker, Felix and Jackson Peter, *The History of London in Maps*, London, Barrie & Jenkins, 1990

Beard, G. W., *Craftsmen and Interior Decoration in England, 1660-1820*, Edinburgh, J. Bartholomew, 1981

Beier, A. L. and Finlay, Roger, eds, *London 1500-1700: The Making of the Metropolis*, London and New York, Longman, 1986

Benevolo, L., *The Architecture of the Renaissance*, 2 Vols, London, Routledge & Kegan Paul, 1978

Berg, Maxine, *The Age of Manufacture, 1700-1820*, London, Fontana Press, 1982

Berg, Maxine, Hudson, Pat and Sonenscher, Michael, eds, *Manufacture in Town and Country Before the Factory*, Cambridge and New York, Cambridge University Press, 1983

Bindman, David and Baker, Malcolm, *Roubiliac and the Eighteenth-Century Monument*, New Haven and London, Yale University Press, 1995

Blomfield, Reginald, *The Formal Garden in England*, 1892, reprinted London, Waterstone & Co., 1985

Borsay, Peter, *The English Urban Renaissance: Culture and Society in the Provincial Town, 1660-1770*, Oxford, Clarendon Press, 1989

Borsay, Peter, ed., *The Eighteenth-Century Town: A Reader in English Urban History, 1688-1820*, London and New York, Longman, 1990

Boulton, Jeremy, *Neighbourhood and Society: A London Suburb in the Seventeenth Century,* Cambridge, Cambridge University Press, 1987

Braudel, F., *Capitalism and Material Life, 1400-1800*, London, Fontana, 1974

Brett-James, Norman, *The Growth of Stuart London*, London, London and Middlesex Archaeological Society with George Allen & Unwin, 1935

Brewer, J., and Porter, R., eds, *Consumption and the World of Goods*, London and New York, Routledge, 1993

Brunskill, R. W., *Illustrated Handbook of Vernacular Architecture*, London, Faber & Faber, 1987

Burke, Peter, 'Popular Culture in Seventeenth-Century London', *London Journal*, Vol. 3, No. 2, 1977, pp. 143-62

Burton, Neil, ed., *Georgian Vernacular: Papers Given at the 1995 Georgian Group Symposium*, London, Georgian Group, 1996

Cannadine, David, 'Urban History in the United Kingdom: The "Dyos phenomenon" and After', in David Cannadine and David Reeder, eds, *Exploring the Urban Past: Essays in Urban History by H. J. Dyos*, Cambridge, Cambridge University Press, 1982

Cannadine, David and Reeder, David, eds, *Exploring the Urban Past: Essays in Urban History by H. J. Dyos*, Cambridge, Cambridge University Press, 1982

Chalkin, C. W., *The Provincial Towns of Georgian England: A Study of the Building Process, 1740-1820*, London, Edward Arnold, 1974

Clark, Peter and Slack, Paul, *Crisis and Order in English Towns, 1500-1700*, London, Routledge & Kegan Paul, 1972

Clark, Peter and Slack, Paul, *English Towns in Transition, 1500-1700*, Oxford, Oxford University Press, 1976

Clarke, Linda, *Building Capitalism: Historical Change and the Labour Process in the Production of the Built Environment*, London and New York, Routledge, 1992

Clifton-Taylor, Alec, *The Pattern of English Building*, London, Faber & Faber, 1972

Coleman, D. C., 'London Scriveners and the Estate Market in the Later 17th Century', *Economic History Review*, 2nd Series, No. 4, 1951, pp. 221-30

Colvin, Howard, 'Gothic Survival and Gothick Revival', *Architectural Review*, March 1948, pp. 91-8

Colvin, Howard, *A Biographical Dictionary of British Architects, 1600-1840*, London, John Murray, 1978

Cooney, E. W., 'The Origins of the Victorian Master Builders', *Economic History Review*, 2nd Series, No. 8, 1955, pp. 167-76

Corfield, P. J., *The Impact of English Towns, 1700-1800*, Oxford, Oxford University Press, 1982

Cox, Alan, 'Bricks to Build a Capital', in Hermione Hobhouse and Ann Saunders, eds, *Good and Proper Materials: The Fabric of London since the Great Fire*, London, London Topographical Society publication No. 140, 1989, pp. 3-17

Crinson, Mark and Lubbock, Jules, *Architecture - Art or Profession?: Three Hundred Years of Architectural Education in Britain*, Manchester and New York, Manchester University Press, 1994

Cruickshank, Dan and Burton, Neil, *Life in the Georgian City*, London, Viking, 1990

Cruickshank, Dan and Wyld, Peter, *London: The Art of Georgian Building*, London, Architectural Press, 1975

Dickson, P. G. M., *The Financial Revolution in England: A Study in the Development of Public Credit*, London, Macmillan, 1967

Downes, Kerry, *English Baroque Architecture*, London, Zwemmer, 1966

Downes, Kerry, 'John Evelyn and Architecture', in John Summerson, ed., *Concerning Architecture*, London, A. Lane, 1968, pp. 28-39

Downes, Kerry, *Sir Christopher Wren: The Design of St Paul's Cathedral*, London, Trefoil in association with the Guildhall Library, 1988

Drury, Paul, '18thC Construction: Joinery', *Architects' Journal*, 14 August 1991, pp. 36-41

Earle, Peter, *The Making of the English Middle Class: Business, Society and Family Life in London, 1660-1730*, London, Methuen, 1989

Earle, Peter, *A City Full of People: Men and Women of London, 1650-1750*, London, Methuen, 1994

Ettlinger, Leopold D., 'The Emergence of the Italian Architect During the Fifteenth Century', in S. Kostof, ed., *The Architect: Chapters in the History of the Profession*, Oxford, Oxford University Press, 1977, pp. 96-123

Forty, Adrian, *Objects of Desire: Design and Society, 1750-1980*, London, Thames & Hudson, 1986

Galinou, Mireille, ed., *London's Pride: The Glorious History of the Capital's Gardens*, London, Anaya, 1990

Gent, Lucy, ed., *Albion's Classicism: The Visual Arts in Britain, 1550-1660*, New Haven and London, Yale University Press, 1995

George, M. D., *London Life in the Eighteenth Century*, Harmondsworth, Penguin, 1965

Girouard, Mark, 'Elizabethan Architecture and the Gothic Tradition', *Architectural History*, No. 6, 1963, pp. 23-38

Girouard, Mark, *Robert Smythson and the Elizabethan Country House*, London, Country Life, 1966

Girouard, Mark, *Life in the English Country House: A Social and Architectural History*, New Haven and London, Yale University Press, 1978

Girouard, Mark, *The English Town*, New Haven and London, Yale University Press, 1990

Glanville, Philippa, 'The Topography of Seventeenth-Century London: A Review of Maps', *Urban History Yearbook*, 1980, pp. 79-83

Goldthwaite, Richard, *The Building of Renaissance Florence: An Economic and Social History*, Baltimore and London, Johns Hopkins University Press, 1980

Goldthwaite, Richard, *Wealth and the Demand for Art in Italy, 1300-1600*, Baltimore, Johns Hopkins University Press, 1993

Grassby, Richard, 'Social Mobility and Business Enterprise in Seventeenth-Century England', in Donald Pennington and Keith Thomas, eds, *Puritans and Revolutionaries: Essays in Seventeenth-Century History Presented to Christopher Hill*, Oxford, Clarendon Press, 1978, pp. 355-81

Gray, Edmund, *The British House: A Concise Architectural History*, London, Barrie & Jenkins, 1994

Harding, Vanessa, 'The Population of London, 1550-1700: A Review of the Published Evidence', *London Journal*, Vol. 15, No. 2, 1990, pp. 111-28

Harris, Eileen, *British Architectural Books and Writers, 1556-1785*, Cambridge, Cambridge University Press, 1990

Harris, John and Higgot, Gordon, *Inigo Jones: Complete Architectural Drawings*, London, Royal Academy of Arts, 1989-90

Harris, John, Orgel, S. and Strong, R., *The King's Arcadia: Inigo Jones and the Stuart Court*, London, Arts Council of Great Britain, 1973

Harvey, J., *The Master Builders: Architecture in the Middle Ages*, London, Thames & Hudson, 1971

Harvey, J., *The Medieval Architect*, London, Wayland, 1972

Hobhouse, Hermione and Saunders, Ann, eds, *Good and Proper Materials: The Fabric of London since the Great Fire*, London, London Topographical Society, 1989

Hook, Judith, *The Baroque Age in England*, London, Thames & Hudson, 1976

Hoskins, W. G., 'The Rebuilding of Rural England, 1570-1640', *Past and Present*, No. 4, 1953, pp. 44-59

Howgego, James, *Printed Maps of London circa 1553-1850*, Folkestone, Dawson, 1978

Jenkins, F., *Architect and Patron: A Survey of Professional Relations and Practice in England from the Sixteenth Century to the Present Day*, London, Oxford University Press, 1961

Jenkins, Simon, *Landlords to London*, London, Constable, 1975

Johnson, Matthew, *Housing Culture: Traditional Architecture in an English Landscape*, London, UCL Press, 1993

Jones, D. W., *War and Economy in the Age of William III and Marlborough*, Oxford and New York, B. Blackwell, 1988

Jones, J. R., *Country and Court: England 1658-1714*, London, Edward Arnold, 1978

Kaye, Barrington, *The Development of the Architectural Profession in England: A Sociological Study*, London, Allen & Unwin, 1960

Kelsall, Frank, 'The London House Plan in the Later 17th Century', *Post-Medieval Archaeology*, Vol. 8, 1974, pp. 80-91

Kingsford, Charles Lethbridge, *The Early History of Piccadilly, Leicester Square, Soho and their Neighbourhood*, Cambridge, Cambridge University Press, 1925

Knoop, D. and Jones, G. P., *The Medieval Mason*, Manchester, Manchester University Press, 1933

Knoop, D. and Jones, G. P., *The London Mason in the Seventeenth Century*, Manchester, Manchester University Press, 1935

Knoop, D. and Jones, G. P., 'The Decline of the Mason-Architect in England', London, RIBA, 1937, reprinted from *Journal of the Royal Institute of British Architects*, Vol. 44, 3rd Series, No. 19, September 1937

Kostof, Spiro, ed., *The Architect: Chapters in the History of the Profession*, Oxford, Oxford University Press, 1977

Kostof, Spiro, 'The Architect in the Middle Ages, East and West', in Spiro Kostoff, ed., *The Architect: Chapters in the History of the Profession*, Oxford, Oxford University Press, 1977, pp. 59-95

Letwin, William, *The Origins of Scientific Economics*, London, Methuen, 1963

Lloyd, Nathaniel, *A History of the English House*, London, Architectural Press, 1931

Longstaffe-Gowan, Todd, 'Gardening and the Middle Classes, 1700-1830', in Mireille Galinou, ed., *London's Pride: The Glorious History of the Capital's Gardens*, London, Anaya, 1990, pp. 122-33

Longstaffe-Gowan, Todd, 'Private Urban Gardening in England, 1700-1830', in John Dixon Hunt and Joachim Wolschke-Bulmahn, eds, *The Vernacular Garden*, Dumbarton Oaks Colloquium on the History of Landscape Architecture, No. 14, 1993, pp. 47-75

Louw, H. J., 'The Origin of the Sash-Window', *Architectural History*, No. 26, 1983, pp. 49-72

Louw, H. J., 'Demarcation Disputes between the English Carpenters and Joiners from the Sixteenth to the Eighteenth Century', *Construction History*, Vol. 5, 1989, pp. 3-20

Lubbock, Jules, *The Tyranny of Taste: The Politics of Architecture and Design in Britain, 1550-1960*, New Haven and London, Yale University Press, 1995

Machin, R., 'The Great Rebuilding: A Reassessment', *Past and Present*, No. 77, 1977, pp. 33-56

McKellar, Elizabeth, 'Architectural Practice for Speculative Building in Late Seventeenth-Century London', unpublished Ph.D., Royal College of Art, 1992

McKellar, Elizabeth, 'Architectural History: The Invisible Subject', in *Journal of Architecture*, Vol. 1, No. 2, Summer 1996, pp. 159-64

McKellar, Elizabeth, 'The City and the Country: The Urban Vernacular in Late Seventeenth and Early Eighteenth Century London', in Neil Burton, ed., *Georgian Vernacular: Papers given at the 1995 Georgian Group Symposium*, London, Georgian Group, 1996, pp. 10-18

McKellar, Elizabeth, 'Palladianism via Postmodernism: Constructing and Deconstructing the "English Renaissance"', *Art History*, Vol. 20, No. 1, March 1997, pp. 154-7

McKendrick, Neil, Brewer, John and Plumb, J. H., *The Birth of a Consumer Society: The Commercialization of Eighteenth-Century England*, London, Europa, 1982

Matless, David, 'Ages of English Design: Preservation, Modernism and Tales of their History, 1926-1939', *Journal of Design History*, Vol. 3, No. 4, 1990, pp. 203-12

Melton, Frank T., 'Sir Robert Clayton's Building Projects in London, 1666-72', *Guildhall Studies in London History*, Vol. 3, No. 1, October 1977, pp. 37-41

Millon, Henry A., ed., *The Renaissance from Brunelleschi to Michaelangelo: The Representation of Architecture*, London, Thames & Hudson, 1994

Morrice, Richard, *The Buildings of Britain: Stuart and Baroque*, London, Barrie & Jenkins, 1982

SELECT BIBLIOGRAPHY

———

Mowl, Timothy and Earnshaw, Brian, *Architecture Without Kings: The Rise of Puritan Classicism under Cromwell*, Manchester, Manchester University Press, 1995

Olsen, Donald J., *Town Planning in London: The Eighteenth and Nineteenth Centuries*, New Haven and London, Yale University Press, 1964

Onians, John, *Bearers of Meaning: The Classical Orders in Antiquity, the Middle Ages and the Renaissance*, Princeton and New Jersey, Princeton University Press, 1988

Pearl, Valerie, 'Change and Stability in Seventeenth-Century London', *London Journal*, Vol. 5, No. 1, May 1979, pp. 3-34

Pevsner, Nikolaus and Cherry, Bridget, *The Buildings of England: London I, The Cities of London and Westminster*, Harmondsworth, Penguin, 1973

Pevsner, Nikolaus and Cherry, Bridget, *The Buildings of England: London III, The North West*, Harmondsworth, Penguin, 1991

Plumptre, George, *The Garden Makers*, Pavilion, London, 1993

Porphyios, Demetri, *On the Methodology of Architectural History*, London, Architectural Design, 1981

Port, M.H., 'The Office of Works and Building Contracts in Nineteenth-Century England', *Economic History Review*, 2nd Series, No. 20, 1967, pp. 94-110

Porter, Roy, *English Society in the Eighteenth Century*, Harmondsworth, Penguin, 1982

Porter, Stephen, *The Great Fire of London*, Stroud, Sutton, 1996

Power, Michael J., 'The Urban Development of East London, 1550-1700', Unpublished Ph.D., University of London, 1971

Power, M.J., 'East London Housing in the Seventeenth Century', in Peter Clark and Paul Slack, *Crisis and Order in English Towns, 1500-1700*, London, Routledge & Kegan Paul, 1972, pp. 237-62

Power, M.J., 'Shadwell: The Development of a London Surburban Community in the Seventeenth Century', *London Journal*, Vol. 4, No. 1, 1978, pp. 29-46

Power, M.J., 'The East and West in Early-Modern London', in E.W. Ives, R.J. Knecht and J.J. Scarisbrick, eds, *Wealth and Power in Tudor England*, London, Athlone Press, 1978, pp. 169-70

Power, M.J., 'The Social Topography of Restoration London', in A.L. Beier and Roger Finlay eds, *London 1500-1700: The Making of the Metropolis*, London and New York, Longman, 1986, pp. 199-223

Quiney, Anthony, 'Thomas Lucas, Bricklayer, 1662-1736', *Post-Medieval Archaeology*, No. 136, 1979, pp. 269-80

Rasmussen, Steen Eiler, *London: The Unique City*, 1934, Cambridge, Mass. and London, MIT Press, 1982

Reddaway, T.F., *The Rebuilding of London after the Great Fire*, London, Jonathan Cape, 1940

Royal Academy of Arts, *Sir Christopher Wren and the Making of St Paul's*, London, Royal Academy of Arts, 1991

Royal Commission on the Historic Monuments, *London: West*, Vol. II, London, HMSO, 1925

Royal Commission on the Historic Monuments, *London: The City*, Vol. IV, London, HMSO, 1929

Royal Commission on the Historic Monuments, *London: East*, Vol. V, London, HMSO, 1930

Rykwert, Joseph, *The First Moderns: The Architects of the Eighteenth Century*, Cambridge Mass. and London, MIT Press, 1980

Rykwert, Joseph, 'On Oral Transmission of Architectural Theory', *AA Files*, No. 6, May 1984, pp. 14-26

Saint, Andrew, *The Image of the Architect*, New Haven and London, Yale University Press, 1983

Saumarez Smith, Charles, 'Eighteenth-Century Man', *Designer*, March 1987, pp. 19-21

Saumarez Smith, Charles, *Eighteenth-Century Decoration: Design and the Domestic Interior in England*, London, Weidenfeld & Nicholson, 1993

Shepherd, Francis, Belcher, Victor and Cottrell, Philip, 'The Middlesex and Yorkshire Deeds Registries and the Study of Building Fluctuations', *London Journal*, Vol. 5, No. 2, 1979, pp. 176-217

Simpson, A. W. B., *An Introduction to the History of Land Law*, Oxford, Oxford University Press, 1961

Solkin, David H., *Painting for Money: The Visual Arts and the Public Sphere in Eighteenth-Century England*, New Haven and London, Yale University Press, 1993

Stone, Lawrence, *The Crisis of the Aristocracy, 1558-1641*, Oxford, Oxford University Press, 1965

Stone, Lawrence, 'The Residential Development of the West End of London in the Seventeenth Century', in B. C. Malament, ed., *After the Reformation*, Pennsylvania, University of Pennsylvania Press, 1980, pp. 167-212

Stone, Lawrence & Fawtier Stone, Jeanne, *An Open Elite? England 1540-1880*, Oxford, Oxford University Press, 1986

Strong, Roy, *The Renaissance Garden in England*, London, Thames & Hudson, 1979

Styles, John, 'Manufacturing, Consumption and Design in Eighteenth-Century England', in J. Brewer and R. Porter, eds, *Consumption and the World of Goods in the Seventeenth and Eighteenth Centuries*, London and New York, Routledge, 1993, pp. 527-54

Summerson, John, *Georgian London*, 1945, Harmondsworth, Penguin, 1962 and subsequent edns

Summerson, John, *Architecture in Britain, 1530-1830*, Harmondsworth, Penguin, 1953, 1983

Summerson, John, *The Classical Language of Architecture*, 1963, London, Thames & Hudson, 1980

Summerson, John, *Inigo Jones*, Harmondsworth, Penguin, 1966

Survey of London, London, Athlone Press, Vols. I -, 1912 -

Taylor, Gladys, *Old London Gardens*, London, B. T. Batsford, 1953

Thompson, F. M. L., *The Rise of Suburbia*, Leicester, Leicester University Press, 1982

Thomson, David, *Renaissance Paris*, London, Zwemmer, 1984

Thornton, Peter, *Seventeenth Century Interior Decoration in England, France and Holland*, New Haven and London, Yale University Press, 1978

Victoria County History, *The County of Middlesex*, Vols I-IX, Institute of Historical Research, London, Oxford University Press, 1969-89

Walker, John A., *Design History and the History of Design*, London, Pluto Press, 1989

Ward, J. R., 'Speculative Building at Bristol and Clifton, 1783-1793', *Business History*, Vol. 20, No. 1, January 1978, pp. 3-18

SELECT BIBLIOGRAPHY

Watkin, David, *The Rise of Architectural History*, London, Architectural Press, 1980

Weatherill, Lorna, *Consumer Behaviour and Material Culture, 1660-1760*, London and New York, Routledge, 1988

Weinreb, Ben and Hibbert, Christopher, *The London Encyclopaedia*, London, Macmillan, 1983

Williams, Raymond, *The Country and the City*, London, Hogarth Press, 1985

Williamson, Tom, *Polite Landscapes: Gardens and Society in Eighteenth-Century England*, Stroud, Sutton, 1995

Wilton Ely, J., 'The Rise of the Professional Architect in England', in Spiro Kostof, ed., *The Architect Chapters in the History of the Profession*, Oxford, Oxford University Press, 1977, pp. 180-208

Wittkower, Rudolf, 'English Literature on Architecture', in Rudolf Wittkower, *Palladio and English Palladianism*, London, Thames & Hudson, 1974, pp. 95-112

Wittkower, Rudolf, *Palladio and English Palladianism*, London, Thames & Hudson, 1974

Worsley, Giles, ed., *Georgian Architectural Practice: Papers Given at the Georgian Group Symposium 1991*, London, Georgian Group, 1992

Wren Society, Vols I- XX, Oxford, printed at the University Press, 1924-43

Wright, Patrick, *On Living in an Old Country*, London, Verso, 1985

Wrigley, E. A., 'A Simple Model of London's Importance in Changing English Society and Economy, 1650-1750', *Past and Present*, No. 37, 1967, pp. 44-70; reprinted in Philip Abrams and E. A. Wrigley, eds, *Towns in Societies: Essays in Economic History and Historical Sociology*, Cambridge, Cambridge University Press, 1978

Wrigley, E. A. and Schofield, R. S., *The Population History of England, 1541-1871*, London, Edward Arnold, 1981

Yeomans, David, 'Structural Carpentry in London Building', in Hermione Hobhouse and Ann Saunders, eds, *Good and Proper Materials: The Fabric of London since the Great Fire*, London, London Topographical Society, 1989, pp. 38-47

Yeomans, David, '18thC Timber Construction: Floor Structures', *Architects' Journal*, 17 July 1991, pp. 46-51

Yeomans, David, '18thC Timber Construction: Roof Structures', *Architects' Journal*, 24 and 31 July 1991, pp. 45-50

Yeomans, David and Cleminson, Anthony, '18thC Timber Construction: Walls and Partitions', *Architects' Journal*, 7 August 1991, pp. 43-6

Index